READINGS

ON

EDMUND HUSSERL'S *LOGICAL INVESTIGATIONS*

READINGS
ON
EDMUND HUSSERL'S
LOGICAL INVESTIGATIONS

edited by

J. N. MOHANTY

MARTINUS NIJHOFF / THE HAGUE / 1977

To
BANI

CONTENTS

44241

EDITOR'S INTRODUCTION

I

Edmund Husserl's *Logische Untersuchungen* is, by any standard and also by nearly common consent, a great philosophical work. Within the phenomenological movement, it is generally recognised that the breakthrough to pure phenomenology — not merely to eidetic phenomenology, but also to transcendental phenomenology — was first made in these investigations. But in the context of philosophy of logic and also of theory of knowledge in general, these investigations took decisive steps forward. Amongst their major achievements generally recognised are of course : the final death-blow to psychologism as a theory of logic in the *Prolegomena*, a new conception of analyticity which vastly improves upon Kant's, a theory of meaning which is many-sided in scope and widely ramified in its applications, a conception of pure logical grammar that eventually became epoch-making, a powerful restatement of the conception of truth in terms of 'evidence' and a theory of knowledge in terms of the dynamic movement from empty intention to graduated fulfillment. There are many other detailed arguments, counter-arguments, conceptual distinctions and phenomenological descriptions which deserve the utmost attention, examination and assimilation on the part of any serious investigator.

With the publication of J. N. Findlay's English translation of the *Untersuchungen*, it is expected that this work will find its proper place in the curriculum of the graduate programs in philosophy in the English-speaking world. This, in its turn, it is hoped, will lead to a better and more careful appreciation of Husserl's style of philosophising as well as of the content of his philosophy. The essays in the present volume are put together with the hope of contributing to that process and providing the beginning reader, the graduate student as well as the instructor with material that bring out, both appreciatively and critically, some of the main problems and issues discussed in, and arising out of, the *Untersuchungen*.

There are two Husserl fragments in this anthology : the first one dating from 1903, is a clarification by Husserl of the sense of his criticism of logical psychologism. The second piece, dating from 1925, is taken from the *Phänomenologische Psychologie*; in it Husserl looks back to the achievements and limitations of the *Untersuchungen* and in particular relates them to Brentano and Dilthey. I have also included two influential reviews of Husserl's works : Frege's review of the *Philosophie der Arithmetik* which is reputed to have led to Husserl's abandonment of his own psychologism (a hypothesis which I have called into question in my essay on the relation between Frege and Husserl). The second is a review of the *Prolegomena* by Paul Natorp, the influential Neo-Kantian of Marburg, in which Natorp seeks to bring out the extent to which the idea of a pure logic is acceptable but needs to be supplemented by the Kantian problematic. Natorp's review is often credited with having influenced the subsequent development of Husserl's thought.

Two of the essays were hitherto unpublished : my "Husserl's thesis of the Ideality of Meanings" and the late Aron Gurwitsch's essay on 'essentially occasional expressions'. I am indebted to Mrs. Alice Gurwitsch for giving me permission to include the latter piece, and to Professor Lester Embree for first drawing my attention to its existence and also for editing it for publication.

For permissions to reprint the various essays in this volume, I am grateful to their respective authors as well as to the editors and/or publishers of the journals or books in which they were originally printed.

II

Several of the essays included in this volume are critical of Husserl, and succeed in raising problems and issues which need to be taken into account. Arne Naess, who is deeply appreciative of the *Untersuchungen*, nevertheless questions the claim of phenomenology to yield apodictic knowledge and asserts that every science courts the radical risk of error. Every *actual* science will be, according to Naess, on the "human side" of the chasm between the real and the ideal and therefore will be subject to the imperfections of the so-called factual sciences. Naess, and also Günther Patzig, questions the claim of evidence to rule out all doubt about truth. In the words of Naess, "the ultimate meeting of human beings with the *Sachverhalt*" cannot effectively rule out the claim of others who do not intuit the *Sachverhalt* but genuinely believe that they do. Likewise Patzig argues that Husserl illegitimately moves from evidence as a *phenomenal* character of certain judgments to evidence as the consciousness of the *actual* truth. Patzig's criticism, developed in great detail, has the merit that it also contains an account of the rationale of Husserl's so-called idealistic turn : for Patzig, this turn corresponds to the shift from the early thesis that evidence is reducible to truth to the later thesis that truth is reducible to evidence, and this latter shift is accounted for as being due to the difficulties inherent in the earlier thesis about the relation of truth to evidence.

If thus Patzig and Naess question the self-evidence theory of truth, the paper by Downes (as also Naess's) is concerned with the theory of apodictic truth. Downes seeks to relate Husserl's conceptions of *a priori* and necessary truth to the contemporary analytical philosophy with which he brings out its basic general agreement. What Husserl's theory lacks is, according to him, a method for investigating the *a priori*. The method Husserl practises is, at its best, implicitly linguistic.

Atwell calls into question the basis on which Husserl's rejection of the referential theory of meaning is grounded; yet one of the central theses of the *Untersuchungen*, i.e. the thesis of the ideality of meanings, rests on this rejection. With regard to the thesis of ideality, Willard emphasises the influence of Lotze on Husserl. This needed to be pointed out, in view of the widely current view as to Frege's influence : the truth would appear rather to be that both Frege and Husserl were under the influence of Lotze. Whereas Willard shows that the relation between mind (or, mental acts) and meaning, for Husserl, is one of instantiation or exemplification, one may add that Husserl seems subsequently to have rejected the treatment of meanings as species, and the relation is still one of intentionality, the *ideal* meaning is still the *content* of the act concerned.

The two papers by Bar-Hillel and Edie, are concerned with one of Husserl's most seminal ideas i.e. the conception of pure logical grammar. Bar-Hillel takes Husserl to task for leaving the linguistic level and seeking to explore the realm of meanings with the help of apodictic evidence. He recognises that Husserl's basic insights (especially with regard to the two kinds of meaninglessness) can be preserved in translating his theses into the purely syntactic idiom. He gives Husserl his due as one of the first to emphasise the role played by the rules of formation in the construction of any language. But he looks upon him only as forerunner of Carnap's more mature and developed conception of logical syntax. Edie corrects some of Bar-Hillel's remarks about the fourth Investigation by taking into account the more developed conception of logical grammar to be found in the *Formal and Transcendental Logic*. In particular, Edie — rightly, I think — insists that unlike Carnap Husserl is concerned, not with ideal constructed languages, but with natural languages. While Bar-Hillel turns to Carnap to bring out the inadequacies of Husserl's seminal conception, Edie turns to transformational grammar to shed light on the Husserlian theme of a universal grammar.

The beauty of Sokolowski's paper (whose theme has now been developed by him in a larger work, *Husserlian Meditations*) is that he takes one central theme from the *Untersuchungen*, the relation of part and whole, and shows, very effectively, not only that it runs through and determines all the six investigations but also that it permeates the entire Husserlian phenomenology. Sokolowski thus succeeds both in dispelling the belief that the investigations are a set of disconnected enquiries and themes and in correcting the widely held belief that for the later and the more developed Husserlian phenomenology, they are of no great importance.

Aron Gurwitsch builds upon Husserl's admittedly incomplete theory of 'essentially occasional expressions' as formulated in the *Untersuchungen*, and taking into account the phenomenon of horizontal consciousness, relates the use of such expressions to the organisational aspect with which the perceptual world presents itself and to the three orders of existence which, according to Gurwitsch, always present themselves in our experience. This essay is a good example of Gurwitsch's own style of phenomenology, and also an example of what can constructively be done on the basis of Husserl's suggestive thoughts.

III

The position of the *Logische Untersuchungen* in the total structure of Husserlian thought has been a matter of some controversy amongst phenomenologists. In fact, this question is part of a wider question concerning the place of philosophical reflections on logic within a phenomenological philosophy. Why is it that Husserl returned to the theme of logic ever anew? Why is it that the breakthrough to pure phenomenology came about in a work on philosophy of logic? Why is it that the first chapter of the early major work introducing pure phenomenology, the *Ideas* I, is devoted to what he calls "logical considerations"? The chapter from *Phänomenologische Psychologie* which is included in this anthology shows Husserl's own evaluation of the role that the logical Investigations played in the development of his thought, and of various historical influences that bore on them. But these remarks also make it clear that even if "fundamental clarity" had not been achieved in the Investigations and even if their subject matter was limited to logical objectivities alone along with their constitutive acts — yet the theses of the Investigations continue to be the abiding basis for the structure of Husserlian thought. As pointed out earlier, Sokolowski's work substantiates this abundantly well, especially with regard to the conceptual framework of the third investigation. But from a still broader perspective, the thematisation of logic would seem to serve two purposes for Husserlian phenomenology : Formal logic, and its correlate, formal ontology lay bare the form of the *world*. In this sense, the 'world' was a theme of Husserlian reflections from the right beginning. In the second place, the ideality of the logical is an important moment of the accomplishments of the life of consciousness. The constitutive function of consciousness is not grasped in its entirety as well as in one of its most essential possibilities, so long as the logical is not grasped in its ideal-objectivity and the acts constituting it are not laid bare. The same holds good also of the life-world thematic : the life-world serves as the foundation for the constitution of the higher order idealities, and the possibility of such constitution is not imposed on the life-world *ab extra* but is inherent in it and in fact defines it as the basis for logical and scientific thinking. The traditional question, if logical thinking distorts reality, is misconceived from the point of view of Husserlian phenomenology. For it is not the case that logic as a tool is found to be there and is taken up by human intellect to engage in its intellectual endeavors to grasp reality. That picture is misleading. Logical forms and objectivities are idealisations of life-world structures and are constituted accomplishments of the life of consciousness. They belong to the total structure of subjectivity and have their rightful place in it. They do not exhaust it, nor are they autonomous in the sense of being the 'first,' presuppositionless beginning. But they are not tools of distortion of misrepresentation of an alien reality. For Husserlian phenomenology, then, reflection on the theme of logic reveals the nature of the constitutive accomplishments of the life of consciousness in one of its most essential moments.

Graduate Faculty of the   J. N. MOHANTY
New School for Social Research,
New York

REVIEW OF DR. E. HUSSERL'S
*PHILOSOPHY OF ARITHMETIC**

by

Gottlob Frege

(*translated by* E. W. Kluge)

The author decides in the Introduction that for the time being he will consider (only) cardinal numbers (cardinalia), and thereupon launches into a discussion of multiplicity, plurality, totality, aggregate, collection, set. He uses these words as if they were essentially synonymous; the concept of a cardinal number [1] is supposed to be different from this. However, the logical relationship between multiplicity and number (p. 9) remains somewhat obscure. If one were to go by the words "The concept of number includes the same concrete phenomena as the concept of multiplicity albeit only by way of the extensions of the concepts of its species, the numbers two, three, four, etc. ...," one might infer that they had the same extension. On the other hand, multiplicity is supposed to be more indeterminate and more general than number. The matter would probably be clearer if a sharper distinction were drawn between falling under a concept and subordination. Now the first thing he attempts to do is to give an analysis of the concept of multiplicity. Determinate numbers as well as the generic concept of number which presupposes them, are then supposed to emerge from it by means of determinations. Thus we are first led down from the general to the particular, and then up again.

Totalities are wholes whose parts are collectively connected. We must be conscious of these parts as noticed in and by themselves. The collective connection consists neither in the contents' being simultaneously in the awareness, nor in their arising in the awareness one after another. Not even space, as all-inclusive form, is the ground of the unification. The connection consists (p. 43) in the unifying act itself. "But neither is it the case that over and above the act there exists a relational content which is distinct

* *Zeitschrift für Philosophie und Philosophische Kritik*, vol. 103 (1894), pp. 313-332. The translator's notes are indicated. E. tr. first appeared in *Mind*, LXXXI, 1972, pp. 321-337. Reprinted here with permission. — J. N. M.
    [1] Henceforth I shall take "cardinal" to be understood. — Trans.

from it and is its creative result." Collective connection is a relation *sui generis*. Following J. St. Mill, the author then explains what is to be understood by "relation"; namely that state of consciousness or that phenomenon (these expressions are supposed to coincide in the extension of their reference) in which the related contents — the bases of the relation — are contained (p. 70). He then distinguishes between primary and mental relations. Here only the latter concern more closely. "If a unitary mental act is directed towards several contents, then with respect to it the contents are connected or related to one another. If we perform such an act, it would of course be futile for us to look for a relation or connection in the presentational content which it contains (unless over and above this, there is also a primary relation). The contents here are united only by act, and consequently this unification can be noticed only by a special reflection on it" (p. 73). The difference-relation, whereby two contents are related to one another by means of an evident negative judgement, is also of this kind (p. 74). Sameness, on the other hand, is (p. 77) a primary relation. (According to this, complete coincidence, too, would be a primary relation, while its negation — difference itself — would be a mental one. I here miss a statement of the difference between the difference-relation and collective connection, where in the opinion of the author the latter, too, is a mental relation because perceptually no unification is noticeable in its presentational content.) When one is speaking of "unrelated" contents, the contents are merely thought "together," i.e. as a totality. "But by no means are they really unconnected, unrelated. On the contrary, they are connected by the mental act holding them together. It is only in the content of the latter that all noticeable unification is lacking." (p. 78) The conjunction 'and' fixes in a wholly appropriate manner the circumstance that given contents are connected in a collective manner (p. 81). "A presentation ... falls under the concept of multiplicity insofar as it connects in a collective manner any contents which are noticed in and by themselves" (p. 82). (It appears that what is understood by "presentation" is an act.) "Multiplicity in general ... is no more than something and something and something, etc.; or any one thing and any one thing and any one thing, etc.; or more briefly, one and one and one, etc." (p. 85). When we remove the indeterminateness which lies in the "etc.," we arrive at the numbers one and one; one, one and one; one, one, one and one; and so on. We can also arrive at these concepts directly beginning with any concrete multiplicity whatever; for each one of them falls under one of these concepts, and under a determinate one at that (p. 87). To this end, we abstract from the particular constitution of the individual contents collected together in the multiplicity, retaining each one only insofar as it is a something of a one; and thus, with respect to the collective connection of the latter, we obtain the general form of multiplicity appropriate to the multiplicity under consideration; i.e. the appropriate number (p. 88). Along with this number-abstraction goes a complete removal of restrictions placed on the content (p. 100). We cannot explain the general concept of number otherwise than by pointing to the similarity which all number-concepts have to one another (p. 88).

Having thus given a brief presentation of the basic thoughts of the first part, I now want to give a general characterization of this mode of consideration. We here have an attempt to provide a naive conception of number with a scientific justification. I call any opinion naive if according to it a number-statement is not an assertion about a concept or the extension of a concept; for upon the slightest reflection about number, one is led with a certain necessity to such conceptions. Now strictly speaking, an opinion is naive only as long as the difficulties facing it are unknown — which does not quite apply in the case of our author. The most naive opinion is that according to which a number is something like a heap, a swarm in which the things are contained lock, stock and barrel. Next comes the conception of a number as a property of a heap, aggregate, of whatever else one might call it. Thereby one feels the need for cleansing the objects of their particularities. The present attempt belongs to those which undertake this cleansing in the psychological wash-tub. This offers the advantage that in it, things acquire a most peculiar suppleness, no longer have as hard a spatial impact on each other and lose many bothersome particularities and differences. The mixture of psychology and logic that is now so popular provides good suds for this purpose. First of all, everything becomes presentation. The references of words are presentations. In the case of the word "number," for example, the aim is to exhibit the appropriate presentation and to describe its genesis and composition. Objects are presentations. Thus J. St. Mill, with the approval of the author, lets objects (whether physical or mental) enter into a state of consciousness and become constituents of this state (p. 70). But might not the moon, for example, be somewhat hard to digest for a state of consciousness? Since everything is now presentation, we can easily change the objects by now paying attention, now not. The latter is especially effective. We pay less attention to a property and it disappears. By this, we let one characteristic after another disappear, we obtain concepts that are increasingly more abstract. Therefore concepts, too, are presentations; only, they are less complete than objects; they still have those properties of objects which we have not abstracted. Inattention is an exceedingly effective logical power; whence, presumably, the absent-mindedness of scholars. For example, let us suppose that in front of us there are sitting side by side a black and a white cat. We disregard their colour : they become colorless but are still sitting side by side. We disregard their posture : they are no longer sitting, without, however, having assumed a different posture; but each one is still at its place. We disregard their location : they are without location, but still remain quite distinct. Thus from each one we have perhaps derived a general concept of a cat. Continued application of this process turns each object into a less and less substantial wraith. From each object we finally derive something which is completely without restrictions on its content; but the something derived from the one object nevertheless does differ from that derived from the other object, although it is not easy to say how. But wait! This last transition to a something does seem to be more difficult after all; at least the author talks (p. 86) about reflection on the mental act of presentation. But be that as it may, the result, at any rate, is the one just indicated. While in my opinion the bringing of an object under a concept is merely the recognition of a relation which previously already obtained, in the present case objects are essentially changed by this process, so that objects brought under the same concept become similar to one another. Perhaps the matter is to be understood thus, that for every object there arises a new presentation in which all determinations which do not occur in the concept are lacking. Hereby the difference between presentation and concept, between presenting and thinking, is blurred. Everything is shunted off into the subjective. But it is precisely because the boundary between the subjective and the objective is blurred, that conversely the subjective also acquires the appearance of the objective. For example, one talks of this or that presentation as if, separated from the presenter, it would let itself be observed in public. And yet, no-one has someone else's presentation but only his own, and no-one knows how far his presentation — e.g. that of red — agrees with that of someone else; for the peculiarity of the presentation which I associate with the word "red," I cannot state (so as to be able to compare it). One would have to have the presentations of the one as well as that of the other combined in one and the same consciousness; and one would have to be sure that they had not changed in the transfer. With thoughts, it is quite different : one and the same thought can be grasped by many people. The components of a thought, and even more so the things themselves, must be distinguished from the presentations which in the soul accompany the grasping of a thought and which someone has about these things. In combining under the word "presentation" both what is subjective and what is objective, one blurs the boundary between the two in such a way that now a presentation in the proper sense of the word is treated like something objective, and now something objective is treated like a presentation. Thus in the case of our author, totality (set, multiplicity) appears now as a presentation (pp. 15, 17, 24, 82), now as something objective (pp. 10, 11, 235). But isn't it really a very harmless pleasantry to call, for example, the moon a presentation? It is — as long as one does not imagine that one can change it as one likes, or produce it by psychological means. But this is all too easily the result.

Given the psychologico-logical mode of thought just characterized, it is easy to understand how the author judges about definitions. An example from elementary geometry may illustrate this. There, one usually gives this definition : "A right angle is an angle which is equal to its adjacent angle." The author would probably say to this, "The presentation of right-angledness is a simple one; hence it is a completely misguided undertaking to want to give a definition of it. In our presentation of right-angledness, there is nothing of the relation to another adjacent angle. True enough; the concepts 'right angle' and 'angle which is equal to its adjacent angle' have the same extension; but it is not true that they have the same content. Instead of the content, it is the extension of the concept that has been defined. If the definition were correct, then every assertion of right-angledness, instead of applying to the concretely present pair of lines as such, would always apply to its relation to another pair of lines. All I can admit is (p. 114) that in this equality with the adjacent angle we have a necessary and sufficient condition for right-angledness." The author judges in a similar way about the definition of equinumerosity by means of the concept of univocal one-one correlation. "The simplest criterion for sameness of number is just that the same number results when counting the sets to be compared." (p. 115). Of course! The simplest way of testing whether or not something is a right angle is to use a protractor. The author forgets that this counting itself rests on a univocal one-one correlation, namely that between the numerals 1 to n and the objects of the set. Each of the two sets is to be counted. In this way, the situation is made more difficult than when we consider a relation which correlates the objects of the two sets with one another without numerals as intermediaries.

If words and combinations of words refer to presentations, then for any two of these only two cases are possible : either they designate the same presentation, or they designate different ones. In the first case, equating them by means of a definition is useless, "an obvious circle"; in the other, it is false. These are also the objections one of which the author raises regularly. Neither can a definition dissect the sense, for the dissected sense simply is not the original one. In the case of the word to be explained, either I already think clearly everything which I think in the case of the definiens — in which case we have the "obvious circle" — or the definiens has a more completely articulated sense — in which case I do not think the same thing in its case as I do in the case of the one to be explained : the definition is false. One would think that the definition would be unobjectionable at least in the case where the word to be explained does not yet have a sense, or where it is expressly asked that the sense be considered non-existent, so that the word acquires a sense only through this definition. But even in the latter case (p. 107), the author confutes the definition by reminding us of the distinctness of the presentations. Accordingly, in order to avoid all objections, one would probably have to create a new root-word and form a word out of it. A split here manifests itself between psychological logicians and mathematicians. The former are concerned with the sense of the words and with the presentations, which they do not distinguish from the sense; the latter, however, are concerned with the matter itself, with the reference of the words.[2] The reproach that it is not the concept but its extension which is being defined, really applies to all the definitions of mathematics. So far as the mathematician is concerned, the definition of a conic section as the line of intersection of a plane with a cone is no more and no less correct than that as a plane whose equation is given in Cartesian co-ordinates of the second degree. Which of these two — or even of the other — definitions is selected depends entirely on the pragmatics of the situation, although these expressions neither have the same sense nor evoke the same presentations. By this I do not mean that a concept and the extension of a concept are one and the same; rather, coincidence of extension is a necessary and sufficient condition for the fact that between the concepts there obtains that relation which corresponds to that of sameness in the case of objects.[3] I here note that when I use the word "same" without further addition, I am using it in the sense of "not different," "coinciding," "identical." Psychological logicians lack all understanding of sameness, just as they lack all understanding of definitions. This relation cannot help but remain completely puzzling to them; for if words always designated presentations, one could never say, "A is the same as B." For to be able to do that, one would already have to

---

[2] On this point please compare my essay "On Sense and Reference" in this journal.

[3] For strictly speaking, the relation does not obtain in the case of concepts. Compare my essay "On Concept and Object" in *Vierteljahrsschrift für wiss. Philosophie* (vol. 16, 1892, pp. 192-205; Trs.)

distinguish A from B, and then these would simply be different presenta-tions. All the same, I do agree with the author in this, that Leibniz's explanation "Eadem sunt quorum unum potest substitui alteri salva veri-tate" does not deserve to be called a definition, although I hold this for a different reason. Since every definition is an equation, one cannot define equality itself. One could call Leibniz's explanation a principle which expresses the nature of the sameness-relation; and as such it is of fundamental importance. I am unable to acquire a taste for the author's explanation that (p. 108) "We simply say of any contents whatever that they are the same as one another, if there obtains sameness in the ... characteristics which at the moment constitute the centre of interest."

Let us now go into details! According to the author a number-statement refers to the totality (the set, multiplicity) of objects counted (p. 158). Such a totality finds its wholly appropriate expression in the conjunction "and." Accordingly, one should expect that all number-statements have the form "A and B and C and ... Q is n," or at least that they could be brought into such a form. But what is it that we get exactly to know through the proposition "Berlin and Dresden and Munich are three" or — and this is supposed to be the same thing — through "Berlin and Dresden and Munich are something and something and something?" Who would want to go to the trouble of asking, merely to receive such an answer? It is not even supposed to be said by this that Berlin is distinct from Dresden, the latter from Munich, and Munich from Berlin. In fact, in the second form at least there is contained neither the difference of Berlin from Dresden nor even their sameness. Surely it is peculiar that this form of number-predica-tion almost never occurs in every-day life and that when it does occur, it is not intended as a statement of number. I find that there are really only two cases in which it is used : in the first case, together with the numbered word "two," to express difference — "Rapeseed and rape are two (different things)" — in the other, together with the number-word "one" to express sameness — "I and the Father are one" —. This last example is particularly disastrous, for according to the author it should read, "are something and something" or "are two." In reality we do not ask "How many are Caesar and Pompei and London and Edinburgh?" or "How many are Great Britain and Ireland?" although I am curious as to what the author would answer to this. Instead, one asks, for example, "How many moons does Mars have?" or "What is the number of moons of Mars?" And from the answer "The number of moons of Mars is two" one gets to know something which is worth asking about. Thus we see that in the question as well as in the answer, there occurs a concept-word or a compound designation of a concept, rather than the "and" demanded by the author. How does the latter extricate himself from this difficulty? He says that the number belongs to the extension of the concept, i.e. to the totality. "It is only indirectly that one can perhaps say that the concept has the property that the number ... belongs to its extension" (p. 189). Herewith everything I maintain has really been admitted : In a number-statement, something is predicated of a concept. I am not going to argue over whether the assertion applies directly to a concept and indirectly to its extension, or indirectly to the concept and directly to its extension; for given the one, the other also obtains. This much is certain, that neither the extension of a concept nor a totality are designated directly, but only by a concept. Now if the author used the phrase "extension of a concept" in the same sense as I, then our opinions about the sense of a statement of number would scarcely differ. This, of course, is not the case; for the extension of a concept is not a totality in the author's sense. A concept under which there falls only one object has just as determinate an extension as a concept under which there falls no object or a concept under which there fall infinitely many objects — where according to Mr. Husserl, there is no totality in any of these cases. The sense of the words "extension of the concept moon of Mars" is other than the sense of the words "Deimos and Phobos"; and if the proposition "The number of Deimos and Phobos is two" contains a thought at all, at any rate it contains one which differs from that of the proposition "The number of the moons of Mars is two." Now, since one never uses a proposition of the latter form to make a statement of number, the author has missed the sense of such a statement.

Let us now consider the ostensible genesis of a totality somewhat more closely (pp. 77ff.). I must confess that I have been unsuccessful in my attempt to form a totality in accordance with the instructions of the author. In the case of collective connections, the contents are merely supposed to be thought or presented together, without any relation or connection whatever being presented between them (p. 79). I am unable to do this. I cannot simultaneously represent to myself redness, the Moon and Napoleon, without presenting these to myself as connected; e.g. the redness of a burning village against which stands out the figure of Napoleon, illuminated by the Moon on the right. Whatever is simultaneously present to me, I present to myself as a whole; and I cannot disregard the connection without losing the whole. I suspect that in my soul there just isn't anything which the author calls " totality," "set," "multiplicity"; no presentation of parts whose union is not presented with them, although it does exist. Therefore, it is not at all astonishing that Dr. Husserl himself later (p. 242) says of a set that it contains a configurative moment which characterizes it as a whole, as an organization. He talks of series (p. 235), swarms, chains, heaps as of peculiar kinds of sets. And no union is supposed to be noticeable in the presentation of a swarm? Or is this union present over and above the collective connection? In which case it would be irrelevant so far as the totality is concerned, and the "configurative moment" could not serve to distinguish kinds of sets. How does the author come to hold his opinion? Probably because he is looking for certain presentations as the references of words and word-complexes. Thus there ought to correspond a presentational whole even to the word-complex "redness and the Moon and Napoleon"; and since the mere "and" allegedly does not express a presentable relation or union at all, neither ought one to be presented. Add to this the following. If the union of the parts were also presented, almost all of our presentations would be totalities; e.g., that of a house as well as that of a swarm or heap. And hereby, surely, one notices only too easily that a number as a property of a house or of the presentation of a house, would be absurd.

The author himself finds a difficulty in the abstraction which yields the general concept of totality (p. 84). "One must abstract completely ... from the particularities of the individual contents collected together, at the same time, however, retaining their connection. This seems to involve a difficulty, if not a psychological impossibility. If we take this abstraction seriously, then of course the collective connection, rather than remaining behind as a conceptual extract, also disappears along with the particular contents. The solution lies at hand. To abstract from something merely means : not paying any particular attention to it."

The core of this exposition clearly lies in the word "particular." Inattention is a very strong lye which must not be applied in too concentrated a form, so as not to dissolve everything; but neither ought it to be used in too diluted a form, so that it may produce a sufficient change. Everything, then, depends on the proper degree of dilution, which is difficult to hit. I, at least, did not succeed in doing so.

Since in the end, the author himself really does admit that I am right after all — that in a number-statement there is contained an assertion about a concept — I need not consider his counter-arguments in more detail. I only want to remark that he evidently has not grasped my distinction between a characteristic and a property. Given his logico-psychological mode of understanding, this is of course not surprising. Thus he comes to foist on me the opinion that what is at issue in the case of number-statements is a determination, the definition of a concept (p. 185). Nothing was farther from my mind.

Three reefs spell danger for naive, and particularly for psychological, views of the nature of numbers. The first lies in the question, how the sameness of the units is to be reconciled with their distinguishability. The second consists in the numbers zero and one; and the third, in the large numbers. Let us ask, how the author seeks to circumnavigate these reefs! In the case of the first, he adduces (p. 156) my words, "If we want to let a number arise by collecting different objects, then we obtain a heap in which the objects are contained with just those properties in which they differ; and this is not the number. On the other hand, if we want to form a number by collecting what is the same, the latter will always coalesce into one and we shall never arrive at a multiplicity." It is clear that I have used the word "same" in the sense of "not different." Therefore the author's charge that I confuse sameness with identity, does not apply. Mr. Husserl tries to blunt this antithesis by means of his hazy sameness: "In a certain respect, sameness does obtain; in another difference. ... A difficulty, or better, an impossibility would obtain only if the expression 'collection of what is the same' (which is intended to describe the genesis of a number) demanded absolute sameness, as Frege mistakenly assumes" (pp. 164, 166). Well, if the sameness is not absolute, then the objects will differ in one or the other of the properties with which they enter into combination. Now with this, compare the following: "The sameness of the units as it results from our psychological theory, is obviously an absolute one. Indeed, already the mere thought of an approximation is absurd, for what is at stake is the sameness of the contents insofar as they are contents" (p. 168). According to the author, a number consists of units (p. 149). He here understands by "unit" a "member of a concrete multiplicity insofar as number-abstraction is applied to the latter" or "a counted object as such." If we consider all of this together, we shall be hard pressed to get clear about the author's opinion. In the beginning, the objects are evidently distinct; then, by means of abstraction, they become absolutely the same with respect to one another, but for all that, this absolute sameness is supposed to obtain only insofar as they are contents. I should think that this sameness is very far indeed removed from being absolute. But be that as it may, the number consists of these units which are absolutely the same; and now there enters that impossibility which the author himself emphasizes. After all, one must assume that this abstraction, this bringing under the concept of something, effects a change; that the objects which are thought through the medium of this concept — these very units which are absolutely the same — are distinct from the original objects, for otherwise they would resemble one another no more than they did at the beginning and this abstraction would be useless. We must assume that it is only through being brought under the concept of a something that these units which are absolutely the same arise, whether they appear through a metamorphosis out of distinct objects or whether they appear in addition to these as new entities. Therefore one would think that in addition to the remaining objects there are also units, sets of units over and above sets of apples. This however, the author most emphatically denies (p. 139). Number-abstraction simply has the wonderful and very fruitful property of making things absolutely the same as one another without altering them. Something like this is possible only in the psychological wash-tub. If the author really has avoided this first reef, then surely he has done so more by way of magic than by way of science.

Furthermore, Mr. Husserl adduces (p. 156) my words, "If we designate each of the objects to be counted by 1, this is a mistake because what differs receives the same sign. If we supply the 1 with differentiating strokes, it becomes useless for arithmetic." To this he makes the following comment (p. 165), "However we commit this mistake with each application of a general name. When we call Tom, Dick, etc., each a human being, this is the same case as that of the 'faulty notation' in virtue of which when counting, we write 1 for each object to be counted." If we did designate Tom by "human being" and Dick likewise, we should indeed be committing that mistake. Fortunately, we do not do that. When we call Tom a human being, we are thereby saying that Tom falls under the concept human being; but we neither write nor say "human being" instead of "Tom." What would correspond to the proposition "Tom is a human being" would be, "Tom is a 1". If we call A, B in the sense of assigning the proper name B to A, then of course everywhere we say "A" we can say "B"; but then we may not give this very name "B" to still another object. This unfortunate expression, "common name," is undoubtedly the cause of this confusion. This so-called common name — better called concept-word — has nothing directly to do with objects but refers to a concept. And perhaps objects do fall under this concept, although it may also be empty without the concept-word referring any less because of this. I have already explained this sufficiently in § 47 of my *Foundations of Arithmetic*. Surely it is obvious that anyone using the proposition "All human beings are mortal" does not want to say anything about a certain chief Akpanya, of whom he has perhaps never even heard.

According to the author, $5+5=10$ means the same thing as "a set (any one, whatever it may be) falling under the concept five, and an other (why other?) set falling under the same concept yield, when combined, a set falling under the concept 10" (p. 202). To illustrate this to ourselves, we are to consider for example the fingers of the right hand as the first set, and a fountain-pen and the fingers of the right hand excluding the thumb as the other. Is it possible that the author has here had Mr. Biermann as a teacher? [4]

We now proceed to the second reef, which consists in the numbers zero and one. The first way out is easily found. One says, "They aren't numbers at all." But now there arises the question, What, then, are they? The author says, negative answers to the question "How many?" (p. 144). Answers like "Never" to the question "When?" "Not-many or 'no multiplicity' is not a particularization of manyness." Perhaps someone might even hit upon the idea that two is not yet a multiplicity but merely twoness (duality as opposed to multiplicity); that none, one and two, therefore, are the three negative answers to the question "How many?" In corroboration of this he would perhaps adduce the fact that two is the only even prime number. It is really asking a lot to want us to consider "one" a negative answer to the question "How many moons does the Earth have?" In the case of zero, the matter has more appearance of being correct. Exactly how are the answers "Never," "Nowhere," "Nothing" to the questions "When?", "Where?", "What?" to be understood? Obviously not as proper answers, but rather as refusals to answer, couched in the form of an answer. One says "I cannot give you a time, a place or an object of the kind wanted because there is none." According to this, an analogous reply to the question "How many?" would be "I cannot tell you such a number because there isn't one." Given my conception of the sense of a number-statement, this is what I should reply for example to the question, "How many are Great Britain and Ireland?" I cannot regard either the answer "One" or the answer "Zero" as answers to the question "How many?" as synonymous with "There is no such number." How is it that there are here two negative replies? If to the question, "Who is Romulus's predecessor on the throne of Rome?" one answers, "No one," then one herewith denies that someone preceded Romulus. Therefore the negation belongs to the predicate, and its fusion with the grammatical subject — whence arises the appearance that "No one" designates a human being just as much as does "Romulus" — is logically incorrect. As is well known, the possibility of certain sophisms rests on this. One would think that such dangers also threaten with zero and one; but these are used just as are all other numbers, without special precautionary measures. Whence this difference? "Zero" is just as little a negative

---

[4] Otto Biermann, Professor of Mathematics at the Deut. Techn. Hochsch. in Brünn; student of Weierstrass. — Trans.

answer to the question "What is the number of Romulus's predecessors on the throne of Rome?" as "Two" would be. One does not thereby deny that there is such a number; rather, one names it. The author says, "To every unit there applies the number one" (p. 170) (presumably as a negative property!), and calls zero and one, concepts (p. 145). Given this, one assumes that unit and one are concepts having the same extension. Or is it not the case that every one is a unit? Wherein do the thoughts of the two propositions, "Tom is one" and "Tom is a unit" differ? To which one, then, does the number zero apply? Unnoticed and in concert with the author, we have again said "the number one!" There are here still many other puzzles left unresolved by the author, and I cannot admit that he has successfully avoided this reef.

We come to the third reef: the large numbers. If numbers are presentations, then the limited nature of our powers of presentation must also carry along with it a limitation of the domain of numbers. Thus, the author states, "It is only under extremely favourable circumstances that we can still have a real presentation of a concrete multiplicity of about a dozen elements" (p. 214). Now, at this point he introduces figurative or symbolic presentations as means of giving information, and the whole second part deals with these. Nevertheless, the author is forced to admit that "Naturally, not even now, when dealing with pure signs, are we completely unbounded; but we no longer feel these bounds..." (p. 274). The finitude of the domain of numbers is thereby admitted. If numbers are presentations which I or someone else must form, then there cannot be infinitely many numbers; and no symbolism can remove this limitation. According to the author (p. 215), a symbolic presentation is a presentation by means of signs which uniquely characterize what is to be presented. "For example, we have a real presentation of the external appearance of a house when we are actually looking at it; we have a symbolic presentation, when someone is giving us the indirect characteristic: the corner-house on such-and-such sides of such-and-such streets." This refers to the case where something objective is present of which I am to make a presentation to myself; and for that very reason, this explanation does not fit our case at all well. To be sure, one cannot help but assume that according to the author, numbers are presentations: results of mental processes or activities (pp. 24, 46). But where is what is objective: that of which a number is a presentation? What is it that here corresponds to the house in the example above? And yet it is precisely this object that is the connecting link between a real and a symbolic presentation; it is this that justifies our saying that the symbolic presentation appertains to the real one, and it is this that is uniquely characterized by the signs when we have a symbolic presentation. The confusion of the subjective with the objective, the fact that no clear distinction is ever made between expressions like "Moon" and "presentation of the Moon", all this diffuses such an impenetrable fog that the attempt to achieve clarity becomes hopeless. I can only say that I have acquired the following impression of the author's opinion : If I want to have a symbolic presentation where I do not have a real one, I *idealize* (p. 251) my powers of presentation; i.e., I imagine or present to myself that I have a presentation which in fact I neither have nor can have; and what I thus imagine would be my symbolic presentation. So, for example, I can form a symbolic presentation by means of the sign "15," by presenting to myself that I am presenting to myself a set consisting of the elements of a set to which the number 10 belongs and the elements of a set to which the number 5 belongs, and then apply to this the procedure which according to the author produces the appropriate number. The presentations of the signs are incorporated into the symbolic presentations. "Here the sensible signs are not mere companions of the concepts, in the manner of linguistic signs. They participate in our symbolic constructions in a much more prominent manner — so much so, that they finally predominate over almost everything else" (p. 273, similarly p. 264). Herewith the author approaches very closely the opinions of Helmholtz and Kronecker. If this were correct, the numbers would change whenever we change the signs. We should have completely different numbers from the ancient Greeks and Romans. But would these symbolic presentations also have the properties which the real ones are supposed to have? Just as little, I think, as my presentation of a green meadow is green. Now, the author does of course note (p. 217) that a real presentation and a symbolic one belonging to it stand in a relation of logical equivalence. "Two concepts are logically equivalent if every object of the one is also an object of the other, and *vice versa.*" He explains that it is on the basis of this, that symbolic presentations can "do proxy for" the corresponding real ones. Here the confusion of presentation and concept interferes with our understanding. If we confine ourselves to the example of the corner-house, we may presume that the "equivalence" is here supposed to consist in the fact that my real presentation and the symbolic one are referred to the same object (that very corner-house). Now, when can the latter "do proxy for" the former? Presumably, when I am talking about the corner-house itself, not about my presentation. In reading this book, I have been able to see how very difficult it is for the sun of truth to penetrate the fog which arises out of the confusion of psychology and logic. Happily, we here see the beginnings of such a penetration. It becomes overwhelmingly evident that our presentations matter very little here, but that instead it is the very thing of which we seek to make presentations to ourselves that is the subject of our concern, and that our assertions are about it. And expressions to this effect occur several times in the second part; which is the more remarkable, the less it really agrees with the author's whole mode of thought. We read (p. 214, bottom), "Even if we have not *really* given the concepts, at least we have given them in a symbolic way." Here, concepts appear as something objective, and the difference between real and symbolic concepts refers only to the way in which they are given. There is talk of *species* of the concept of number which are not accessible to us in any real sense (p. 265), and of *real* numbers, of numbers in themselves which are inaccessible to us in general (p. 295). We read (p. 254) about symbolic formations of numbers which belong to one and the same real number. Given the opinion of the author, one should expect "non-existent" instead of "real"; for if a number were a real presentation, in this case there would not be one. What are these "numbers in themselves" (p. 294), these "real numbers" if not objective numbers which are independent of our thinking; which exist even when they are not accessible to us (p. 296)? The author says (p. 295), "Any number whatever can be uniquely characterized... by means of diverse relations to other numbers, and each such characteristic provides a new symbolic presentation of this very number." Here the objective number "in itself" clearly plays the role of the corner-house in our example of the latter. It is not my presentation that is the number; rather, I form one or several presentations of one and the same number, or a least I try to do so. A pity that the author does not try to keep the expressions "A" and "presentation of A" clearly distinct. But if my presentation of a number is not that number itself, then the ground is herewith cut out from under the psychological mode of consideration insofar as the latter's aim is to investigate the nature of numbers. If I want to investigate a presentation, I have to keep it as unchanged as possible — which, of course, is difficult to do. On the other hand, if I want to investigate something objective, my presentations will have to conform as much as possible to the matter at hand, to the results of this investigation; in general, then, they have to change. It makes a tremendous difference to the mode of investigation whether the number-presentation is itself the object of the investigation, or whether it is merely a presentation of the real object. The author's procedure fits only the first case, whereas the last passages adduced above can only be interpreted as instances of the second. If a geographer were to read a work on oceanography in which the origin of the seas were explained psychologically, he would undoubtedly receive the impression that the very point at issue had been missed in a very peculiar way. I have the same impression of the present work. To be sure, the sea is something real and a number is not; but this does not prevent it from being something objective; and that is the important thing.

In reading this work, I was able to gauge the devastation caused by the influx of psychology into logic; and I have here made it my task to present this damage in a clear light. The mistakes which I thought it my duty to show reflect less upon the author than they are the result of a widespread philosophical disease. My own, radically different, position makes it difficult for me to do justice to his achievements, which I presume to lie in the area of psychology; and I should like to direct the attention of psychologists especially to Chapter XI, where the possibility of momentary conceptions of sets is discussed. But I consider myself insufficiently qualified to pass judgement in that area.

HUSSERL AND FREGE:
A NEW LOOK AT THEIR RELATIONSHIP*

by

J. N. MOHANTY

(New York)

Husserl's explicit rejection of psychologism as a theory of the origin of the logico-mathematical entities and his advocacy of a conception of pure logic as a science of objective meanings were first expounded in the *Prolegomena to Pure Logic* (1900), and Husserl tells us that the *Prolegomena*, in its essentials, is a reworking of lectures he had given at Halle in the year 1896.[1] Føllesdal, in his careful study of the relation between Frege and Husserl during these years, asks the question, at what point of time between 1890 (the year of publication of the *Philosophie der Arithmetik*) and 1896 did this change in Husserl's mode of thinking take place?[2] The papers published during 1891-1893 do not, according to Føllesdal, bear testimony to any such change. In the paper "Psychologische Studien zur Elementaren Logik" of the year 1894, Husserl is still found to believe that the foundations of logic can be clarified with the help of psychology. Accordingly, the change must have occurred between the years 1894 and 1896. Frege's famed review of the *Philosophie der Arithmetik* appeared in the year 1894. Føllesdal therefore conjectures that it is Frege's review which must have led Husserl to a complete revision of his prior mode of thinking.[3] This view about the Frege-Husserl relationship is shared by many writers. A recent writer even speaks of Husserl's "traumatic encounter with Frege."[4]

In this paper I wish to argue that the basic change in Husserl's mode of

---

* First appeared in *Research in Phenomenology*, V, 1975. Reprinted here with permission. J. N. M.

[1] Husserl, E. *Logical Investigations*, E. tr. by J. N. Findlay, Vol. I, New York : Humanities Press, 1970, p. 47.

[2] Føllesdal, D. *Husserl und Frege*, Oslo : I Kommisjon Hos H. Aschehoug & Co., 1958, p. 23.

[3] *Ibid.*, p. 25.

[4] Solomon, R. C., "Sense and Essence : Frege and Husserl," *International Philosophical Quarterly*, 10, 1970, p. 380.

thinking which by itself could have led to the *Prolegomena* conception of pure logic had already taken place by 1891. This change may be discerned in Husserl's review of Schröder's *Vorlesungen über die Algebra der Logik*.[5] It also underlies the program of *Inhaltslogik* worked out in "Der Folgerungs-kalkül und die Inhaltslogik" of the same year.[6] If pure logic is defined in the *Prolegomena* in terms of the concept of ideal objective meanings,[7] then already the 1891 review of Schröder's work contains this concept. If the major burden of Frege's 1894 review of the *Philosophie der Arithmetik* is the lack of distinction, in that work, between the subjective and the objective,[8] between *Vorstellung* and *Begriff* and between both and the object, then Husserl already had come to distinguish between *Vorstellung*, meaning and object in his 1891 review. If this be so, then another historical judgement — connected with the above — needs to be revised. It has been held by many authors that Husserl's distinction, in the *Logische Untersuchungen*, between meaning and object of an expression is Fregean in origin. Thus, for example, Hubert Dreyfus writes : "Husserl simply accepted and applied Frege's distinctions... The only change Husserl made in Frege's analysis was terminological." [9] Now, if Husserl's review of Schröder already contains that distinction, then it surely antedates the publication of Frege's celebrated paper "Über Sinn und Bedeutung" of 1892, and Husserl must have arrived at it independently of Frege.

---

[5] Published in *Göttingische gelehrte Anzeigen*, 1, 1891, pp. 243-287.

[6] Published in *Vierteljahrsschrift für wissenschaftliche Philosophie*, 15, 1891, pp. 168-189, 351-356.

[7] *Logical Investigations*, Vol. I, p. 322.

[8] Thus writes Frege : "First of all, everything becomes presentation. The references of words are presentations ... Objects are presentations ... concepts, too, are presentations." A little later on : "Everything is shunted off into the subjective." (Frege, G., "Review of Dr. E. Husserl's *Philosophy of Arithmetic*" E. tr. by E. E. W. Kluge, *Mind*, LXXXI, 1972, pp. 321-337; esp. 323-324.)

[9] Embree, Lester E., *Life-World and Consciousness, Essays for Aron Gurwitsch*, Evanston : Northwestern University Press, 1972, pp. 139-140 (in H. Dreyfus, "The Perceptual Noema : Gurwitsch's Crucial Contribution"). In a footnote on p. 140, Dreyfus rejects Gurwitsch's claim that Husserl discovered the distinction between real mental states and ideal meanings and refers to "Husserl's explicit attribution of this distinction to Frege" in the *Logical Investigations*, I (Findlay edition), p. 292. This reference however is misleading. First, this is not the place where Husserl first introduces the distinction. The distinction is introduced, first, in the 1891 Schröder review as this paper will argue. Secondly, at this place, Husserl is only referring to Frege's different terminology.

I

Referring to Schröder's distinction between univocal and equivocal names, Husserl writes :

... he lacks the true concept of the meaning of a name. That requirement of univocity is also expressed in the form : "The name shall be of a ... constant meaning." (48) However, according to the relevant discussions on pages 47-48, the author identifies the meaning of the name with the representation (*Vorstellung*) of the object named by the name, from which the striking consequence follows, to be sure, that all common names are equivocal. It is not as if the author had overlooked the distinction between equivocal and common names — and besides, who could overlook it! But to see a distinction and to apprehend its essence are two different things. Moreover, he uses the term "meaning" (*Bedeutung*) itself equivocally, and that in an already intolerable degree. In the above quotation, in spite of mutually opposed and false explanations, what is intended is the ordinary sense. On another occasion, however, what is actually meant is the object named by the name; how otherwise, e.g., could, in verbal contradiction with the above mentioned requirement, the common names be as such characterized as being such that "several meanings are true of them with the same right and justification!" (69) And even that is not enough; the class corresponding to the common name is also called its meaning (69 fn.). It is therefore understandable that the author is not able to formulate the essence of equivocation precisely... It is further connected with unclarity in the concept of meaning that Schröder regards names such as "round square" as meaningless (*unsinnige*) and sets them apart from univocal and equivocal names. Obviously he confuses here between two different questions : (1) whether there belongs to a name a meaning (*ein* "*Sinn*"); and (2) whether an object corresponding to a name exists or not.[10]

This paragraph clearly shows that Husserl did distinguish, already in 1891, between :

    (1) the sense or meaning of a term (for which he is using both '*Bedeutung*' and '*Sinn*', though in the *Logische Untersuchungen* he will prefer '*Bedeutung*'),

    (2) the object (*Gegenstand*) which the name may designate in case the object exists,

and (3) the representation (*Vorstellung*) of such an object.

Representations may vary, but the meaning or *Sinn* may remain the same. Further, there may be no object that is designated, and yet a name may have meaning. Even when there are objects that are designated, the multiplicity of objects does not imply multiplicity of meanings. He therefore has a clear distinction between *Vorstellung*, *Gegenstand* and *Bedeutung* or *Sinn*.

It is true that these remarks do not contain the thesis of the *ideal* objec-

---

[10] *Göttingische gelehrte Anzeigen*, I, 1891, p. 250.

tivity of meanings, but they certainly do not confuse meaning with *Vorstellung* and therefore testify to an awareness of the *objectivity* of meanings as contrasted with the subjectivity of the *Vorstellungen.*

Could Husserl have derived this threefold distinction from any of Frege's earlier writings? If anywhere in Frege's writings before 1891, we are to look for it in *Die Grundlagen der Arithmetik* (1884). But Frege writes in his letter to Husserl of May 24, 1891 that he had not yet in the *Grundlagen* drawn the distinction between meaning and reference.[11] It is unlikely then that Husserl took it from him. It is more likely then that both arrived at the distinction independently as Husserl writes back to Frege : "I also notice, that in spite of essential points of divergence, our points of view have many things in common. Many observations which forced themselves on me, I find had been expressed by you many years earlier." That seems in principle to be a true account of their relationship at this stage, though it would seem that on this point, i.e. the distinction between meaning and reference, Husserl and Frege must have arrived at it about the same time and independently of each other.

What is of importance for our present purpose, however, is that Husserl's overcoming of subjectivism in favor of an objective theory of meaning and the consequent theory of logic is already foreshadowed in the 1891 review of Schröder's work and three years prior to Frege's review of the *Philosophie der Arithmetik.* The other 1891 paper, i.e. the one on *Inhaltslogik* more clearly brings this out.

II

Amongst the major theses which Husserl puts forward, in so far as his conception of logic at this point is concerned, we may mention the following :

(1) A calculus quâ calculus is not a language : "the two concepts are fundamentally different. Language is not a method of systematic-symbolic inference, calculus is not a method of systematic-symbolic expression of psychic phenomena."[12]

---

[11] Thiel considers the terminology of 'sense' and 'reference' obligatory for all Frege works after 1890. Cp. Christian Thiel, *Sense and Reference in Frege's Logic*, Dordrecht-Holland : D. Reidel, 1968, p. 44. Angelelli finds the distinction already in the *Begriffsschrift* ("only the famous terminology ... is lacking here") and in the *Grundlagen*, § 67. Cp. Ignacio Angelelli, *Studies on Gottlob Frege and Traditional Philosophy*, Dordrecht-Holland : D. Reidel, 1967.

[12] *Göt. gel. Anz.*, I, 1891, pp. 258-259.

(2) A logic quâ logic is not a calculus. A calculus is a technic, a *Zeichentechnik*. Logic is concerned, not with mere signs, but with conceptual contents.[13]

(3) Deductive logic is not the same as a technic of inference, nor is it exhausted by a theory of inference. There are deductive operations other than inferring. A deductive science does not consist only in inferences. It may involve e.g. the operation 'computing' (*Rechnen*) which is not inferring.[14]

(4) It is not true that only an extensional calculus of classes is possible. A calculus of conceptual contents, or intentions, is also possible.[15]

(5) An *autonomous* extensional logic of classes is not possible, for every extensional judgement (*Umfangsurteil*) is, in truth, an intensional judgement (*Inhaltsurteil*). The concept of class presupposes the concepts of 'conceptual content' and 'object of a concept.' [16]

(6) Every judgement has two aspects : logical content and 'algorithmic content.' [17] The logical content is the judged content (*Urteilsgehalt*) i.e. that which it states (*das, was sie behauptet*). When a categorical judgement is reduced to relation of subsumption amongst classes, this brings out its algorithmic content. The two are equivalent, but not always identical. They are identical when the judgement is a judgement about classes.

(7) A judgement by itself is directed not towards classes or conceptual contents, but towards objects of concepts (*Begriffsgegenstände*).[18]

(8) Geometrical thinking is not operation with signs or figures. The signs are mere 'supports' for the 'conception of the truly intended operations with concepts and with respective objects of those concepts.' [19]

Most of these theses are retained, with modifications and shifts in emphasis no doubt, in the *Prolegomena* and the *Investigations*. Pure logic is the science of meanings. "Everything that is logical falls under the two correlated categories of meaning and object." [20] Algorithmic methods spare us genuine deductive mental work by "artificially arranged mechanical operations on sensible signs" [21] and "their sense and justification depend on validatory thought." [22] Certainly, Husserl has now,

[13] *Ibid.*, p. 247.
[14] *Op. cit.*, p. 246.
[15] *Vierteljahrsschrift f. wiss. Phil.*, 15, 1891, pp. 169, 171.
[16] *Gött. gel. Anz.*, I, 1891, p. 257.
[17] *Ibid.*, p. 262.
[18] *Viert. f. wiss. Phil.*, 15, 1891, p. 178.
[19] *Gött. gel. Anz.*, I, 1891, p. 249.
[20] *Logical Investigations*, I, pp. 322-325.
[21] *Ibid.*, p. 69.
[22] *Ibid.*, p. 69.

in the *Prolegomena*, much more sympathetic understanding of the "mathematicising theories of logic" and he has come to regard the mathematical form of treatment as the only scientific one which alone offers us "systematic closure and completeness." [23] But he is still cautioning us that "the mathematician is not really the pure theoretician, but only the ingenious technician, the constructor, as it were, who looking merely to formal interconnections, builds up his theory like a technical work of art." [24] But this note of warning is mollified by the assurance that what makes science possible is not essential insight but "scientific instinct and method," [25] and that philosophical investigation should not meddle in the work of the specialist but should seek to "achieve insight in regard to the sense and essence of his achievements as regards method and manner." [26] The thesis that extension of a concept presupposes its intension is developed in the Second Investigation, though there is more explicit emphasis on the ideal objectivity of meanings and there is the talk of the *Inhalt* as a *species*.

III

Husserl sent copies of his 1891 papers to Frege. We know of this from the correspondence between the two men. It is worthwhile therefore to find out, what Frege's responses to the Husserl papers were. In his letter of May 24, 1891, after acknowledging receipt of Husserl's *Philosophie der Arithmetik* and the papers on Schröder and *Inhaltslogik*, Frege emphasises that the two have many ideas in common, and renews his own decision to write down his own thoughts on Schröder's book.[27] He agrees with some of Husserl's criticism of Schröder, e.g. of Schröder's definitions of '0', '1', 'a+b' and 'a—b'. Referring to the *Philosophie der Arithmetik*, Frege hopes that sometime in the future, time permitting, he may reply to Husserl's criticisms of his own theory of number. He draws attention to one major difference between them, and that concerns how a common name relates to its objects. Frege illustrates his own view with the help of the following scheme :

---

[23] *Ibid.*, p. 244.
[24] *Ibid.*, p. 244.
[25] *Ibid.*, p. 245.
[26] *Ibid.*, p. 245.
[27] Frege, G., "Kritische Beleuchtung einiger Punkte in E. Schröders Vorlesungen über die Algebra der Logik," *Archiv für systematische Philosophie*, I, 1895, pp. 433-436.

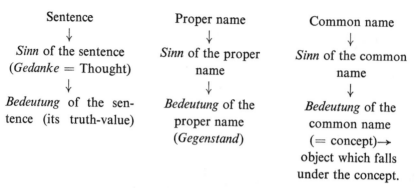

Sentence	Proper name	Common name
↓	↓	↓
Sinn of the sentence (*Gedanke* = Thought)	*Sinn* of the proper name	*Sinn* of the common name
↓	↓	↓
Bedeutung of the sentence (its truth-value)	*Bedeutung* of the proper name (*Gegenstand*)	*Bedeutung* of the common name (= concept)→ object which falls under the concept.

In the case of common names, one step more is needed — according to Frege — to reach the object than in the case of proper names. Further, in the case of common names, the concept may be empty i.e. there may be no object without its ceasing thereby to be scientifically useful. In the case of proper names, however, if a name does not name anything i.e. lacks an object, it is scientifically useless. This refers to Frege's well-known and controversial thesis that concepts constitute the reference, not the *Sinn*, of common names. Frege contrasts with this Husserl's view that the *Sinn*, (or, in Husserl's language, the *Bedeutung*) of a common name is the concept expressed by it and its reference is constituted by the object or objects falling under the concept. The letter makes it clear that Frege does recognise that Husserl had the distinction between *Sinn* and *Gegenstand*, only he does *not* ascribe here to Husserl a distinction between *Vorstellung* and *Sinn*.

Husserl writes back to Frege on July 18, 1891. He admits the great intellectual stimulus he had received from Frege's theories, and he goes on to express his views about the many points of agreement between them — to which reference has been made earlier. Amongst these points of agreement, Husserl refers to his own distinction between 'language' (*Sprache*) and 'calculus' which he now finds in Frege's 1883 paper on "Über den Zweck der Begriffsschrift" [28] where he distinguishes between the concept of "calculus ratiocinator" and the concept of "lingua characteristica." It appears to him that the *Begriffsschrift* is intended to be a lingua characteristica and not a "sign language constructed in imitation of the arithmetical." He concludes the letter by expressing agreement with Frege's rejection of "formal arithmetic" as a *theory* of arithmetic, however important it may be as an extension of the arithmetical technic. Husserl is referring to Frege's "Über formale Theorien der Arithmetik" [29] whose copy Frege had just sent him. The sense of 'formalism' in which Frege rejects it as a theory of arithmetic is that according to which the signs for numbers like '1/2,' '2/3', 'π' are empty, meaningless signs (*leere Zeichen*). According to this theory, as Frege understands it, these empty signs themselves are numbers and they constitute the proper subject matter of arithmetic.[30] That Husserl should concur fully with Frege's total rejection of such a theory of arithmetic should be obvious from the foregoing summary of his views. The *Prolegomena* however shows much greater understanding of the significance of formalism, but even there his philosophy of arithmetic is not formalistic. His formal logic is there correlate of formal ontology, and in large parts of the work he is concerned not with a specific formal science but with the form of theory in general.

From the above survey of the Frege-Husserl correspondence of 1891 [31] it becomes clear that Frege did not quite show any recognition of the presence of the *Vorstellung-Sinn* distinction in Husserl's Schröder review. However, as we have already seen, this distinction is there, which suggests that Husserl was already on his way, independently of Frege's 1894 review, towards the objective conception of logic of the *Prolegomena*.

IV

Let us now look at other comments by Frege on the Husserl papers of 1891. We know that in his May 24, 1891 letter to Husserl, Frege writes that Husserl's Schröder review had made him decide to publish his own thoughts on Schröder's book, and that his comments on it may appear in the *Zeitschrift für Philosophie und philosophische Kritik*. However, Frege's "Kritische Beleuchtung einiger Punkte in E. Schröders Vorlesungen über die Algebra der Logik" finally appeared four years after in the *Archiv für systematische Philosophie*.[32] In this review, Frege, amongst other things, brings out the essential points of difference between Schröder's concept of '*Gebiet*' (domain) and the logical concept of class, and points out how Schröder unknowingly oscillates between the two. In so far as the logical concept of class is concerned, Frege considers it entirely mistaken to take

für das Jahr 1885, Jena: Fischer, 1885/86, pp. 94-104, (now reprinted in Ignacio Angelelli (ed.), Freges *Kleine Schriften*, Hildesheim : Georg Olms, 1967, pp. 103-111).

[30] Frege, *Kleine Schriften*, p. 105.

[31] I am indebted to Professor F. Kambartel of the University of Konstanz, director of the Frege-Archiv, for making these available to me.

[32] See fn. 27 above.

a class as consisting in individual things, as a collection of individuals — a mistake which, according to him, derives from Schröder's attempt to extend his *Gebietekalkül* to the logic of classes.[33] And yet, asks Frege, how else is a class constituted if one abstracts from common properties? "Only through the fact that the classes are determined by the properties which their individuals should have, only through the fact that one uses expressions such as 'the class of objects which are b,' is it possible to express general thoughts when one states relations amongst classes; only through this that one comes to logic."[34] Thus Frege agrees with Husserl's comments : the extension of a concept presupposes the intension of the concept. In Frege's own words : "In reality I hold the view that the concept logically precedes its extension, and I consider it a mistake to attempt to found the class, as extension of a concept, not on the concept itself but on the individual things."[35] However, despite this agreement with Husserl's point of view, Frege refuses to side with *Inhaltslogik* as against the so-called *Umfangslogik*, and adds : "Nevertheless, I am in many respects possibly closer to the author (i.e. to Schröder) than to those whom one could call, in opposition to him, logicians of content (*Inhalt*)."[36] He has obviously Husserl in mind. The question naturally arises : why does Frege reject the conception of an *Inhaltslogik* even though he does not agree with a purely extensional analysis of classes?

The reasons become partly clear when one considers his remarks on *Inhaltslogik* in the "Ausführungen über Sinn und Bedeutung"[37] which possibly belongs to the period 1892-95. Frege writes :

Even if one has to concede to the *Inhalts*-logicians that the concept itself, as contrasted with its extension, is the foundational, nevertheless it should not for that reason be understood as the meaning (*Sinn*) of the concept-word, but as its reference, and the *Umfangs*-logicians are nearer the truth in so far as they locate in the extension (*Umfang*) an essential meaning (*Bedeutung*) which, though not itself the concept, is yet very closely connected with it.[38]

We have already found that the *Inhaltslogik* is a logic of meanings. Although Frege regards the concept as primary and extension as derivative, he also considers the concept itself to be the *reference* of a concept-word. A logic of concepts then would be a logic, not of *Sinn* but of *Bedeutungen*

---

[33] Frege, *Kleine Schriften*, p. 207.
[34] Frege, *Kleine Schriften*, p. 208.
[35] *Ibid.*, p. 209.
[36] *Ibid.*, pp. 209-210.
[37] In Frege, G., *Nachgelassene Schriften*, Hamburg : Felix Meiner, 1969, pp. 128-136.
[38] *Ibid.*, p. 134.

(in Frege's senses of those words) and hence closer to an extensional logic. The following paragraph further clarifies Frege's argument :

They (i.e. the *Umfangs*-logicians) are right when, because of their preference for the extension of a concept to its intension, they admit that they regard the reference of words, and not their meaning, to be essential for logic. The *Inhalts*-logicians only remain too happily with the meaning, for what they call "*Inhalt*", if it is not quite the same as Vorstellung, is certainly the meaning (*Sinn*). They do not consider the fact that in logic it is not a question of how thoughts come from thoughts without regard to truth-value, that, more generally speaking, the progress from meanings (*Sinne*) to reference (*Bedeutung*), must be made; that the logical laws are first laws in the realm of references and only then mediately relate to meaning (*Sinn*).[39]

Also in the same "Ausführungen," Frege makes reference to Husserl's distinction between whether a name has a *Sinn* and whether an object corresponding to it exists or not. But he finds this distinction insufficient, for Husserl does not distinguish between proper names and concept-words and as we saw earlier Frege differs widely from Husserl on this point. Again there is no reference to Husserl's distinction between *Vorstellung* and *Sinn*. The one likely recognition of this is the covert statement that the *Inhalt* of the *Inhalts*-logicians, if it is not *Vorstellung*, must be the *Sinn*.[40]

V

We may sum up our conclusions in so far as the Frege-Husserl relationship about the years 1891-94 is concerned :

1. The two men arrived at the *Vorstellung-Sinn*-reference distinction independently of each other.

2. Husserl's overcoming of psychologism and acceptance of a theory of objective pure logic was fundamentally independent of Frege's 1894 review of the *Philosophie der Arithmetik*. The basic change had occurred in 1891. That this should have occurred in the very year of publication of the *Philosophie der Arithmetik* is made all the more plausible by the following note by Husserl, belonging to a much later date :

Ich las viel in der "Philosophie der Arithmetik." Wie unreif, wie naiv und fast kindlich erschien mir dieses Werk. Nun, nicht umsonst peinigte mich bei der Publikation das Gewissen. *Eigentlich war ich darüber schon hinaus, als ich es publizierte.* Es stammte ja im wesentlichen aus den Jahren 86/87.[41]

[39] Frege, G., *Nachgelassene Schriften*, p. 133.
[40] *Ibid.*, p. 133.
[41] Husserl, E., "Persönliche Aufzeichnungen", edited by W. Biemel, in *Philosophy and Phenomenological Research*, XVI, 1956, 293-302, esp. 294. (Italics mine). — J. N. M.

3. (a) Frege agrees with Husserl that the concept of a class presupposes the concept of concept, that the extension of a concept presupposes the intension.

(b) Nevertheless, while Husserl went on to develop the idea of an *Inhalts-logik* and subsequently a logic of meanings (though he did not quite reject *Umfangslogik*, to be sure, but wavered between (i) asserting a bare equivalence between the two logics and (ii) asserting the primacy of the *Inhalts-logik*), Frege sides with *Umfangslogik* and that for two reasons : (α) his belief that logic is concerned not with mere consistency of thoughts but with their truth-value, and (β) his theory that the reference of concept-words is the concept itself (as contrasted with Husserl's view, which may also be said to be the standard view, that the concept is the *Sinn* of the concept-word.)

We cannot here undertake a discussion of the questions whether these two Fregean theses are acceptable or not. But we know now where exactly the two men stood in relation to each other between the years 1891 and 1894.

A REPLY TO A CRITIC OF MY REFUTATION OF LOGICAL PSYCHOLOGISM *

by

EDMUND HUSSERL

(translated by DALLAS WILLARD, Los Angeles)

One does not need to read very far in this work to see that its content deviates fundamentally from its title. Namely, it does not really give a general treatment of the quarrel between the psychologistic and the formalistic logicians. Rather, it deals only with my quarrel with Psychologism in my *Logische Untersuchungen*, which appeared in 1900. It is the author's intent to oppose the "formalistic tendency in modern logic" (p. 5), the "precipitous, retrograde movement which writes on its banner the war cry — 'Away from psychology' "! He will oppose the "formalistic danger" of an "unfruitful and sterile formalism" (p. 1). Thus he puts his task quite generally, in his "Introduction." But then, as we proceed, we immediately hear also that Bolzano is to be regarded as "the true originator of modern formalism in logic"; and we are reminded that Husserl is, so far, the only modern logician who has linked his positions to Bolzano's *Wissenschaftslehre* in essential points. Then we further notice that the author mentions no other formalists. Rather, his attacks — some in particular chapters, and some in the form of sorties interspersed throughout the text — relate solely and only to Husserl. So we must, so far as this work is concerned, form the equation : Modern Formalists = Husserl. If, now, the malice in the tone preferred by the author does not suffice to keep me form complying with the kind invitation of the editor of this journal to review this work, it is in order that I might fulfill the obligation, which every serious worker has, not to let his work fall victim to attacks that would distort it.

* This is a translation of Husserl's review of *Der Streit der Psychologisten und Formalisten in der modernen Logik*, by Melchoir Palágyi, published in Leipzig by Engelmann in 1902. The review appeared in volume 31 (1903) of *Zeitschrift für Psychologie und Physiologie der Sinnesorgane*, pp. 287-294. It is especially valuable because it responds to typical criticisms which followed Husserl throughout his career, and is one of the very few times when Husserl explicity undertook to meet his critics. All footnotes have been added by the translator. (E. tr. first appeared in *The Personalist*, vol. 53, 1972, no. 1, pp. 5-13, reprinted by permission. — J. N. M.)

My logical investigations place themselves against the dominant current of logical and epistemological persuasion : — at least as an irksome impediment. It is indeed conceivable how a work which, like the one before us, energetically guarantees to have done away with the impediment, or proven it to amount to nothing, can calculate on easy laurels of victory; and how it might easily transmute present inclination into agreement with itself, and thereby mislead many readers into orienting themselves about my point of view according to the author's statements, instead of according to my writings. But I must keep this from happening. In his very orientation (toward my standpoint) Mr. Palágyi employs a peculiar, though certainly quite convenient, method. He is satisfied with a cursory reading of a few chapters or paragraphs of volume one of my *Logical Investigations*.[1] All of the rest is, for him, non-existent. Of volume two, which appeared fully three-quarters of a year before his work, he says not a word, regardless of the relevant points it might bring to bear on the discussion. The astounding thoroughness of the author, together with an equally astounding incapacity to grasp the plain sense of any sort of conceptual distinction, brings it about that he — and this is to be taken quite literally — also is unable to report on even one of my or Bolzano's theories without twisting it into something which is unbelievable.

This is immediately revealed by his general characterization of my position. He repeatedly ascribes to me the tendency "to allow Logic to sink, where possible, into Mathematics" (p. 9), the "struggle" to "tear Logic loose" (p. 43) from Psychology and to "split the blanket between Logic and Psychology" (p. 37), and so on. Of course he is silent about the distinction — one of which is decisive for the simple understanding of the sense of my tenets, and has been justified in detail — which I make between "Logic" in that most inclusive sense which it has as a practical discipline, and "pure Logic," as the theoretical system of purely formal (categorial) truths. He also does not mention that I abundantly approve of a logic which has that tendency toward being a methodology exhibited in the logics of Mill, Sigwart and Wundt. Nor does he remark that I in no wise contest the founding of logic, in this common sense, upon empirical psychology, but even require that such a founding be extensively provided. He does not mention that "pure" or "formal Logic" is for me only a title introduced to aid in understanding historical traditions and tendencies; one joined to a certain class of propositions (*Sätze*) which are called 'logical' in the fullest sense, and of which I sought to show the following : — that they

---

[1] *Logische Untersuchungen*, 2 vols., Max Niemeyer Verlag, Halle a. S., 1900 and 1901.

belong to a distinct discipline which is *a priori* and independent of all psychology, and that this discipline, through a natural extension, also takes in formal mathematics (its theories being *a priori*, and foreign to psychology in the same sense), and is ultimately identical with *mathesis universalis* in the generalized sense coined by Leibniz. Whoever takes his directions from the author must assume that I intend, in any case, to reduce it to a 'class logic' (*eine 'Umfangslogik'*) in the style of the Boolean school. That I laid bare the follies of extensional (*quantifizierenden*) logic over twelve years ago in a very detailed critique (see the *Göttingische gelehrte Anzeigen* for 1891) might be unknown to Mr. Palágyi. But he cannot be ignorant of the distinctions just stressed, the neglect of which can only have the effect of transforming the sense of my views into nonsense.

Mr. Palágyi is also quiet about my distinction between the mere technique which is associated with theories of formal logic, (and which can be consigned to the mathematicians), and, on the other hand, the sphere of genuinely philosophical tasks, *viz.* elucidation (*Aufklärung*) of the primitive concepts and propositions of pure logic through comprehensive, descriptive-psychological (or "phenomenological") analyses. He is silent on how — as is to be seen from volume two of my *Logische Untersuchungen* — I have worked at these philosophical tasks, and especially at the descriptive phenomenology of the experience of thought, at lengths scarcely ever gone to before. My work shows that my struggle against Psychologism is in no wise a struggle against the psychological grounding of Logic as methodology, nor against the descriptive-psychological elucidation (*Aufklärung*) of the source (*Ursprungs*) of the logical concepts. Rather, it is only a struggle against an epistemological position, though certainly one which has had a very harmful influence upon the way in which *Logic* is done. — So *that* struggle is what Mr. Palágyi, manifesting an exemplary reliability, characterizes as "splitting the blanket" between Logic and Psychology.

If, now, we go in sequence through the four polemical sections of the work which follow the *Introduction*, we find that the first bears the title, "Facts and Truths." All of my arguments against Psychologism rest — so the author says — on the proposition *that truth is no fact*. I.e., the proposition that the act of judging correctly is indeed a temporal process, but truth is not. Now, out of this mere distinction of reason (*begrifflichen Unterscheidung*) between the act and the content of the judgment — thus, that distinction in virtue of which we speak, for example, of *the* proposition, $2 \times 2 = 4$, whoever may express *it*, one and the same thing — there arises, under the hands of the author, a real distinction between two allegedly connected moments (*Momente*) : "Husserl supposes that, after *subtraction* of the judgment content, he can retain as *remainder* a psychic act." (p. 14, cf. p. 47 among others) And now the critique is worthy of the interpretation : — Not a psychic act, but rather a "mechanical process," is what is left over after "subtraction" of the judgment content; and so my view wavers "in an unceasing equivocation, between the physical and psychical." (p. 15) After this searching probe there probably is no need to go into the other twists through which Palágyi seeks to support his darling objection to the effect that I confuse psychology and physics (science of fact). Having previously decided to read all sorts of absurdities out of my statements, he no longer comes to them in order genuinely to read them according to their sense and interconnection.

In the next two sections of his work, Palágyi concerns himself with plugging up the source of "modern Formalism". These sections are directed against Bolzano's theories about concepts (*Vorstellungen*), propositions (*Sätze*), and truths (*Wahrheiten*) in themselves. Here I must first mention the suggestive manner in which Palágyi conceives of my relations with Bolzano. In a series of hints which would be insignificant taken separately, but which are efficacious when taken in sequence, he gives the reader no less a notion that I have exploited Bolzano in a dishonest manner and have kept silent about my dependence upon him. Suppressing judgment on the author's procedure, I note, for the benefit of the uninformed, that not only — as the author once mentions (p. 16) — have I "remembered" Bolzano and "named" him one of the greatest of logicians. Rather — in an 'appendix' to chapter 10 of *Logische Untersuchungen*, Vol. 1, an appendix specifically devoted to this purpose — I have pointed out the significance of the *Wissenschaftslehre* as one of the Foundation works of logic, and have stressed the necessity of building upon this work and studying it with the greatest care. This I have done in such a detailed manner, and with such emphasis, as has never before occurred, either in earlier times or contemporary. And, not satisfied with that, I expressly designated Bolzano as the one (along with Lotze) by whom I have been "decisively influenced." These words I quote from *Logische Untersuchungen*, Vol. 1, p. 226 (1st ed.).

As to my concept of "ideal" significations, and "ideal" contents of representations and judgments, to speak specifically, they originally derive, not from Bolzano at all, but rather — as the term "ideal" alone indicates — from Lotze. In particular, Lotze's reflections about the interpretation of Plato's theory of forms (*Ideenlehre*) had a profound effect on me. Only by thinking out these ideas (*Gedanken*) of Lotze — and in my opinion he failed to get completely clear on them — did I find the key to the curious conceptions of Bolzano, which in all their phenomenological naivity were at first unintelligible, and to the treasures of his *Wissenschaftslehre*.

If, like all earlier readers of Bolzano, his "propositions in themselves" ("*Sätze an sich*") previously appeared to me as mythical entities, suspended between being and nonbeing, it then became clear to me, with one stroke, that here we basically have a quite obvious conception which traditional logic did not adequately appreciate. I saw that under "proposition in itself" is to be understood, then, what is designated in ordinary discourse, which always objectifies the ideal, as the "sense" ('*Sinn*') of a statement. It is that which is explained as one and the same where, for example, different persons are said to have asserted the same thing. Or, again, it is what, in science, is simply called a theorem, e.g., the theorem about the sum of the angles in a triangle, which no one would think of taking to be someone's experience of judging. And it further became clear to me that this identical sense could be nothing other than the universal, the species, which belongs to a certain *moment* present in all actual assertions (*Aussagen*) with the same sense, and which makes possible the identification just mentioned, even where the descriptive content of the individual experiences (*Erlebnisse*) of asserting varies considerably in other respects. The proposition thus relates to those acts of judgment (*Urteilsakte*) to which it belongs as their identical meaning (*Meinung*) in the same way, for example, as the species redness relates to individuals of "the same" red color. Now with this view of things as a basis, Bolzano's theory, that propositions are objects which nonetheless have no "existence," comes to have the following quite intelligible signification : — They have the "ideal" being (*Sein*) or validity (*Gelten*) of objects which are universals ("*allgemeiner Gegenstände*") — and thus, that being which is established, for example, in the "existence proofs" of mathematics. But they do not have the real being of things, or of dependent, thing-like moments — of temporal particulars in general. Bolzano himself did not give the faintest intimation that these phenomenological relationships between signification, signification moment, and full act of signifying [2] had been noticed by him. And this notwithstanding the fact that he treats the psychology of knowledge in great detail in Vol. III of his *Wissenschaftslehre*. Indeed, everything indicates just the contrary — that his conception of the *Satz an sich* wound up unclarified, in spite of all his efforts to avoid it.

---

[2] "*Bedeutung, Bedeutungsmoment und vollem Akt des Bedeutens.*" There is no more fundamental analysis in Husserl than that of the concrete individual, whose essence is to be temporally located, into quality, quality phase or moment, and whole individual. See the opening paragraph and section 19 of the second "logical Investigation," and also the second sentence of the fifth "Investigation". Also, the first chapter of the third "Investigation" and section 3 of the fourth "Investigation."

Now as to Mr. Palágyi, he has adopted my view, or that from it which was immediately intelligible to him, without qualification. He interprets Bolzano's concepts through my ideas and expressions, but does it as if he drew directly upon Bolzano, and also as if the corresponding statements by me were only just borrowings — underhanded borrowings, moreover — from Bolzano. He adopts my theory of the identical, ideal sense (*Sinn*), without mentioning it in his *ever* so friendly statements. But this *sense* he makes out to be an identical, ideal *moment* of experience. Then the distinction, stressed by me, between the species and particular, between the sense as the *Idea* (*Idee*) which becomes an object for us through species-abstraction (*spezifizierende Abstraktion*) and the sense *moment* (*Sinnesmoment*) of descriptive psychology : this distinction Palágyi overlooks or does not understand. Then, since I make a distinction of reason between the identical signification and the signifying act (in the sense in which, say, the quality-species (*Qualitätsspezies*) redness is distinct from a red thing), he has the concrete, psychic experience of judging consisting of two *moments* — of the supra-temporal (!) sense-moment and the act. After this distortion, he objects to Bolzano and to me, that we would tear the sense-moment away from the act. As if his sense-moment (which inconsistently with its being a moment, he characterizes as ideal and supra-temporal) were identical with Bolzano's "proposition in itself," or with the sense as species! Obviously the author could have spared himself the effort of emphasis — hauled out with ceaseless repetition — upon the indissolubility of the sense moment from the act, by which he thinks to refute us so decisively, through mere quotations from my *Logische Untersuchungen*.

Of the same nature and value are the other objections which Palágyi advances in these sections. Thus, for example, the reference to propositions of a kind with "I am now thinking" (25 ff.), which include in their objective content a reference to the one judging — in a word, the 'occasional' propositions [3] already treated in detail in Vol. III of my *Logische Untersuchungen* — is of no use whatsoever in somehow calling into question that "independence" which is characteristic of the species *vis-à-vis* the singular case, and thus of the proposition *vis-à-vis* the fortuitous act of judging. It is of no use, that is, unless — deceived by the ambiguity of the phrase "content of judgement" — one follows Palágyi in confusing *proposition* (*Satz*) with *fact* (*Sachverhalt*). Again, the "intrinsic contradiction in Bolzano's philosophy," which with no little pathos is brought forth in subsection #4, is in truth a contradiction between what Bolzano is supposed,

---

[3] Cf. Hans Reichenbach's notion of "token reflexive" terms, in *Elements of Symbolic Logic*, § 50.

according to Palágyi, to have maintained, and what he really did maintain. One is immediately convinced of this by comparison of Palágyi's remarks with the passage concerned (*Wissenschaftslehre*, Vol. I, sub-section 25). While, according to the clear sense of his repeated statements, Bolzano taught that to the "truth in itself" (i.e. the truth in that quite common sense in which we designate, not an act of judging, but rather a *proposition* (*Satz*) as a truth) being thought or, more precisely, being judged or known is *non-essential*, the author has him teaching that being *un*thought of or *un*known is essential to it. Bolzano's careless use of the ambiguous expression "proposition thought" ("*gedachten Satz*") offers the author a handhold for ascribing, here and further on, a series of crude inconsistencies to this exceptionally clear thinker. Of the duties of a fair interpretation, or of a careful reading which compares passage with passage, Mr. Palágyi is ignorant. And so, throughout two long sections, one must patiently endure such utterly untenable statements : statements which, of course, are supposed equally to uproot the whole of Bolzano's philosophy and my *Logische Untersuchungen* — as if they did not go their own peculiar ways.

In section IV Palágyi again turns himself directly and exclusively against my *Logische Untersuchungen*, and especially against my distinction between laws of the real and laws of the ideal, which I bring to bear upon logic. The basic error of Psychologism consists, according to my view, in its obliteration of this fundamental distinction between pure and empirical generality, and in its misinterpretation of the pure laws of logic as empirical laws of psychology. Of course our author finds obvious absurdity in this view : So our actual course of thinking is supposed to be governed by two sorts of laws, is it? And by laws which belong to two worlds separated by an "infinite abyss"? But it is simply impossible to see how extra-temporal laws of the ideal could come to have some sort of causal efficacy. Such an estrangement of the real and the ideal means the utter impossibility of any knowledge at all (pp. 41f.). Or so says Mr Palágyi.

Unfortunately, the author has read too selectively. Otherwise he would have stayed on guard against misinterpreting the contrast between ideal and real as lack of relation. Since the ideal significations are instanced (*sich ... vereinzeln*) in acts of signifying, each pure law of logic (*rein logisches Gesetz* [4]) expresses a universal connection which *eo ipso* can be referred to the ideal extensions of the respective signification species, and thus to

---

[4] "Purely logical law" does not get at what Husserl intends, since a law may be a rule or law of logic without being one of *pure logic* or a *non-empirical* law of logic. See chapters 2 and 3 of *Logische Untersuchungen*, vol. 1 on this point. Hence, here and elsewhere the phrase, "*rein logisches Gesetz*," has been translated as above.

possible acts of thought in the realm of the real. Thus, as I have sufficiently explained, there can be derived from any ideal law whatsoever (e.g. any arithmetical law) universal truths about ideally possible or impossible connections of psychic fact. The character of these ideal laws, as truths of reason (*vérité de la raison*), is transmitted to such derivations and is not affected by them. All of the forceful expressions with which the author embellishes his criticisms cannot change the fact that he is passing judgment upon matters which he has not sufficiently studied.

It is hardly worthwhile to enter into his further objections, which often evince a striking lack of intelligence. Thus, a contradiction of my contrast between real and ideal law is supposed to proceed from the fact that I myself allow law contents to function as thought motives in judging. Through this function, Palágyi supposes, the ideal law in fact attains the significance of a real law of our thinking (p. 45). Thus, according to this way of reasoning, the law of gravitation, where it guides the thinking of the engineer, and likewise any law that guides us in practice would attain the significance of a law of thought.

And what is one supposed to say to the objection that, through my separation of the laws of pure logic, as laws of the ideal, from laws of psychology, as laws of the real, these latter laws "appear to fall into the same category as the laws of mechanics, and that then one at least no longer knows wherein the psychic could be distinguished from the physical" (p. 43)? Likewise for the objection that the truth is simply one, so that the separation of truths into two classes, separated by an "unbridgeable abyss," is impossible (p. 52)? Likewise to the misconception related to these objections, that — as it would not be possible for me to do otherwise — I base that distinction of laws just referred to upon a distinction between modes of human knowledge (namely, knowledge through "induction" and through "Insight"); and that I thus perpetually confuse two sorts of laws with two ways of knowing one law (p. 53)? I need not say that I do hold the distinction between the two kinds of laws to be grounded solely in the essence of their signification (*in ihrem bedeutungsmässigen Wesen*), but that with that essence there is connected a phenomenological distinction in the mode of knowledge of the states of affairs (*Sachverhalte*), of the one and the other sort, corresponding to laws. In the context of the critiques in the "Prolegomena," [5] the phrase "law of the real" does not signify just any arbitrary universal proposition referring to the real, but rather a universal fact (*allgemeine Tatsache*); or at least a proposition which, in the manner of our

---

[5] I.e. Vol. I, *Logische Untersuchungen*.

assertions of natural laws, is weighed with factual content. So my point here essentially comes down to the distinction between factual truths and purely conceptual truths (i.e. ideal laws, or laws in the most narrow and rigorous sense of the word). Were the world so made that all of the spheres in it were red, then, arriving at an inductive belief that this is so, we would speak of a "natural law" to that effect. However, in itself it would be no (genuine) law, no proposition grounded in the conceptual essence 'sphere' and 'red'; rather, it would be a universal fact (*allgemeine Tatsache*). It is precisely this objective distinction, which is fundamental for both logic and epistemology, between what Hume called "relations of ideas" and "matters of fact" that our author surely rejects as invalid. But the inadequacy of his polemic against this great thinker works an immediate embarrassment, since he does not once grasp the sense of the distinction in question. Palágyi objects, against Hume's well-known statements, that even facts come under the principle of contradiction. For, he says, the opposite of a fact is never possible. The fact can never be undone. As if Hume doubted that! Is it really so difficult to understand that Hume's referral of the principle of contradiction to his "relations of ideas" is intended to mean no more than that truths about relations of ideas are rooted precisely in the ideas (*Ideen*) alone (i.e. merely in the relevant concepts), and therefore cannot be denied without contradiction; whereas negations of factual truths are indeed false, but not self-contradictory?

After this fruitful search into the innumerable absurdities which he imputed to his adversaries, in the concluding section of his book the author explains his own views about the relationship between Logic and Psychology. On page 72 he distinguishes knowing (*Wissen*) as a general or abstract (!) psychic function — to the character of which it belongs to stand in the most intimate of relations to the remaining psychic functions — from sensing, feeling or willing as "concrete" (!) psychic functions, or as "isolated psychic functions" ("*psychische Sonderfunktionen*"), which lack the capability of relating to other psychic functions or to themselves. The investigation of the former function falls to Logic. The investigation of the latter function falls to Psychology. In other words, what we have here is a division of what everyone calls psychology into "Logic" and "Psychology" : — namely, into the psychology of knowing and the psychology of the remaining psychic functions. The author is thus so naive as to suppose he can settle, through a slight displacement of terminology, such a weighty epistemological question as that about the relationship between Logic and Psychology. A formula with the ring of profundity to it is supplied to the author, for the expression of his views, by the new terminological distinction between 'unreflected' and 'reflected' consciousness (e.g. the seeing of the red and the knowledge (*Wissen*) of this seeing), and by the — not precisely unheard of — introjection of the notion (*Gedankens*) of the furtherance of knowledge into the concept of Logic. Then it is said (p. 81) that Logic "reflects on the reflected consciousness, and endeavours to raise our knowing processes to a higher power by investigating the laws of our reflected consciousness. Psychology, on the other hand, will try to carry reflection raised to a higher power by Logic over into the investigation of unreflected consciousness."

THE PARADOX OF LOGICAL PSYCHOLOGISM: HUSSERL'S WAY OUT*

by

Dallas Willard

(Los Angeles)

I

Logical Psychologism is the view that the non-normative statements made by logicians engaged in their business both are about, and draw their evidence from the examination of, the particular conceivings, assertings, and inferrings of particular persons — a range of facts commonly thought to belong ultimately to the science of psychology alone. This view enjoyed wide acceptance during the last half of the 19th century, being advocated by such men as John Stuart Mill in England, and Sigwart and Erdmann in Germany. More recently, and due as much to misunderstandings and an unfavorable press as to the essential incredibilities it contains, it has suffered an eclipse which is almost total. A part of the purpose of this paper is to show how this eclipse hinders understanding of what Logic is about.

What is here called the "paradox" of Logical Psychologism arises when one sees that, while (i) the class of statements mentioned — we might call them "logicians' truths" — are indeed, in some very important sense, about and applicable to such particular events in personal careers as referred to above, (ii) they nonetheless, as Husserl, Frege, and others have shown, do *not* draw their evidence from the examination of such events. Now this seems paradoxical. For *how* can claims about a certain sort of thing fail to draw their evidence from the examination of things of that sort? There seem to be good reasons for believing both (i) and (ii). And yet the truth of (i) or (ii) seems each to exclude the truth of the other. Thus we have a paradox or antinomy in the classical sense. This paper also proposes to consider a way of resolving the paradox without calling either (i) or (ii) into question.

II

Logicians today are likely to feel uneasy about (i). In this respect we seem

* Reprinted from *American Philosophical Quarterly*, 9, 1972, by permission. — J. N. M.

to be the inverse of most 19th century philosophers, who easily accepted (i), but had difficulty with (ii). We today have heard or read many snappy announcements that the laws of logic are not expressions of how we actually *do* think, but of how we *ought* to think. And then — with these ringing in our ears — we fail to notice that logicians in fact fill up large volumes without once saying that anyone ought to do anything at all : — Just try counting the "oughts" in Quine's *Methods of Logic*, or Mate's *Elementary Logic*. We fail to see that "valid," "invalid," "tautologous," "consistent," "inconsistent," "derivable," and the other terms which form the core of the logician's vocabulary are not used by him at his trade to commend or condemn, to praise or to blame, to exhort or to direct, at all. That an argument, or argument form, is valid or invalid is a point of mere information or misinformation, to which some positive or negative value may or may not be attached. Value considerations have nothing at all essentially to do with whether or not an argument is valid or invalid, or with whether or not an expression is L-determinate.

It is, of course, true that terms from, or closely related to the core vocabulary of the logician are often given a normative use — are often used to commend or condemn — in the contexts of actual thinking and talking. An example would be the common claim that a certain person at a certain point in an essay or lecture advanced an invalid (or valid) argument, or on a certain occasion made an invalid (or valid) inference. But it is still true here that the normative use is accidental only. A particular instance of the Barbara syllogism, for example, is valid — i.e., no argument of its sort has or can have true premises and false conclusion — regardless of what value may or may not be placed upon it; and, of course, also regardless of how anyone's beliefs may be arranged around the premises and conclusion. *It* is valid, and is known to be valid. That is, the logician's claims (about validity in this case) apply to *it*, the *particular* event of thinking or speaking in the life of a *particular* person. And persons who are logically informed and trained can *know* that *it*, and not merely Barbara syllogisms in general, is valid.[1]

Without this kind of application there would simply be no use at all for what the logician has to teach. If he denies the possibility of such appli-

---

[1] Quine, for one, explicitly says that what admits of truth and falsity — and, by implication, of logical relations — are, "individual events of statement utterance." (*Methods of Logic*, rev. ed. (New York, 1959), p. xi.) Unfortunately, this statement forms no homogeneous part of his logical theories, but rather is forced upon him by his theory about logic, and his general epistemological views. One who knew only what Quine has said in developing logical theories would not have the least inkling that the theories were theories about utterance events.

cation, he talks himself out of a job. But there is no real danger of that. No logician — even the most hide-bound of anti-Psychologists or Formalists — will assure those whom he would teach that what he has to say is irrelevant to the thinking and speaking which they, or at least *some* persons, may happen to do or meet with. He may have no ready account of *how* it is relevant to actual thinking and speaking, and may — as many teachers and texts do today — either simply avoid the subject, or content himself with a few remarks about its obscurity (or utter impossibility). But that the remarks he makes at his trade are assumed by him to apply to the actual thought and discourse of himself and others is shown by how he *uses* the logical tools which he has sharpened. He *does* analyze particular arguments and inferences, and he does it *with* the principles and techniques which he has developed. Further, he *expects* others — especially if he has taught them — to do the same. No doubt most students of logic fail to know *why* or *how* what their instructor or text has told them applies to actual thinking and talking; and that is probably why only a minuscule percentage of them do in fact ever make *any* use whatsoever of what they learned from their study of logic.[2] But instructors and texts in logic do yet convey to them the assumption that what they are being taught applies to and informs on actual thinking and talking. To this assumption Logical Psychologism did full and explicit justice; but, with very few exceptions, such as John Dewey, logicians of this century have not even faced up to it.

III

But while a logician working today would, perhaps with some uneasiness, agree with Psychologism so far as to own up to (i), he certainly would also reject Psychologism by asserting, with (ii), that the *evidence* which he has for the truths he teaches does not arise from an examination of particular episodes of thinking and speaking. He would assert this simply because he *has* evidence for his truths, but he did not get it in that way prescribed by Psychologism, and because he feels that the *sort* of evidence he has cannot be empirically derived. If Psychologism were correct, then

---

[2] As a matter of simple fact, few courses more totally — though perhaps many equally — waste the student's time, so far as his own self-betterment is concerned, than university courses in logic. The irony is that the greater waste is usually made by the very courses which are technically more rigorous. A nice, sloppy course mainly dealing with so-called "informal fallacies" often gives the student a critical handhold (usually involving insight) on some things he subsequently thinks or hears.

when a logician is speaking, in general and non-normative terms, about propositions, statements, proofs, arguments or inferences, his claims could have only that degree of probability provided by actual *observation* of instances from the classes of psychical or linguistic facts to which he refers. But he very well knows that his claims are not probability statements at all, and that they are never tested by observation of instances.

For example, Quine says, at the opening of "Part One" of his *Methods of Logic* :

The peculiarity of *statements* which sets them apart from other linguistic forms is that they admit of truth and falsity, and may hence be significantly affirmed and denied. To deny a statement is to affirm another statement, known as the *negation* or contradictory of the first.

If, now, we were to approach this (quite non-normative) passage with a consistently psychologistic attitude, the following sorts of questions would have to be asked : How are these claims which Quine makes known to be true? How did he discover them? What are the data upon which these claims rest? When were the relevant observations made? What kind of person was making the statements, the denials, the affirmations, etc., observed? And was the observer qualified or trained in the making of such observations? Did he correctly record his observations? Is a margin of error to be allowed for in such observations? If not, why not? If so, what is it? And was it correctly handled in the observations here in question? What were the conditions under which the observations relevant to Quine's statements were made? Were the conditions sufficiently varied to insure that the correlation to be drawn is indeed just between the classes mentioned (e.g., statements, truths, denials, etc.) and not some others? — *If* non-normative logicians' truths belong to psychology — and perhaps, more specifically, to the psychology of linguistic behavior — and *if* psychology is a science in which evidence is ultimately drawn from observations of fact, *then* these questions *must* be asked. Otherwise there simply is no evidence for the logicians' truths in question. And they must, of course, be asked with reference to *all* of the non-normative truths of logic, not only those stated by Quine above : truths such as, "No proposition (or sentence or statement or utterance) is both true and false," "Arguments with inconsistent premises are valid, but never show their conclusion to be true," "The universal quantifier validly distributes through a conjunction, but not through a disjunction," and so on. *All* of the evidence for the truth of these and like claims, as well as for their falsity, must ultimately derive from observation of instances of the appropriate classes of experiences, linguistic and otherwise, if Psychologism is true. But, of course, it simply does not do so. Hence, Psychologism is false. It is wrong about where and how the logician obtains evidence for the truths he teaches.

IV

All of which leaves us with the puzzle of how (i) and (ii) can be shown consistent with each other. It is interesting that many philosophers seem not to have been aware of this puzzle, much less worked out any solution for it. Frege, for example, distinguishes very clearly between what he calls an "idea" (a temporalized segment of the experience of some particular person) and what he calls a "thought." [3] As is well known, he takes certain complex 'thoughts' to be the bearers of truth, and assigns "to logic the task of discovering the laws of truth, not the laws of asserting or thinking." [4] But as to an elucidation of *how* these "thoughts" and "ideas" are related to one another, especially in such a way that the laws of the former allow us to ascertain (as we constantly do) the logical character of the latter, e.g., valid, inconsistent, etc. — on this Frege has nothing helpful to say. He agrees that something in the individual consciousness must be "aimed at" the thought for us to think it or have it.[5] But he has no analysis of this metaphor of "aiming." He gives the name "apprehension" (*Fassen*) to the relation of mind or "idea" to the thought, but of course has to acknowledge that this too is a metaphor.[6] The puzzle of how logicians' truths apply to and inform us about certain aspects of actual thinking and asserting is left unresolved by Frege, if, indeed, he had any clear perception of it at all. And in this respect he is typical of many of the best logicians and philosophers of recent decades.

Husserl, on the other hand, was driven to work out a solution to this puzzle by his attempts to understand, from what was at first a strongly psychologistic point of view, the anti-Psychologistic view of the *proposition*, as presented by Bolzano.

The pattern for the standard, anti-Psychologistic view of propositions (and concepts as well) was set by Bolzano's "*Satz an sich*," established by Frege's "*Gedanke*," and naturalized in Anglo-Saxon countries in the "proposition" of Russell, Moore, W. E. Johnson, L. S. Stebbing, R. M.

[3] "The Thought : A Logical Inquiry," in P. F. Strawson, ed., *Philosophical Logic* (Oxford, 1967), pp. 26-29; and "Der Gedanke," in Gottlob Frege, *Logische Untersuchungen*, Günther Patzig, ed. (Göttingen, 1966), pp. 40-43.
[4] Strawson, *op. cit.*, p. 19; and Frege, *op. cit.*, p. 31.
[5] Strawson, *op. cit.*, p. 35; and Frege, *op. cit.*, p. 50.
[6] Strawson, *op. cit.*, p. 35n; and Frege, *op. cit.*, p. 49n.

Eaton, and many other writers. In this pattern (and it is necessary here to think of a *pattern*, which allows some variation in the way it is specified by each writer) a proposition has the following main features :

1. The proposition is not located in space or in time, as, for example, sentences, or events involving sentences, are. This is in part what is meant by saying that they do not have *actual* or *real* existence, but only *ideal being*.

2. The proposition is not identical with a sentence, but the meaning or sense of an (indicative) sentence is a proposition. Propositions may, thus, be "expressed" by sentences, though it is not *essential* to them that they be so expressed.

3. The proposition is not something which can be sensuously perceived — even as a faint "glow" upon meaningful sentences or "living" words — thought it is, of course, *somehow* known, or, to use Frege's term, "apprehended."

4. The *same* proposition can be somehow grasped by the minds of *many* persons. In this capacity the proposition has been invoked as the intersubjective basis of the phenomena of communication and of the objectivity of scientific knowledge.

5. But it *need not* be grasped by the mind of any person at all. Its *esse* is not *percipi*. As Frege says, "In thinking we do not produce thoughts but we apprehend them... The work of science does not consist of creation but of the discovery of true thoughts." [7]

6. When the proposition is related to a mind, its relation is, or principally is, that of an *object* of thought or of the so-called "propositional attitudes," such as belief or doubt. It is "before" the mind. This is sometimes obscurely expressed by saying that it is the "content" of a belief or judgment.

7. Description of a proposition does not *essentially* involve a reference to any particular mind or act of thought with which it may be involved. Its truth value or what it refers to is never affected by such involvement, unless it happens to be a proposition which *refers* to such involvement.

8. But its description does essentially involve mention of its references *to*, or intendings or meanings *of*, certain things, plus description of how these references are related to one another. A proposition essentially consists of a more or less complex set of references, intentions, or meanings, plus the mode of their combination.

9. Finally, the proposition is what is underivatively true or false, while opinions or sentences or statements are true or false only because they have a certain relationship with a proposition.

---

[7] Strawson, *op. cit.*, p. 35; Frege, *op. cit.*, p. 50.

It would not be worthwhile here to document each point of this pattern in all of the writers mentioned above. The whole pattern appears in subsections 19, 25-26, 34, and 48-50 of vol. I of Bernard Bolzano's *Wissenschaftslehre*. In Frege's paper on "The Thought," already referred to, the pattern once again appears whole. It is almost whole in Moore's *Some Main Problems of Philosophy*, chap. 3; in chap. 1 of W. E. Johnson's *Logic*, Pt. I; on pages 6-24 of R. M. Eaton's *General Logic*; and on pages 17-20 of Max Black's *Critical Thinking* (2nd edition). Bertrand Russell's "On propositions : What They Are and How They Mean," in his *Logic and Knowledge*, as well as chap. 12 of his *Analysis of Mind*, presents important phases of the pattern, as well as some modifications of it. So does C. I. Lewis in chap. 3 of *An Analysis of Knowledge and Valuation*. Husserl's *adaptation* of the pattern is nowhere presented more clearly than in chaps. 7 and 8 of Vol. I, and in subsections 28-35 of the first "Investigation" in Vol. II of his *Logische Untersuchungen*.

V

And it obviously is with an *adaptation* or *modification* of the anti-Psychologistic pattern that we must be concerned, if its concept of the proposition is to be used in a resolution of the paradox at hand. It is clear that, if logicians' claims are fundamentally about the "propositions" described, then evidence for those claims could not be derived from a mere inductive survey of particular thinkings and speakings, to which, in the pattern, propositions have only a quite extrinsic and contingent connection. Thus, the pattern supports our (ii), and Husserl strongly concurs with it in this respect. But it is equally clear that the pattern, as it stands, gives us no help in reconciling (ii) with (i). It gives not the least suggestion of how logicians, having the source and sort of evidence they do have for their claims, do nonetheless succeed in saying something about the actual thinking and speaking of particular human beings. Where in the anti-Psychologistic pattern does the problem lie?

According to Bolzano — and point six of the anti-Psychologistic pattern — the relation between the mind and the propositions which it "thinks" or "grasps" is that of *intentionality*. That is, the proposition is the mind's object; or, to use one of Frege's terms it "stands over against" (*gegenübersteht*)[8] the mind thinking it. L. S. Stebbing expresses this view of the

---

[8] In "Die Verneinung : Eine Logische Untersuchung," in Gottlob Frege, *op. cit.*, p. 58.

proposition's relation to mind in words frequent in logical writings of her time, by saying that "a proposition is anything that is believed, disbelieved, doubted or supposed." [9] Of course the objections to this position on propositions are quite well known. They are stated, for example, on pages 35-36 of Vol. I of McTaggart's *The Nature of Existence*, and more fully on pages 105-111 of Gilbert Ryle's paper, "Are There Propositions?" [10] Perhaps the main points in these objections may be summed up by saying that the alleged "objective" propositions are a queer, or at least superfluous, sort of entity, and that they *are not* always, if they are ever, the objects of our beliefs, doubts, etc.

In fact, these are precisely Husserl's objections to objective propositions. He thought of Bolzano's "propositions in themselves" as "mythical entities, suspended between being and non-being." [11] And he held that when "we make an assertion, we judge about the fact concerned, and ... not about the judgment in the logical sense," [12] i.e., about the proposition. However, what is principally of interest here is not Husserl's objections to objective propositions, but rather his way of avoiding those objections, while still retaining the essence of anti-Psychologism in *his* view of the proposition and, simultaneously, resolving the paradox of Logical Psychologism.

VI

In the review just quoted from, Husserl indicates that the key for his revision of Bolzano's theory of propositions came from his study of yet another revision : Lotze's revision of Plato's theory of forms.[13] Plato's forms had, like Bolzano's propositions, been persistently called both queer and useless; and the queerness and uselessness alleged seemed mainly to follow upon their being located in something at some sort of "distance" from their instances — in some void or Divine Mind or Τόπος οὐράνιος. Lotze saw that this odd kind of "localization" was not required by the various argu-

---

[9] *A Modern Introduction to Logic* (London, 1961), p. 33. Cf. pp. 4-7 of W. E. Johnson, *Logic*, Pt. One (New York, 1964).

[10] *Proceedings of the Aristotelian Society*, vol. 30 (1929-1930) pp. 105-111.

[11] From page 290 of Husserl's review of *Der Streit der Psychologisten und Formalisten in der modernen Logik*, by Melchoir Palágyi (Leipzig, 1902). This review appeared in vol. 31 (1903) of *Zeitschrift für Psychologie und Physiologie der Sinnesorgane*, pp. 287-294. An English translation of this review appeared in *The Personalist*, 1972. (Included in this volume. — J. N. M.)

[12] *Logische Untersuchungen*, 5th ed., vol. 2, Pt. One, p. 103.

[13] Herman Lotze, *Logic*, ed. and trans. by Bernard Bosanquet (Oxford, 1884), Bk. III, chap. II, pp. 433-449.

ments for universals, and that it indeed made no sense anyway. He held that to say that blueness or triangularity, for example, "exists" or "is" is not to say that a certain color or plane figure is located somewhere nor is it to imply this.[14] It is only to say that certain discriminable elements of things have certain (always non-spatial and non-temporal) determinations of their own : — e.g., blueness is a color which is darker than yellowness (though no blue thing is), and triangularity is a plane figure involving fewer straight lines than squareness (though no triangular object is). One — really not quite correct — way which Lotze (and later Husserl) had of saying this was to say that for universals to exist means only that certain propositions about them are true.[15] To mark this point of connection between their existence and truth, Lotze said that universals do not have *real* existence, or *Wirklichkeit*, but only *ideal* being, which he also called *Geltung* or *validity*.[16]

Now Husserl does not detail for us precisely how this revision of Plato's theory of forms led to his revision of Bolzano's theory of the proposition "in itself." One can see, however, an attractive route which he may have traveled : — If universals can avoid the charges of queerness and superfluity by the assignment of ideal being or *Geltung*, then possibly propositions can escape by being regarded as universals. Such an identification of propositions with universals (of a certain sort) must have been rendered more attractive by observing that it conflicted with the anti-Psychologistic pattern for the proposition only on point six, and that the other points either do not conflict with it or actually seem to strengthen it, as does point four.

In any case, Husserl came to regard the propositions of which logicians speak, and for the truth of which, according both to him and Frege, they discover laws, as complex, *referential qualities*, which may or may not be instanced in minds, but which — following Brentano — are never instanced by any physical thing. He said that upon reading Lotze he

... saw that under "proposition in itself" is to be understood, ... what is designated in ordinary discourse — which always objectifies the ideal — as the "sense" of a statement. It is that which is explained as one and the same where, for example, different persons are said to have asserted the same thing ...

And it further became clear to me that this identical sense could be nothing other than the universal, the species, which belongs to a certain moment or phase

---

[14] *Ibid.*, p. 443.

[15] *Op. cit.*, pp. 439-446. And for Husserl see *Logische Untersuchungen*, Vol. II, Pt. I, p. 101.

[16] Of course, this is no more *in rebus* or *post rem* doctrine of universals. To deny that universals exist in some place apart from their instances is not at all to hold that they exist only (or at all) in their instances or in minds which have beheld their instances. Nor is it to say that they in any way depend, for their being known, upon their instances.

present in all actual assertions (*Aussagen*) with the same sense, and which makes possible the identification (of sameness) just mentioned, even where the descriptive content of the individual experiences (*Erlebnisse*) of asserting varies considerably in other respects. The proposition (*Satz*) thus relates to those acts of judgment (*Urteilsakte*) to which it belongs as their identical intention (*Meinung*) in the same way, for example, as the species redness relates to individuals of "the same" red color. Now with this view of things as a basis, Bolzano's theory, that propositions are objects which, nonetheless, have no "existence" (*Existenz*), comes to have the following quite intelligible signification : — They have the "ideal" being (*Sein*) or validity (*Gelten*) of objects which are universals (*allgemeiner Gegenstände*); and, thus, that being which is established, for example, in the "existence proofs" of Mathematics. But they do not have the real being (*reale Sein*) of things, or of dependent, thing-like moments — of temporal particulars in general. Bolzano himself did not give the faintest intimation that these phenomenological relationships between signification, signification moment, and full act of signifying had been noticed by him.[17]

And elsewhere Husserl says :

... In the actual experience of signification there corresponds to the unitary signification [18] an individual aspect as singular instance of the signification species : in the same way as in the red object the red-moment corresponds to the specific difference, red. If we actualize the act of signifying and, as it were, live in it, then we naturally mind the act's object and not its signification. When, for example, we make an assertion, we judge about the fact concerned, and not about the signification of the indicative sentence involved, not about the judgment in the logical sense. This latter becomes an object for us only in a reflective act of thought, in which we do not merely look back upon the *real*-ized assertion, but rather carry out the required abstraction (or, better said, ideation). This logical reflection is not ... an act which occurs under certain artificially induced conditions. Rather, it is a normal constituent of logical thinking.[19]

We may, therefore, sum up Husserl's revision of Bolzano's view of the proposition as follows : For Bolzano (and most anti-Psychologists) the relation of mind to proposition is *intentionality*, while for Husserl it is *instantiation* or *exemplification*.[20] The obviously increased intimacy of the connec-

---

[17] From p. 290 of the review of Palágyi.

[18] A "proposition" was one type of "signification" (*Bedeutung*) for Husserl, as it was one type of "sense" for Frege.

[19] *Logische Untersuchungen*, Vol. II, p. I, p. 103.

[20] The similarity between the views of Husserl and those of Gustav Bergmann on propositions should now be obvious. See Bergmann's *Logic and Reality* (Madison, 1964), p. 34 and elsewhere. The American psychologist R. S. Woodworth also advocated similar views early in this century. On p. 706 of his "Imageless Thought" (in *The Journal of Philosophy* for 1906) he says : "There is a specific and unanalyzable conscious quale for every individual and general notion, for every judgment and supposition. These qualities recur in the same sense as red and green recur."

tion as viewed by Husserl is the essence of his resolution of the paradox of Logical Psychologism.

VII

It seemed paradoxical that logicians could succeed in saying something true of particular events of thinking and speaking, since they do not develop their theories by inductive or empirical analysis of such events. Given Husserl's revision of the concept of the proposition, this fact may be explained as follows : Propositions, on his view, are not particular acts of thought, but complex, referential characters or qualities *of* such acts. These referential qualities also have determinations, among which are truth and falsity and conditions of truth and falsity. But these determinations do not merely have some quite extrinsic and contingent connection with the concrete acts of thinking and speaking which instance their immediate subjects, i.e., propositions. Somewhat as, since red is a color, a red thing, though no color, is necessarily a colored thing, so, we might say, an act of thought or speech which instances a true proposition, though itself no truth, is nonetheless a true judgment or utterance. And the various logical relations which hold between the truth conditions of propositions can similarly be given a natural extension to apply to the acts of belief or inference which involve instantiation of the proposition in question. The proposition, or set of propositions, introduces its determinations (properties and relations) into the individual acts which instance it.[21]

Because of this connection between universals and their instances, truths about universals, including, of course, truths about concepts and propositions,[22] entail corresponding truths about the corresponding individual things or events.[23] To take examples from logic, the proposition that the

[21] *Logische Untersuchungen*, 5th edition, Vol. I. See the sentence spanning pp. 142-143 and the sentence ending the paragraph on p. 151. Cf. p. 140 of Bertrand Russell's paper "The Limits of Empiricism" (*Proc. of the Arst. Society*, Vol. 36), where he discusses cases of *perception* of "facts about universals," and points out how this perception extends our knowledge of individual entities beyond the range of those that have been examined in sense experience. Russell here adopts precisely the view of Husserl about how knowledge of the properties of universals yields knowledge of the things which instance the universals in question.

[22] On p. 342 of *Logische Untersuchungen*, Vol. II, Husserl says : "As to all ideal units (i.e., universals), so there correspond to significations real possibilities and, perhaps, actualities. To significations *in specie* there correspond acts of signifying; and, indeed, the former are nothing but aspects of the latter, taken as ideal (*als Ideal Gefasste*)."

[23] See subsections 7 and 8 of Husserl's *Ideas* (New York, 1962), for elaboration of this claim. A clear exposition of essentially the same position is found in H. W. B. Joseph, *An Introduction to Logic*, 2nd ed. (Oxford, 1916), pp. 282-285.

proposition that Nixon is a Republican is true, has its transform in the proposition that all judgments or statements to the effect that Nixon is a Republican are true. Or again, the proposition that the premises of a certain syllogism of type Barabara imply its conclusion has its transform in the proposition that all actual inferences from those premisses to that conclusion are valid.

What the logician's truths are *primarily* about are, therefore, not mental or linguistic acts, but characters of acts; and it is from the analysis of the truth conditions of these characters (which, as universals, are always the same, no matter what their instances may be) that he obtains evidence for his claims. But his truths also apply informatively to particular acts, and do so precisely because they are about the characters *of* such acts. And *this* is Husserl's way out of the paradox of Logical Psychologism. It is unfortunate that it has been so universally neglected or misunderstood; for it concerns a central issue in the philosophy of logic, and there is perhaps no other philosopher who has worked out a way of reconciling our (i) and (ii) that is remotely as plausible as Husserl's way.[24]

---

[24] I must add that the above account is by no means the whole story on Husserl's view of propositions. In *Ideas*, Vol. I (see especially subsection 93) and in *Formal and Transcendental Logic* (The Hague, 1969), one finds an immensely — and, I think, unfortunately — more complex theory of propositions, which returns to an essentially Bolzanian or "neomatic" proposition.

ON THE QUESTION OF LOGICAL METHOD
IN RELATION TO EDMUND HUSSERL'S
*PROLEGOMENA TO PURE LOGIC**

by

PAUL NATORP
(Marburg)

translated by J. N. MOHANTY)

The problem of the method of logic has received a new and thorough treatment in the book by Edmund Husserl mentioned in the title of this paper. To attempt a critical review of it here is all the more appropriate because the problem obviously concerns also the "Criticism of Knowledge" of Kant and his successors. For, the task which Husserl ascribes to 'pure logic' is basically the same as that which the Kantians today call "Criticism of Knowledge."

The problems which the book wants to resolve are (p. 56) : whether logic is a purely theoretical or a practical discipline; whether or not logic is dependent on other sciences, especially psychology and metaphysics; whether it is concerned with the mere form of knowledge or also with its matter; whether it arrives at its theorems through *a priori* demonstration or empirically through induction. According to the author, there are fundamentally only two alternatives : one which looks upon logic as theoretical, independent of psychology, formal and demonstrative, and the other which considers it as practical, dependent on psychology, material and empirical. — This may, to a great extent, be true of the present state of the science. In itself, however, it is not clear that the purely theoretical, demonstrative logic which is independent of psychology can simply be only formal and cannot be in any sense material; Schuppe and the "transcendental" logic of Kant immediately suggest themselves as counter-instances. Also connected with this is the question about the relation of logic to metaphysics which has remained unnoticed in the contrast of the "two alternatives." One who holds it to be possible to ground a logic of objective truth purely theoretically and independently, would not easily allow for the possibility of a

* Edmund Husserl, *Logische Untersuchungen.* 1 Teil. *Prolegomena zur reinen Logik.* Halle : Niemeyer. 1900. XII, 285 p. (*Logical Investigations* vol. I, E. tr. by J. N. Findlay, New York : Humanities Press, 1970. Page references within the text are to the Findlay edition. Translated and reprinted from *Kant-Studien*, 6, 1901, with permission — J. N. M.)

metaphysics besides it; he would rather maintain that metaphysics is thereby resolved into logic, exactly as Kant said of the old 'ontology' that it was 'resolved' into the 'Analytic of pure understanding' — completely disregarding the fact that criticism of knowledge as fundamental philosophical discipline has a well justified claim to the title of a πρώτη φιλοσοφία. We shall come back to this point later on.

After this introduction to the problem (*Introduction*), the enquiry begins (ch. 1) with the question, whether logic is a normative science. The answer is in the affirmative : logic is the art or technology (Kunstlehre) of scientific knowledge. But now first arises the further question (ch. 2) regarding the theoretical foundation of this technology. Is it to be sought after outside of logic itself, in accordance with a point of view that is dominant today, in psychology, or has logic itself to do this job? In other words, is there a 'pure' logic i.e., theoretical logic that is built up entirely on its own basis and which serves as the foundation of logic as technology? The major part of the book is devoted to an attack on the first point of view, called by the author 'psychologism'; and he would seem to succeed in seriously shaking up this view which appears today to be so certain of itself and which has taken a firm root, in the last decades, through a series of works that are valuable in their own ways, insofar as Husserl does not restrict himself to proving the untenability of the view with the help of a barely sufficient deduction even if the latter touches the heart of the matter, but rather does not spare any effort to dislodge it from all sides, to follow their attempted defense to all possible hiding places, and to cut off, for them, all means of retreat.

The movement of thought of psychologism is somewhat as follows (ch. 3) : logic has to do only with psychic activities, how then can psychology not constitute its foundation? One of course contends that logic deals not with the actual but with the necessary employment of understanding, with thought as it ought to be, not as it is. The distinguishing mark can only be a psychological one. It is self-evidence (*Evidenz*). If one raises the objection that what logic enquires into is not the causality of thinking, but the conditions of its truth, then one can only mean the conditions of that psychological feature viz. self-evidence which must in any case be psychological conditions. The argument that logic cannot depend upon psychology since the latter, on the contrary, already presupposes the laws of logic, does not also appear to be a decisive point against psychologism, for every justification of the logical claims must also be in accordance with the logical laws themselves, and to that extent presuppose them. (See p. 94; the author believes that thereby he has met my remarks in *Philosophische Monats-*

hefte XXIII, p. 254f. In fact, he makes use of my discussions on p. 179. The discussions agree with those of the author in ch. 8. See further below.)

Psychologism thus appears in a favorable light. What in the first place makes it equally well unacceptable to the author is its sharp empiricistic consequences (ch. 4). Psychology is a science of facts, and so empirical. It can establish only approximate regularities of coexistence and succession, and these cannot provide the foundation for the logician truths insofar as the latter claim exact validity. The correctness of thinking shall be brought about by a peculiar sort of causality; but thereby one negates logical insight, for "how are we to have insight into causal laws?" Logical lawfulness is certainly not causality. Logical law never appears as a member in the chain of causation. One confuses between logical ground and causal bringing about an effect when one interprets logical ground as a constraint of thought. No logical law involves a fact or is a law of facts. To be sure, one comes to be aware of logical laws only in factually given cases, but the content of logical insight is not a consequence of the psychological particularity. All knowledge certainly begins with experience, but does not therefore arise from it. If there are "insightfully known" laws, they cannot therefore be laws of psychological facts. "No truth is a fact" i.e., something temporally determinate; if that were so, then a consequence would be the countersense that the law itself comes into being and goes out of existence — and that in accordance with a law. — The argument is weighty, in fact totally devastating, but clearly under the presupposition that one is already convinced that there are strict laws at least in logic and mathematics. And yet it is this consequence which the defender of psychologism finds himself forced to admit, i.e., to give up all strict laws, which does not correspond to the intentions of the great majority of the psychological logicians. Psychologism to skepticism, in order to be able to assert anything. Ch. 7 will show how the author will not let it be in peace even in this last resort; in the next two chapters, he continues to follow the path suggested in ch. 4 insofar as he subjects the psychological interpretation of the fundamental principles of logic (ch. 5) and the theory of syllogism (ch. 6) to more specific examination.

Extreme empiricism does not shrink from the consequence that even the ultimate principles of logic are only vague generalizations of psychological experiences. The principle of contradiction shall then say : two mutually contradictory acts of belief cannot co-exist. But this proposition is incomplete : one has to say, under what circumstances this is not possible. For, such co-existence does in fact occur. What is meant is : under normal circumstances, in the case of human beings, etc.. But there is still lacking every

secure delimitation, one does not even attempt it once. Concerning the ultimate foundations of all science, one is satisfied with quite vague presuppositions. The proposition which is to support the entire structure of knowledge is itself the model of a crudely inexact and unscientific proposition.
But that is not any more the proposition of logic; for, the latter asserts
that two contradictory propositions, under no circumstances, can both be
true — in absolute strictness and exclusiveness. Husserl convincingly formulates Hume's defect thus : mediate judgments of fact permit no rational
justification, but only psychological clarification, but what justifies this
clarification? Since it rests on only mediate judgments of fact, it is itself
incapable of a rational justification. And the author passes the following
judgment on Mill : where one is concerned with the fundamental basis of
his empiricistic prejudices, this so deeply ingenious man is, as it were,
forsaken by all the gods. One says, contradictory propositions exclude
each other in thought, but one means : in correct judging. But that is a
tautology, nothing is proved therewith for the impossibility of real co-existence. Or, one says they exclude each other in consciousness, and means
the over-temporal ideal consciousness; that again is only a reformulation of
the logical principle which has nothing to do with psychology. Or : "nobody
can" simultaneously think contradictories — namely, no one who is
rational : the others we call irrational. For those who judge correctly, and
for no one else, does this impossibility hold good. In brief, quite unjusti-
fiedly one puts 'non-coexistence' in place of 'not being able to be true
together.' One confuses objectively determined incompatibility with subjective incapability of performing the unification. — If one applies the theory
to the theory of syllogism, then is not every fallacious inference a counter-
instance? A contradiction that is noticed would of course be eliminated,
but does not the 'law of contradiction' hold also for the unnoticed ones?
Occasionally, one speaks in the same breath of striving after contradiction-
free thought and of the impossibility of thinking what is self-contradictory.
What does it mean to strive after something whose opposite is impossible,
etc.?

As pointed out, chapter 7 will demonstrate more decisively the skeptical
consequences of psychologism. The theory transgresses the evident conditions of the possibility of a theory in general. The conditions are two-fold :
the subjective possibility of distinguishing evident from blind judgments
('noetic' condition), and the objective constituents of a theoretical unity in
general ('logical' conditions). Husserl defines skepticism as the denial of
either the logical or the noetic conditions of the possibility of a theory in
general. Scepticism in this sense — which goes beyond the metaphysical

scepticism with regard to the knowability of "things in themselves," and does not necessarily tie itself to it — is directly counter-sensical. (Perhaps only if one wants a strict theory at any cost. The sceptic will probably say that he also wants it, but then finds it to be an unattainable ideal. Besides, the doubt arises again whether the question about the object can at all be separated from the question about the logical principles; whether in fact the latter say nothing about the object in any manner, since there is no knowledge that is not of objects. The author himself asserts the 'objectivity' of the logical in the sense of non-subjectivity; but can subjectivity be overcome without the object being thereby posited? 'Thing in itself' means, however, nothing but : unlimited objectivity.) Husserl now examines more exactly scepticism or sceptical relativism in its individualistic formulation : for him, it "is refuted, no sooner than it is stated," — for one to whom the objectivity of everything logical is evident. (But this precisely is what is contested.) He devotes more detailed examination to B. Erdmann's "specific" i.e. anthropological relativism. This too is counter-sensical, insofar as it wants to leave open the possibility that what is true for one species is false for another. But the logical principles express only what belongs to the meanings of the words 'true' and 'false.' If they were true only for a species, then there could possibly be for a species no truth at all, or it could possibly be true that nothing is true, and so on. The presuppositions of every theory cannot certainly be rendered doubtful by any theory, without thereby annulling itself as a theory. Psychologism however, in every form has relativism as its consequence; truth becomes psychological experience. It is rather an 'Idea' (in a quite Platonic sense, p. 149).

Chapter 8 will directly refute the arguments of psychologism directly, not — as the preceding one — from its consequences. 1) One contends that the norms for regulating psychic activities must themselves be psychologically founded. As against this, Husserl definitely states : the idea of norm does not essentially belong to the content of logical propositions; one may equally well express mathematical propositions in the form of prescriptions, although they certainly are purely theoretical. One does not, therefore, counter psychologism correctly when one plays off, as against it, the normative character of logic; what is rather relevant is its purely theoretical character. And here Husserl himself makes use of arguments which apparently were rejected by him earlier : truths which are grounded purely in the content or meaning of those concepts which constitute the idea of science as objective unity, cannot themselves belong to the domain of any one of the special sciences such as psychology. That on the contrary the logical laws should hold good for the construction of logic itself, may be paradoxical but certainly not logically objectionable. What truly contrasts with natural law is not normative law but ideal law which is purely theoretical. — 2) Logic speaks of representations, concept, judgments, inferences, proofs; all these are psychic structures; how then could the propositions relating to them not be psychological? — Reply : The same argument would transform mathematics (and all sciences in general) into psychology. Rather, the objects of pure logic, as much as those of mathematics, are 'ideal species'; their fundamental concepts have no empirical extension (factual singularities, individuals), they consist in purely ideal singularities (like the numbers of mathematics). But in present-day logic one speaks confusingly of representations in the psychological sense and of contents of representations, of judgments as psychic acts and of the contents of judgments (proposition), etc. One does not distinguish between psychological interconnection of the acts of knowing in which science is subjectively realised, the interconnection of the facts that are known and that constitute the region of science, and the logical structure. (The second coincides with the third in the case of pure logic and arithmetic.) — 3) One understands evidence (Evidenz) as a psychological property, and makes logic into a causal theory of such evidence. — Here Husserl concedes that logical propositions do in a certain sense contain the psychological conditions of evidence; but the propositions themselves do not state them, but take on this significance only through psychological application and transformation. From every pure logical proposition, it is possible to derive psychological conditions of evidence; for the evidence of judgments is subject on the one hand, to the merely psychological conditions such as concentration of interest, mental alertness, training, etc., but, on the other to the ideal conditions which are valid for every possible (and so also for any given) consciousness. (I must confess that the issue does not seem to me to have been fully settled thereby. Husserl himself has, on earlier occasions, so energetically and correctly denied that logical and ideal laws could enter into the chain of causation, that it can only be due to an obscurity of expression that it appears to be otherwise. What I mean is that, a purely theoretical logic has nothing at all to say about the psychological experience of evidence; it says only that there are relations of agreement amongst unities of thought which are conditioned by such and such determinate contentual (*inhaltlichen*), fundamental relations. The relations obtain, which means not that they occur in the experiences of the thinking mind, but that they subsist atemporally like the relation $1+1=2$. Certainly, we would not have known anything of such atemporal being if there were no temporal experience of 'insight' in which, according to Husserl's manner of speaking, the 'ideality' is 'realised' for us; but nothing of the temporal character of this experience affects the content of what we thus perceive in time. "Truth is an Idea, whose individual instance, in evident judgment, is actual experience," says Husserl (p. 194). That needs to be explained, if it is not to be metaphysically misunderstood. Or should one take it as metaphysical? Then it would appear that it is not logic, but the settlement of the border dispute between logic and psychology, which depends upon metaphysics. Similarly, when he says, "Where there is nothing, one can see nothing," or also "Where there 'is' no truth, nothing would be seen as truth" — whereby it is sought to be proved that the truth of the content of a judgment is the essential pre-condition of the 'feeling' of evidence — the logical law would appear to enter into the chain of causation, for what else can the pre-condition of a 'feeling' be other than condition in the causal sense?

Also the biological foundation of logic (attempted by Mach and Avenarius, later assimilated by Cornelius entirely into psychologism) from the standpoint of 'economy of thought' is subject to a special examination (in chapter 9). It rests on a ὕστερον πρότερον. In itself, pure logic precedes economy of thought. It is countersensical to found the former in the latter. The reasons against such an attempt are essentially the same as those against psychologism.

A concluding consideration to this entire critique (ch. 10) touches upon historical antecedents which, in so far as they concern critical philosophy, will be examined by me at the end. Amongst the advocates of psychologism — to note this here — Mill, Sigwart, Erdmann and Heymans are treated in most details, Wundt, considering his great influence, receives too little attention, Riehl hardly any, Lipps no more than they. Schuppe, who has already entered into an argument with the author, should have been given a more decisive assessment. (*Archiv für systematische Philosophie*, VII, p. 1ff. Compare also my report on Schuppe's *Grundriss, ibid.*, III, pp. 103ff., and on Wundt's criticism of Schuppe, VI, pp. 214ff.)

In the last chapter (ch. 11), the author develops his own positive conception of pure logic. What is sought after is the unity of science as objective and ideal interconnection, and therewith the unity of objectivity or of truth — these two being, to be sure, not identical, but separable only by abstraction. What however determines the unity of science? The unity of grounding interconnections (*Begründungszusammenhanges*), of the interconnection of laws. This must, in the purely theoretical ('nomological') sciences, lead to fundamental principles. The concrete or factual sciences derive their theoretical content from the sciences of principles (*Gesetzwissenschaften*). The fundamental problem of logic then concerns the conditions of possibility of science in general, of theory in general, of truth in general, of deductive unity — the necessary generalisation of the Kantian question regarding the conditions of the possibility of experience, for this meant, as Husserl recognises, the unity of objective lawfulness. The 'conditions' sought after are naturally to be understood as ideal, as concerning only the content, but not in the subjective sense. The question therefore arises, what are the primitive 'possibilities' out of which the 'possibility' of theory is constituted, i.e. what are the primitive 'essential concepts' from which the essential concept of theory itself is constituted. All logical justification of our concepts must go back to this ultimate foundation. Pure logic then is the theory of theories, the science of sciences. In particular, it has to be asked : what are all those primitive concepts which make possible the connection of knowledge in objective respect for the theoretical connectedness, or which constitute the idea of theoretical unity? What are the purely formal objective 'categories,' independent of the specificity of any and every cognitive matter, under which all concepts specially appearing in thought, all objects, propositions, states of affairs must order themselves? They are to be discovered through reflection on the human thought functions, they are then to be separately fixed and investigated in their logical, not psychological, origin. (Later on, he will not allow the word 'origin' because of the risk of psychologistic interpretation. But he could not avoid speaking of 'primitive' concepts. One generally opposes the original to the derived, not only in a psychological sense. When one speaks of a derivation or deduction, one cannot help speaking of origin.) Next to be considered are the laws that are founded in the categorial concepts and that concerns not only their complications but also their objective validity. To this belongs not merely the foundation of syllogistic, but also the basic propositions of pure arithmetic. There must however be a closed number of primitive or basic laws which are immediately founded in the categorial concepts and which, by virtue of their homogeneity, constitute an all-comprehensive theory. Finally, one has to move forward to the essential types or forms of theory, and then to its differentiation into possible theories, which also has to be executed purely *a priori* through compelling deduction. A partial realisation of the idea is to be found in mathematical theory of sets. In general, the development of logical theory leads everywhere to pure mathematics. Thus there arises here a new border issue to which logicians have given the least thought : the question about the border line between logic and mathematics. Construction of theories is always left to mathematics which, already since a long time, does not see its own limitations in number and quality, which has, in particular, completely made itself the master of the syllogistic and has given it an unexpected extension at a time when one had taken it to have been closed. But the mathematician is not a pure theoretician, but an ingenious technician, a constructor. Precisely for that reason, his work deserves special epistemological criticism which is a task of the philosopher. If science — for the author, as for Plato and Kant, already the same as mathematics — constructs theories, then philosophy enquires into the theory of theories. The discussion wants to show thereby that actually something is achieved which mathematics as such could not achieve and which yet needs to be done. — Empirical science should not be reduced to pure theory. All theory in the empirical sciences is merely presumptive theory; it explains not from 'insightfully certain,' but from 'insightfully probable' principles. Even the facts themselves are only probabilities. But probability itself again has its own laws; these must be comprehended within pure logic in its completeness. Yet Husserl will, to be sure, limit his investigations primarily to the domain of pure knowledge.

It seemed appropriate to the importance of the subject matter that the author be permitted to express himself in his own words, with only few occasional interruptions through critical remarks. When I come to add some remarks to it as a whole, critically and possibly by way of carrying the author's thesis forward, it should appear obvious — not merely to the readers of the *Kant-Studien* — that I seek to relate the efforts of the author to those of Kant as also of present-day critical philosophy. For this relationship lies tangibly present in the nature of things and is not completely concealed from the author himself. In fact, he believes that Kant and his school are still deeply imprisoned in psychologism. He certainly concedes (p. 122, fn. 1) that Kant's theory of knowledge "has aspects which strive to go beyond the psychologism of *mental faculties as sources of knowledge* and in fact succeed in doing so"; but they have also "strongly noticeable aspects which fall within psychologism." A large number of the Neo-Kantians belong, according to him, "to the sphere of psychologising epistemologists, however little they may fancy the name. Transcendental psychology also is psychology." Unfortunately, he only names one of them i.e. Lange whose reduction of the *a priori* to the 'organisation' has long since been recognised as wrong and decisively rejected by Cohen as well as by those who have learnt from Cohen. If nevertheless, for example, even Cohen does not scrupulously avoid phrases which are psychologically oriented, that happens because he trusts that the explanations given rule out all suspicion of psychologism. One who wants to find the psychological, will find it everywhere, also in Husserl. It does not help him at all, that he (p. 214) repeats those cheap pleasantries about "those misleading mythical concepts which Kant so much loves... the concepts of Understanding and Reason," which "in the proper meaning of faculties of the soul" do not make us any more smarter than if we, in an analogous case, wanted to explain the art of dancing by the faculty of dancing, or the art of painting by the faculty of painting, and so on. It does not help him at all, when he himself, with no less preference, uses the words 'insight,' 'insightful,' and even 'rational,' which are no less open to the charge of psychologism. That he at all speaks of an 'a priori,' as if no one could thereby suspect something psychological, suffices to place him totally in the same damnation along with transcendental philosophy. This would mean that if only he extended a small finger towards the devil, he would surely have to give away the entire hand. But if one reads in Kant 'concept' for 'Understanding,' 'Idea' for 'Reason,' and so all throughout, then one will not only succeed in understanding, but would very soon recognise, that Kant, in his concepts 'Understanding,' 'Reason,' etc., would not like to settle even a secondary issue of his transcendental philosophy, not to speak of one of its fundamental issues. Why, for what reason, did he devote such great effort to the purification of the list of categories, to the 'deduction' of the pure concepts of the understanding and the principles. Why did he express the sharp warning, in connection with the 'Postulates,' that to claim that any synthetic proposition whatsoever is "immediately certain, independent of any justification," to "ascribe to it without *deduction*, and in view of its own claim, unlimited validity" would certainly amount to frustrating all criticism of understanding and to giving up understanding to every fancy or delusion? Why at all did 'Understanding' and 'Reason' need a criticism, if through them, as given psychological instances, any question in philosophy of knowledge could have been answered? They serve everywhere only to actually exhibit and exactly delimit the *problems*, never to solve those problems. In psychological respect, they say nothing more than that the objective content of knowledge must somehow represent itself in the subjective course of knowing, which is the same as what, in Husserl, receives the far more questionable, because metaphysically sounding, formulation that the 'Ideal' 'realises' itself in the experiences of mental life.

Husserl has made an understanding of Kant impossible, an understanding which is so necessary for his purpose, especially because of the fact that as a logician he has chiefly depended upon Kant's 'pure logic,' especially on the summary of lectures made by Jäsche in a sufficiently "brief and dry" manner, whereas in fact Kant's decisive contribution to logic has to be sought for in "transcendental" logic. If one completely separates from this latter all psychological elements, i.e. the subjective deduction which Kant himself so definitely distinguishes from the 'objective' deduction, and keeps before one's mind the pure structure of the content of the "transcendental" logic as such, then it would correspond, in all purity, to the ideal outlined by Husserl. He moves forward from fundamental concepts to fundamental principles, and from them to fundamental sciences, exactly as Husserl requires it and as Plato, the true discoverer of logic had clearly seen. (See my discussion in Hermes, XXV, 411-426.) And thereby Kant answers the question regarding the "possibility" of actually given sciences, which Husserl himself states as the ultimate and the purest formulation of the basic question of logic. It should not be hard to come to an agreement about this, especially after I have to thank the author for his explicit agreement with the general consequences which I have drawn exactly on this basis in the article "Über objektive und subjektive Begründung der Erkenntnis" (*Philosophische Monatshefte*, XXIII, 257ff., 1887) and have defended in my *Einleitung zur Psychologie* (1888) and often in occasional, chiefly critical discussions (with regard to "Psychologism," especially on Lipps in *Gött. gel. Anz.* 1885, March 1).

Or, is the continuing distrust of critical philosophy perhaps a symptom of a deep-lying difference? Already the question has been raised above, why does in fact Husserl insist on the 'formal,' not the material character of logic? It is all the more remarkable because Husserl, on the other hand, intends to prove the 'objective' validity of the logical laws, but he is not thereby wanting to restrict it to what has been up till now called 'formal' logic but includes the entire pure mathematics within it when every advocate of 'formal' logic has taken mathematics to be the 'matter' of the sciences. With respect to its scope as well as content, the 'formal' seems accordingly to coincide with the 'pure' and at the same time 'objective' i.e. with the *transcendental*. There also remains unresolved, in Husserl, the *opposition* between formal and material, *a priori* and empirical, and along with it that between the logical and the psychological, the objective and the subjective; or, to put it in one word and at the same time in his own terminology : the ideal and the real. The material, empirical, psychological i.e. the 'real' remains an uncomprehended, irrational surd; the question about the *relation*, the inner, epistemological and also the *logical* bond between the two is not at all raised, but with their sharp and pure *separation* the problem is laid to rest. And therefore in spite of all the extraordinary lucidity of each special logical discussion — I venture to say — the reader is left with a certain logical dissatisfaction. One follows the dramatically tense struggle between the two opponents, and yet does not see, where precisely is the root of their opposition, what precisely is that which makes this life and death battle necessary; but therewith an exact reciprocal relationship, even an inseparable belonging together between the two shows itself more and more, which is all the more surprising since one is allowed at the beginning only to witness their antagonism. Now while the author of the drama, in clear partisanship, sides with the 'Ideal' and in this truly Platonic sense pays allegiance to 'Idealism,' the 'real' remains alien, confused, and yet as a surd that cannot be done away with. The 'idealism' however wanted to ground the real in the ideal, the *onta* in the *logoi*; the same in Plato, in Leibniz, in Kant — who with special clarity recognises the problem of *object* (*Gegenstand*) itself as the central problem of his new 'transcendental' logic and even constructs the entire concept of the object from the formal components of knowledge, out of the logical in the deepest sense. The only intelligible consequence is : that the opposite of the objective, the subjective, the quasi-object of psychology, appears the mere reverse, and at the same time the 'reflection,' of the objective; what would be explained is, why is it that the deepest investigation into the constitution of objectivity cannot avoid taking subjectivity into consideration. I have tried not so much to interpret, as to further develop Kant in this direction; and I presume, that when the development of his logical investigations will, as is unavoidable, bring him face to face with this problem which has been left unresolved in his 'Prolegomena,' and in fact hardly recognized now, Husserl will find himself forced to move in the same direction. A bond, a *logical* connection *must* be set up between the super-temporal being of the logical and its temporal actualization in the experience of the mind, if the words 'Realization of the Ideal, are not to remain an enigma, a metaphysical locution of the most suspicious sort. If such a connection is to be possible, then that can only be from the side of the super-temporal and through the mediation of (in itself still super-temporal) the *Concept* of Time itself. The 'realization' then means no more a mystical metaphysical act, but a strictly intelligible logical transition from one mode of consideration to another, which ultimately was already implicit in it. And then it becomes first clear what the psychological truly 'is,' what is the source of its collision with the logical, and in which ultimate mediation, itself logical, this conflict is reconciled. The drama must be led towards this climax (*Peripetie*), till then the curtain should not fall.

But we have before us only the 'First Part'; it was certainly advantageous for the instruction of the logical investigation to completely lay aside the psychological. We are therefore thankful for what has been achieved, and should expect still more positive advancements from the continuation of the investigations which, since these lines were written, have already appeared and shall be afterwards critically evaluated here.

HUSSERL ON THE APODICTIC EVIDENCE
OF IDEAL LAWS*

by

ARNE NAESS

(Oslo)

It is now more than 50 years since the publication of Husserl's *Logische Untersuchungen*. His argumentations are formulated with such care, thoroughness and vigour, and many of his conclusions are so well substantiated by later research, that the book is justly regarded as one of the philosophy classics of our century.

There is a quality in the *Logische Untersuchungen* which is not often commented upon, but which deserves unreserved praise : the fairness and unbiasedness, the *Sachlichkeit* of his exposition of the doctrines criticised, especially those of psychologism. No charge is directed against imaginary adversaries, but against amply quoted assertions in definite texts. Considering the passion and consequence with which Husserl hammers out his views, this fairness is most admirable and makes his contribution singularly adapted to philosophical analysis.

In this article, some reflections are made about the character of the phenomenological approach. They do not conclude in any criticism of the main thesis of *Logische Untersuchungen*, but interpret them in the light of a philosophy of philosophy which is diametrically opposite to that of Husserl.

Husserl continues the tradition of those philosophers who try to bring certain fundamental disciplines *in den sicheren Gang einer Wissenschaft* by starting from apodictically certain, definitely established, intuitively grasped truths. The present article represents the tradition of those who believe that the status of science will, if at all, be reached by continuation and expansion of that kind of research which has provided us with matter-of-fact knowledge, tentative hypotheses and laws with different degrees of high probability.

Husserl attacks "psychologism" and "extreme empiricism." The first

* Reprinted from *Theoria*, 20, 1954, with permission — J. N. M.

term is defined in § 17 of the first volume of *Logische Untersuchungen*, as a kind of theory about the relation of psychology to formal logic. "Die wesentlichen theoretischen Fundamente (der Logik) liegen in der Psychologie, — Die Logik verhält sich zur Psychologie wie irgendein Zweig der chemischen Technologie zur Chemie, wie die Feldmesskunst zur Geometrie u. dgl." [1] "In theoretischer Beziehung verhält sich also die Logik zur Psychologie wie der Teil zum Ganzen. Ihr Hauptziel ist es zumal, Sätze der Form herzustellen : Gerade so und nicht anders müssen sich — allgemein oder unter bestimmt charakterisierten Umständen — die intellektuellen Betätigungen formen, anordnen und zusammenschliessen, damit die resultierenden Urteile den Character der Evidenz, der Erkenntnis im prägnanten Sinne des Wortes erlangen." [2]

The imposing development of symbolic logic as an independent science in recent decades and also its close connection with mathematics makes it difficult for us to understand how eminent thinkers such as St. Mill, Sigwart und Erdmann could embrace the plainly untenable doctrines of psychologism. The development has no striking parallel in causal sciences having human reasoning in logic and mathematics as their subject-matter. The belief of St. Mill, Sigwart, Erdmann, Lipps, Cornelius that such sciences under the leadership of the new psychology should be able to explain genetically and causally the development of the formal sciences, was unwarranted or at least premature. The traditions of empiricism suffered from the defeat, and it is characteristic that many philosophers of our day who strongly emphasize their empirical and "anti-metaphysical" leanings (Russell, Carnap a. o.) are severe in their criticism of the dominant trends in empirical theory of knowledge of the 19th Century.

The mistake of psychologism is only a consequence of a much deeper and more common mistake, according to Husserl. "Die psychologistischen Logiker verkennen die grundwesentlichen und ewig unüberbrückbaren Unterschiede zwischen Idealgesetz und Realgesetz, zwischen normierender

---

[1] *Logische Untersuchungen* ("L.U."), I, p. 51. All quotations are from the 2nd edition, Halle, 1913. ["The essential theoretical foundations of Logic lie in psychology... Logic is related to psychology just as any branch of chemical technology is related to chemistry, as land-surveying is to geometry etc." Findlay edition, I, p. 90.]

[2] L.U., I, p. 57. ("Theoretically regarded, Logic therefore is related to psychology as a part to a whole. Its main aim is, in particular, to set up propositions of the form : Our intellectual activities must, either generally, or in specifically characterized circumstances, have such and such a form, such and such an arrangement, such and such combinations and no others, if the resultant judgments are to have the character of evidence, are to achieve knowledge in the pointed sense of the word." Findlay Edition, I, pp. 94-95.)

Regelung und kausaler Regelung, zwischen logischer und realer Notwendigkeit, zwischen logischem Grund und Realgrund." [3]

The psychologists seemed to believe that the *principium contradictionis* can be *validated* by an inference with psychological or, more generally, factual premises. Many premises were offered. We cannot at the same time both believe and not believe in the same proposition. If we deny the laws of thought, we reaffirm them in our very denial. The principle of contradiction evokes in us complete evidence.

Because of and on the basis of these or other *Tatsachen* concerning human beings and their thinking, the *principium contradictionis* is valid — according to psychologism. It would be possible to reformulate pure logic as a factual science, a kind of anthropological discipline.

Husserl maintains that a "reformulation" along these lines annihilates formal logic, and there is scarcely anybody who would disagree with him today on that point. From the invalidity of p & q. &. ~ (p & q) in the propositional calculus, one could not after the "reformulation" rigorously infer any other proposition, let us say p & q. &. p v q. From the unableness to think the former does not "follow" the unableness to think the latter. There may be constant confirmation of both instances of inability, and this justifies an inductive inference, but no proof of the propositional calculus could be formulated on that basis.

On the other hand — and this is often forgotten in the laudable effort to stamp out every trace of psychologism — the programme of a science of science remains. A science of science must include research dealing with human scientific activity and its products — including pure logic, pure mathematics and pure theory of knowledge in the sense of Husserl. Among the objects studied, we find the calculus of propositions in various modifications and all the proofs, axioms, rules, metamathematical devices developed in recent times. It is part of the task of empirical philosophy to explore the possibilities of a *kausale Tatsachenwissenschaft*, of establishing *reale Notwendigkeiten* and *Realgründe*. On the basis of such research it is in principle legitimate to expect *predictions* of experiences of apodictic evidence and the establishment of *die Logik als normative und praktische Disziplin* (L.U. I, chapter I). And all this without committing empirical philosophy to any form of psychologism.

Husserl does not reject the possibility of such sciences of the real — he

---

[3] L.U., I, p. 68. ("The psychologistic logicians ignore the fundamental, essential, never-to-be-bridged gulf between ideal and real laws, between normative and causal regulation, between logical and real necessity, between logical and real grounds." Findlay Edition, I, p. 104.)

only emphasizes that their laws neither can prove nor disprove any strict law, e.g., of the kind we require in order to develop formal sciences.

In the realm of the ideal laws in the sense of Husserl, there is necessity and complete exactness of content. And in so far as sentences are intended to express ideal laws and their interconnections, their *claims* must be to express necessary connections and complete exactness of content.

A researcher in pure mathematics may feel uncertain whether the proofs in his latest publication are all valid, he may even sincerely believe that the probability is less than 0.99 that all conclusions follow in complete strictness from the premises. But this will not induce him to change the claims from that of a strict proof to that of a reasonable argumentation. He stands or falls with his *proofs*.

We do not know which claims of living mathematicians and logicians are warranted and which are not. The only way of substantiating any claim is to go through the proofs repeatedly and increase their completeness and explicitness. If we as part of this activity make assumptions such as that oneself or the author of a text (actually) follows his definitions, or that he (actually) has certain intentions, these assumptions do not belong to the proofs. They cannot add or diminish the validity of conclusions. According to Husserl the validity is either apodictic or not of the kind required in an exact science. Any matter-of-fact assumption about definitions being followed introduces, it seems to me, something foreign to apodictic reasoning.

So much about pure and factual sciences in general. Let us then ask for instances satisfying the requirements of being parts of sciences. It is comparatively easy to give instances satisfying the modest requirement of factual sciences, but, if we are right in our interpretation of Husserl, there are formidable difficulties confronting those who will establish parts of a pure science beyond doubt.

Husserl argues that we have apodictical evidence of pure or ideal laws, such as *modus barbara*. But the assertion that he or any other has this evidence, does not belong to pure logic or any other pure or formal science. It belongs to a factual science concerning the relation of logicians (and others) to pure sciences. It is not necessary to conceive this to be psychology. It is enough for our argumentation that it is a science of facts or more generally, a science about the real rather than the ideal.

Any assertion *that* a sentence interpreted as intended by a logician (or by myself, or by any other person) expresses an ideal law (and therefore something completely exact and of apodictic validity) is a sentence in principle belonging to the *Tatsachenwissenschaften*. It does not belong to pure science (*reine Wissenschaftslehre, reine Erkenntnistheorie*) but to a part of science concerned with certain kinds of objects and asserting things about those objects which may be true or false, depending on our shifting abilities of thinking and observing.

Factually existing sentences in treatises of pure logic may — as Husserl says — have the claim to express ideal laws. But from a claim does not follow its own satisfaction. Which sentences actually express ideal laws, is a question admitting different answers, contradicting each other. The products of logicians are human products and whatever their aspirations, the adequateness of their relations to the entities of the realm of the ideal is not apodictically evident. They must be established inductively.

If it is objected that certain strict laws such as the *principium contradictionis* cannot be doubted because its very denial reaffirms the principle, the argumentation is already within the realm of *Tatsachenwissenschaften* : it is asserted something about the possibility or impossibility of certain acts of thinking, doubting etc. The arguments against psychologism are applicable to such an attempt to validate that ideal law which Husserl gives the name *principium contradictionis*.

The objection is also ill-conceived, because no argument in the foregoing paragraphs has been directed against the apodictic validity of the ideal laws. The subject-matters under consideration are the products of existing mathematicians and logicians in their relation to ideal laws. Does any such product express an ideal law?

In the foregoing we have mentioned how Husserl conceives the difference between the real and the ideal sciences. We shall now consider what he offers as a criterion by which we can know beyond doubt to have reached knowledge in the strict sense of the word, *Wissen im strengsten Sinne*. The criterion is *evidence*. Husserl elucidated what he means by "Evidenz" by calling it (defining it?) *unmittelbares Innewerden der Wahrheit selbst* and "*die lichtvolle Gewissheit, dass ist, was wir anerkannt, oder nicht ist, was wir verworfen haben.*" [4] Evidence is, of course, to be distinguished from one's merely being completely convinced about something. The difference is itself evident in certain special situations, namely when we concentrate on ideal relations such as those expressed by the pure science.

Let us quote a passage in which Husserl describes how we as human beings can meet and grasp ideal existences and reach apodictic certainty. "Indem wir nun einen Erkenntnisakt vollziehen oder, wie ich es mit

---

[4] L.U., I, p. 13. ("an immediate intimation of truth itself," and "the luminous certainty that what we have acknowledged *is*, that what we have rejected *is not*." Findlay Edition, I, pp. 60/1.)

Vorliebe ausdrücke, in ihm leben, sind wir, 'mit dem Gegenständlichen beschäftigt,' das er, eben in erkennender Weise, meint und setzt; und ist es Erkenntnis im strengsten Sinne, d.h. urteilen wir mit Evidenz, so ist das Gegenständliche originär *gegeben*. Der Sachverhalt steht uns jetzt nicht bloss vermeintlich, sondern wirklich vor Augen und in ihm der Gegenstand selbst, als das, was er ist, d.h. genau so und nicht anders, als wie er in dieser Erkenntnis gemeint ist : als Träger dieser Eigenschaften als Glied dieser Relationen u. dgl." [5]

This passage, with its many striking metaphors, is as good as any in calling to attention what sometimes happens when we assert such a truth as *modus barbara* or "dass die drei Höhen eines Dreieckes sich in einem Punkte schneiden." (L.U., II, 44.) And I doubt that anybody with truth could say that he never has the experience of "Erkenntnis im strengsten Sinne." If he is inclined toward skepticism he may get rid of that experience relating to a particular assertion, but in extricating himself from what he considers an illusion of absolute or apodictic knowledge, he runs the risk of having a new experience of the kind he just subjected to scrutiny.

On the other hand, there is nothing in the description by Husserl that eliminates the possibility of mistaking knowledge of less than the strictest kind for a piece of knowledge of the strictest kind. The history of pure mathematics and doctorate theses turned down illustrates this point. There is nothing in the description of how we arrive at and judge apodictic knowledge that can help people who do not *really* have a *Sachverhalt wirklich vor Augen* but are fully convinced that they have.

From this I conclude that it is not possible to describe the intimate meeting of human beings with the *Sachverhalt* in such a way that it can be effectively described for the benefit of those who doubt that they have the power to distinguish those meetings from others.

Husserl seems to rely not so much on the description of the crucial meeting as on the exemplifications. He points to assertions which are apt to cause such meetings if grasped in their exact meaning. Of such examples he offers us many, 'allgemein gilt für beliebige Klassentermini A, B, C, dass, wenn alle A B und alle B C sind, auch alle A C sind,' 'Die drei Höhen

---

[5] L.U., I, p. 229. ("If now we perform an act of cognition, or, as I prefer to express it, live in one, we are 'concerned with the object' that it, in its cognitive fashion, means and postulates. If this act is one of knowing in the strictest sense, i.e. if our judgment is inwardly evident, then its object is *given* in primal fashion (*originär*). The state of affairs comes before us, not merely putatively, but as actually before our eyes, and in it the object itself, *as* the object that it is, i.e. just as it is intended in this act of knowing and not otherwise, as bearer of such and such properties, as the term of such relations etc." Findlay Edition, I, p. 226.)

eines Dreieckes schneiden sich in einem Punkte,' 'Zwei kontradiktorische Sätze sind nicht beide wahr,' and others referred to by names such as *der Bernoullische Schluss con n auf n+l*. A list of these examples, together with a list of examples of assertions which should not cause the crucial happening — let us say, "One cannot at the same time believe and not believe in the same proposition," and others — might furnish a kind of test similar to certain color-tests.

The appeal to examples which actualizes the meeting as a happening is based on the assumption that they are definitively established and that their exact meaning can be communicated to the reader. If the reader does not grasp the exact meaning, but believes he does, and he therefore also believes he experiences the crucial meeting, he may be misled permanently. He will try to fix his experience in his memory and use it as a standard. He will use it in judging future assertions, thus perverting whatever ability he has had to discern knowledge of the strictest kind from that of the less strict.

Even if he grasps the exact meaning and gets the *Sachverhalt wirklich vor Augen*, this will happen as a matter of fact, as *eine Tatsache, d. i. ein zeitlich Bestimmtes* (L.U., I, p. 76). That it happens under certain conditions, would constitute *eine reale Notwendigkeit*, not as a strict law in the sense of Husserl. It is not contradictory to suppose that such a meeting never has been granted to any human being, not even to Husserl himself. I am convinced that the supposition is false, but I may be mistaken in my convictions.

Shall we then, as many would do who are empirically minded, dismiss pure phenomenology and the search for apodictic knowledge, for pure intuitive, ideal knowledge?

Yes and no. To be dismissed is the programme of a science of *Wissenschaftslehre* in the shape of a system of apodictic knowledge. As soon as a science is said to be science of or about something, there is a radical risk of error; it partakes in the imperfections of the sciences of the real.

Not to be dismissed is the invitation of pure phenomenology to explore the ideal, the infinite domain of forms and structures including the domain of contradictions. This exploration has considerable autotelic value. Husserl was inspired by the *allgemeine Mannigfaltigkeitslehre*, and it certainly is well suited as a stepping stone toward free engagement in contemplation of mere possibilities of forms and structures, independent of any purpose to create a *Lehre* or science. The field of exploration will include *the domain of the not real, not pretended real and not contradictory*.

The term 'not contradictory' in the last sentence is preferred to such terms as 'evident' or 'apodictic,' because of the difficulties of obtaining a concept of evidence unconcerned with the real, and because if we obtain it, it is scarcely discernible from a concept of consistency or non-contradiction. Instead of 'ideal,' the term 'not-real' is used, in order to avoid too many associations with certain conceptions of platonic idealism. The term 'real' is used synonymously with "what is as a matter of fact," using "a matter of fact" for *eine Tatsache, d. i. ein zeitlich Bestimmtes.*

The domain to be explored is in part the same, as far as I can see, as the realm of the ideal as conceived by Husserl. It will include pure logic and pure theory of knowledge in so far they strictly belong to that realm. All truths, those discovered and those undiscovered, belong to the domain. Truth, in the sense of Husserl, *ist über alle Zeitlichkeit erhoben* (L.U., I, 77). Further all falsehoods in the sense of *kontradiktorisches Gegenteil einer Wahrheit* will belong to it. They also are *über alle Zeitlichkeit erhoben.*

Let us return to Husserl as the architect of a system.

Husserl conceives his programmatically pure theory of knowledge and his logic as two systems of truths which rigidly exclude other systems as rightful candidates to the same titles. There is according to Husserl, if I am not mistaken, *one* pure logic, the one apodictically evident. It is obtained directly from the fountain of strict knowledge, the meetings with the *Sachverhalt* in pure intuition. The same exclusiveness holds good of his pure theory of knowledge. As a system of assertions expressed in human language, it may show variation due to homonymity. "Die Bedeutungen" as ideal entities would, however, be identical. A law about the real, according to Husserl, is *eine von unzähligen theoretischen Möglichkeiten einer gewissen, obschon sachlich abgegrenzten Sphäre.* A pure logical law is *die eine und alleinige Wahrheit, die jede andersartige Möglichkeit ausschliesst.*[6]

Now, considering the plurality of ways in which formal logic can be built up as a system, and considering how *ideale Bedeutungen* of each formula or proposition because of implicit definitions are dependent upon the system as a totality, there is no strong reason to expect any development toward one single system as *the* system. The question of whether the different systems of signs really is one considering their *ideale Bedeutungen* seems incapable of clear formulation. A third body of propositions and rules would be needed in order to compare systems of *ideale Bedeutungen.* There is, however, not any one definite such body which might be singled out as the "correct" one and used as a basis for the comparison. Consequently there is no reason to expect one definite result of the comparison.

---

[6] L.U., I, p. 73. ("one of countless theoretical possibilities within a certain factually delimited sphere" ... "the single, sole truth which excludes all other possibilities." Findlay Edition, I, p. 107.)

Similarly, with regard to the postulate of one definite system of pure theory of knowledge. In the domain of the real, different, mutually inconsistent theories may be equally well confirmed. In the domain of the real, a multiplicity of structures are possible, but not necessarily inconsistent or even comparable with each other.

Rigid exclusion of reference to the empirically real does not tend to narrow down the range of different systems.

A system of pure knowledge is as such completely indifferent toward any trait whatsoever of human knowledge, in the sense that at no single place in the system is anything implied concerning the question whether there exists human knowledge and, if it exists, of what kind it is. No reference is made to mathematics and symbolics as actually developed by mathematicians and logicians. All existent systems as actual systems may contain formidable mistakes or exclusively pure truths. The systems are irrelevant in so far as they are real, i.e. in so far as they exist as products of an activity, for instance intentions, of human beings.

The criticism of Husserl against psychologism and the emphasis on the *fundamental* difference between real and ideal is taken for granted in this article. So is also his emphasis on evidence of the apodictic variety, as a requirement in pure mathematics and logic. The only difference is that we apply the rigid distinction between real and ideal to any historical system erected, e.g., by Husserl, and given the attribute "pure." They are situated on the human side of the *ewig unüberbrückbares* chasm between real and ideal. They are actually intended systems, products of intentional and ideational activity carried out by Husserl and others in the 20th century. They will be real and their properties will have some properties which by definition do not belong to the realm of the ideal. They may or may not represent systems of truth. Human thinking sometimes seems to be, sometimes seems not to be adequate to the tasks in hand. There is no one to tell when adequate, and when not. The judges are members of our own species. We may actually have a great deal of apodictic knowledge, but it cannot be known (in the strict sense of Husserl) that we have.

The conception of pure phenomenology as exploration in the ideal does not exclude its use in research in factual science of science, just as Riemann's phantastic exploration of structures with certain analogies to physical geometry, but totally unconcerned with that geometry as a science of the real, has not excluded its usefulness in factual science. On the contrary, this conception of pure phenomenology makes such use more understandable, because subsumable under a kind of use exemplified since the dawn of geometry and celestial mechanics as exact sciences.

HUSSERL'S THESIS OF
THE IDEALITY OF MEANINGS

by

J. N. Mohanty

(New York)

1. No other thesis of Husserl, in his philosophy of meaning, has been subjected to more unfavorable criticism than the view, which he yet never seems to have taken back, that meanings are ideal entities. And yet it would seem that by that rather misleading locution he was trying to capture an essential moment of our experience of meanings and our commerce with them. That moment may perhaps be described by the following propositions: first, discourse, and more so logical discourse requires that meanings retain an identity in the midst of varying contexts; secondly, meanings can be communicated by one person to another, and in that sense can be shared; further, in different speech acts and in different contexts, the same speaker or different speakers can always return to the same meaning. Now any satisfactory theory of meaning should be able to take care of these inter-related phenomena. The theories that reduce meaning to the private experiences of the speaker or the hearer cannot explain how it is possible for private experiences (images, for example) of one to be communicated to, and shared by, another. Any criterion of identity with regard to such private experiences by which one could say, for example, 'This is the same image as I had last evening' is difficult to come by. It may be argued that there is in truth no real communication of meaning at all, so that each person is enclosed within his own world of private experiences. Such a radical scepticism is different from that moderate scepticism which doubts if we *always* do understand each other. The latter position not only does not rule out, but rather presupposes, that sometimes we do succeed in communicating or understanding. The radical scepticism however is a position which can hardly be coherently stated, for it would frustrate the possibility of public language, and has to meet all the difficulties connected with the notion of private language combined with the additional troubles arising out of the denial that there is any public language at all. The so-called Platonic theories of meaning are motivated by the theoretical need for taking into account

the identity, communicability and repeatability and, in that sense, objectivity of meanings. But they err by sundering meanings apart from the concrete meaning experiences (intending, speaking, understanding, etc.), by hypostatising them into entities that one supposedly inspects when understanding or meaningfully using appropriate expressions; in effect, they reduce expressions to conventional signs for those entities. Thus they cut off meaning from both the subjective life of persons and from the expressions that bear them.

A satisfactory theory of meaning then should take cognisance of the facts : (1) that meanings are characterised by a sort of identity, context-independence, intersubjective sharability and communicability that make it legitimate to say of them that they are objective; (2) that on the other hand they stand internally related to the mental life (thoughts, feelings and intentions) of the persons participating in them; (3) that in spite of their sort of identity which suggests they do not belong to the real order of temporally individuated events, they nevertheless serve as mediums of reference to things, events, persons, places and processes in the world; and finally, (4) that they are incarnated in physical expressions, words and sentences which from one point of view are conventional signs and so extrinsic to the latter, and from another, united with the meanings they signify in such a manner that they both form a most remarkable sort of wholeness.

Husserl's thesis regarding the ideality of meanings has to be understood in this total context, and not in an isolated manner i.e., only in view of the first of the above-mentioned facts.

2. There is no doubt that on occasions Husserl does speak of meanings in an ontological mode. He divides all beings into the real and the ideal, the mark of reality being temporality.[1] He then divides ideal objects into those that are meanings and those that are not.[2] In a rather famous passage, he characterises meanings as species or universal entities :

As a species, and only as a species, can it (a meaning) embrace in unity ($\xi\upsilon\mu\beta\grave{\alpha}\lambda$-$\lambda\epsilon\iota\nu$ $\epsilon\grave{\iota}s$ $\overset{"}{\epsilon}\nu$), and as an ideal unity, the dispersed multiplicity of individual singulars. The manifold singulars for the ideal unity of Meaning are naturally the corresponding act-moments of meaning, the *meaning-intentions*. Meaning is related to varied acts of meaning... just as Redness *in specie* is to the slips of paper which lie here, and which all 'have' the same redness.[3]

---

[1] LI, I, p. 353. (The references to the *Logical Investigations* are to J. N. Findlay's English translation.)

[2] LI, I, pp. 331, 325.

[3] LI, I, p. 330.

Now this ontological mode of speech is gradually mellowed down.[4] To be sure, the meanings are ideal, their ideality is nothing but 'unity in multi-plicity' [5] but they are mediums of reference, not objects of reference. When in an act of reflection they are made objects, they cease to function as meanings. Thus meanings quâ meanings cannot also be objects, and when made into objects they cease to be meanings and are referred to through some other meanings. Further, all Husserlian essences are not meanings. It is important, for example, to bear in mind the distinction between the meaning of 'Redness' and the essence Redness. When Husserl extends the concept of meaning to all acts and gets the concept of noema, he tells us that the concern with noemata is possible in a phenomenological attitude while the concern with essences is said to belong to an ontological attitude.[6] In *Experience and Judgment*, the characterisation of meanings as species is explicitly and unambiguously taken back :

The irreality of objectivities of understanding must not be confused with generic universality... it is a great temptation to think that the proposition belongs to the various acts of which it is the sense by virtue of its generic universality, as, for example, many red things belong to the generic essence 'redness' ...

But one must say in opposition to this : certainly, the proposition... is not general in the sense of generic universality i.e., *the generality of an "extension"* ...; it is, therefore, not general in the manner of essences...

... the proposition itself is, for all these acts and act-modalities, *identical as the correlate of an identification and not general as the correlate of a comparative coincidence*. The identical sense does not become particular in individuals; the generic universal in coincidence has particulars under it, but the sense does not have particulars under it.[7]

3.   If the ideality of the meaning is not that of a species or an essence, it is also to be distinguished from a presumptive ideality of the linguistic entity itself. The same word 'the' recurs. It is a word of the English language, though it has infinitely many occurrences. But one may also return from the written to the spoken word, and yet be aware that it is the same word. Purely physicalistically considered, of course, each inscription is a distinct physical object, each uttered sound a distinct event, and there seems to be no way of bringing them under the same linguistic item, 'the same word.' The idea of sameness here needs the concept of ideality. Only what is irreal can defy individuation by spatio-temporal location, and can maintain

---

[4] For the following, see my "On Husserl's Theory of Meaning" (*The Southwestern Journal of Philosophy*, V, 1974, pp. 229-244.)

[5] LI, I, p. 331.

[6] E. Husserl, *Ideen* III (*Husserliana*, Bd. V) p. 86.

[7] *Experience and Judgment*, 64(d), esp. pp. 261-263, also FTL, § 57(b).

identity in multiplicity. It is these considerations that lead Husserl to speak of the ideality of language and of the linguistic.[8] Language has an objective, spiritual being that is handed down by tradition as a persisting, abiding system. The word, the grammatical sentence, considered purely in respect of its 'spiritual corporeality' is an ideal unity. The same holds good of a symphony in relation to its reproductions or performances.

This ideality is not the same as that of the meanings which those words and sentences express. One cannot but help asking, at this point, if we really need to accord recognition to two orders of ideality in the constitution of an expression : a 'corporeal' and an incorporeal. Is it not possible to take care of the use of 'same' with regard to a word or a sentence in its purely 'corporeal' aspect by taking recourse to the distinction between 'type' and 'token?'

4.   The ideal meanings are 'contents' of the acts which are called meaning-intending or also meaning-conferring acts. Both these names are misleading. There is a perfectly ordinary sense in which we may say of a person that he intends to mean such and such by using the words he is using. His intention is relevant to determine what he means when what he says does not quite show what he means. Husserl does not want to use 'meaning intending' in this sense. The other expression 'meaning conferring' is equally misleading. One may speak of an act that it confers a certain right or a certain title on a person — the act, for example, of closing a deed. It is not as if what Husserl calls meaning conferring act confers meaning on a string of meaningless noises or inscriptions. The metaphors then are liable to mislead. The metaphors however, like all metaphors, are intended to be illuminative only in certain respects, within certain limitations. In order to be able to see what Husserl means let us recall some other characterisations he gives of these acts and their functions.

First, we have to bear in mind that for Husserl meaning is always and primarily meaning of an act i.e., of an intentional experience. The senses in which a physical inscription or a thing are or may be said to be meaningful are derivative from this primary sense inasmuch as we posit some act or other as being the source of that meaningfulness. If Husserlian meanings, like the Fregean *Sinne*, are intensional entities,[9] what I am emphasising is that for Husserl intensionality derives from intentionality. To say that an act is intentional is to say that an object is intended in it in a certain

---

[8] FTL, § 2.

[9] Cp. D. Føllesdal, "Husserl's Notion of Noema," *The Journal of Philosophy*, LXVI, 1969, pp. 680-687.

manner as being such and such : this is to ascribe to it a sense or a meaning and a reference. It was therefore only in the fitness of things that in the *Ideas* I the results of the First Investigation were extended over the entire domain of acts.

Secondly, Husserl says that meanings are contents of acts. If I am perceiving a thing and on the basis of that perception say 'This is white,' the meaning of the sentence I utter is a content of my act of (perceptual) judgment. If I simply utter the words 'The victor at Jena' understanding what they mean, the act I would be giving expression to is an act of representing to me a certain thing in a certain manner or satisfying a certain description : the meaning of the words is a content of that act. The talk of 'content' may mean : either real components of an experience such that each such component itself is a real bit of that experience, or intentional correlates which necessarily accompany an act, as does the percept (the perceived quâ perceived in the precise manner in which it is perceived) accompany an act of perceiving, or a proposition accompany an act of judging. The meaning is a content in the latter sense, it is not a real part of an act and so is not a private particular. It is not also, for reasons which are well known, the object towards which an act may happen to be directed. It is called an ideal content. It is not, as it were, that within the corpus of an experience there are elements that are variable and changing and a core of invariant structure which is the meaning.[10] That would have made the ideal meaning a real component of an experience in the same sense in which a sensation, an image, a feeling may be said to be, which indeed is absurd.

Third, subtract from the understanding of a verbal expression (or meaningful use of one) the uncomprehended hearing (or, uttering) of it, the surplus is the meaning-conferring act. Or, begin with hearing a string of noises which then grows into comprehension of a structure of meanings : what supervenes is a meaning conferring act. Husserl therefore often calls such an act an act of 'understanding' [11] which "shines through the expression" and "lends it meaning and thereby relation to objects." [12] A clearer statement is this :

The soliloquising thinker 'understands' his words, and this understanding is simply his act of meaning them.[13]

---

[10] F. H. Bradley held that the logical idea is a part of the content of the psychological idea or image. See his *The Principles of Logic*, 2nd rev. edn., Oxford, 1963, esp. pp. 6-8. For a criticism of Bradley's view, see B. Blanshard, *The Nature of Thought*, vol. I.

[11] LI, I, pp. 302, 327.

[12] LI, I, p. 302.

[13] LI, I, p. 309fn.

At this point, the following question may be raised : a word or sentence is meaningful, no matter whether I understand it when it is being uttered or not. Likewise if I utter a sentence belonging to a language that I do not understand but which I have learned to articulate, the sentence that I utter is meaningful even if I do not comprehend its meaning. How then can one say that my understanding — whether as the utterer or as the hearer — contributes to making a string of meaningless noises into meaningful expressions? If the expressions are meaningful, they are so because of reasons other than the acts of understanding by those who may happen to understand them. They may, for example, be meaningful because there *are* rules for their use.

Compare the following with the situation we are in : a physical object is a physical object, irrespective of whether some one perceives it or not. My perceiving it does not make it a physical object, nor does my failure to perceive it make it cease to be one. Or, take a specific type of physical object, a tool e.g., a hammer. It is, and continues to be a hammer even if no one uses it as one. In what sense, then, its 'being hammer' is determined by its use by some one in the prescribed manner?

I think these questions are pertinent, for they bring out the real nature of a phenomenological theory of meaning. It is often recognised that phenomenology is concerned not with things but with meanings. It is, for example, concerned not with physical objects (as the natural sciences are, or even a naive metaphysics would be), but with their sense as physical objects. It seeks to clarify that sense by returning to those intentional experiences in which it is constituted. The same applies to the other concerns of phenomenology. A phenomenological theory of meaning is then concerned not with meanings directly but with *their* sense as 'meanings' : it asks, how is *this* sense constituted? If the sense of the predicate 'physical object' is constituted in perceptual experiences of various sorts interrelated in certain more or less determinate manners, similarly the sense of 'meaning' is constituted in acts of understanding and certain correlations between 'understanding use' of expressions by speakers and 'understanding grasp' by auditors. It is in this kind of act-structure that the predicate 'meaningful' is constituted. A phenomenological theory of meaning, then, would trace the constitution of meanings as ideal unities to the acts in which these unities come to the sort of givenness appropriate to them by virtue of their sense as 'meanings.' What about meanings that are not understood? or, physical objects that are not perceived? Of course, there are unperceived physical objects, and that there are such unperceived physical objects may even be regarded as being, not an empirical truth,

but a truth that follows from the sense of 'physical objects.' Since constitutive phenomenology has to be guided by the sense of the constituted, part
of the explication of the sense of 'physical object' is to make room for that
component of the sense from which the existence of unperceived physical
objects appears to follow analytically. Similarly, it belongs to the sense of
'meaning' that meanings are not only understood, but may be misunderstood and even be silently passed 'by. A phenomenological theory that
meanings are constituted in acts of understanding has to be so understood
that these possibilities are taken care of.

The comparison with 'perception' was very much in Husserl's mind.[14]
Meanings are given in acts of understanding, as much as physical objects
are given in acts of perception. If in the case of perception it is appropriate
to say that the sensations that are the primary data are 'interpreted' to
signify such and such perceptual object, so in the experience of meanings
such and such inscriptions or sounds are 'interpreted' to signify such and
such meanings. Thus the meaning-conferring acts are not only acts of understanding but also acts of interpretation.[15] Just as in relation to the tree or
the pencil, my perceptual experience is a 'presentation,' but in relation to the
sensory data an 'interpretation,' so in the case of meanings it (i.e., my act
of understanding) is both an intuitive grasp and an act of interpretation.[16]

[14] E.g., LI, II, pp. 565-566.
[15] E.g., LI, I, pp. 310-365.
[16] LI, II, p. 568.

HUSSERL ON SIGNIFICATION AND OBJECT *

by

JOHN E. ATWELL

(Philadelphia)

In the first investigation of his *Logische Untersuchungen* [1] Edmund Husserl puts forth an analysis of expression from the standpoint of mental acts. This rather unusual procedure results in a curious and interesting account of the relation between the signification (*Bedeutung*) of an expression and its object or referent (*Gegenstand*). My purpose is to examine the aspects of this account which help determine where Husserl stands with respect to the so-called referential theory of meaning (signification).[2] A proponent of this theory, I shall suppose, subscribes to the general statement that "for an expression to have meaning is for it to refer to something other than itself," and to the specific view that "the meaning of an expression is that to which the expression refers." [3] Now Husserl denies — at least verbally — both the specific view and the statement that an expression's referring to an object gives it a signification; hence he appears to deny *in toto* the

* Reprinted from *American Philosophical Quarterly*, 6, 1969, with permission — J. N. M.

[1] Edmund Husserl, *Logische Untersuchungen* (5th ed.; Tübingen, 1968). References in the text and subsequent footnotes are to volume II/i. The original work was published in 1900-1901, with substantial changes made in the second edition (1913) and retained in later editions.

[2] In reporting and criticizing Husserl's views I use "mean" and "meaning" to translate, respectively, his terms "meinen" and "Meinung." "Sense," which Husserl uses synonymously with "signification" (p. 52), I use to translate "*Sinn*." For readers of Frege's essay, "Über Sinn und Bedeutung" (*Zeitschrift für Philosophie und philosophische Kritik*, Band 100), it should be noted that, roughly, Frege's term "*Sinn*" is equivalent with Husserl's terms "*Sinn*" and "*Bedeutung*," and his term "*Bedeutung*" is fairly close to Husserl's term "*Gegenstand*." Unlike Frege, however, Husserl does not regard the "*Bedeutung*" of a true statement as "the true," but rather as a "truth in itself." With the publication of *Ideen I* (1913), Husserl begins to treat "*Sinn*" and "*Bedeutung*" as non-synonymous (but not in the manner of Frege) : the former term is there applied to sensory objects, and the latter is reserved for logical or word signification (see sections 124-127). The notion of "Sinn' (or "sens") of objects is taken over and stressed by M. Merleau-Ponty, *Phenomenology of Perception*, tr. by Colin Smith (London, 1962).

[3] William Alston, *Philosophy of Language* (Englewood Cliffs, N. J., 1964), pp. 12-13.

referential theory of meaning. I shall argue, however, that he has no justification for either denial.

I

Since Husserl's L.U. has received relatively little attention, at least in most quarters, it will not be unfitting, I trust, to recall briefly a few of its more prominent themes. But I mention only those which have a direct bearing on the topic of this paper.

One of Husserl's primary concerns in the first investigation is to distinguish the signification of an expression (or statement) [4] from those features of expressions which are frequently, but in his view erroneously, regarded as significations. Advocates of psychologism tend to identify significations (concepts and propositions) with certain mental experiences ("acts of thinking"), as well as the relations between significations with the relations between mental experiences; consequently, they confuse necessary laws of logic with contingent laws of psychology. But no less mistaken, Husserl claims, are those philosophers who identify the signification of an expression (or statement) with that to which the expression refers, its object or referent. In full accord with his critique of psychologism, carried out in the *Prolegomena* (L.U., I), and with his conception of "pure logic," Husserl is most anxious to insure the uniqueness and irreducibility of significations. For they alone are the "true objects" of logical inquiry (p. 2).

Nevertheless, belonging to an expression are all three of the aforementioned features : the signification, the object, and the mental experience (or "act"). Every expression has, in other words, three functions : it signifies something, it refers to something, and it manifests or announces something (viz., one or more mental acts). Now Husserl recognizes that expressions which have no actual object, e.g., "the golden mountain" and "the round square," are perfectly significant, which means for him that they have signification. But to say that an expression has no actual object is not to say that it has no reference to an "object" or that it is non-referential : "Every expression not only enunciates something, it also talks about something; it not only has its signification, it also refers to certain objects... However, the object and the signification never coincide" (p. 46). Furthermore : "To use an expression with sense and to refer expressively to an object (to present the object) are one and the same. It does not matter at

---

[4] Husserl does not fail to distinguish expressions and statements; for though every statement is an expression, not every expression is a statement. For our purposes, the distinction plays no crucial role.

all whether the object exists, whether it is fictional, or even impossible"
(p. 54). In virtue of the mental act which is (if degrees are proper) most
essential to an expression and which accounts for its having signification,
every expression has reference to an "intentional object." Every mental
act has an intentional object, according to the tradition of Brentano, hence
every act of signifying or every act of meaning something "expressively"
has an intentional object. But by definition an intentional object need not
actually exist.

For Husserl this is by no means a mysterious way of saying that the
intentional object need not exist except in the mind or "immanently." He
stresses, again and again, that it need not exist at all, or anywhere. For
example :

I present the god Jupiter, that is, I have a certain presentational experience; in
my consciousness there occurs a presenting-of-the-god-Jupiter. One may dissect
by descriptive analysis this intentional experience in any way one pleases, but one
will naturally not find anything like the god Jupiter; the "immanent," "mental"
object does not belong therefore to the descriptive (real) constituency of the experience, thus it is really not immanent or mental. Of course it is also not *extra
mentem*, it does not exist at all. But that does not affect the fact that the
presenting of-the-god-Jupiter is actual... (p. 373)

And so it is with meaning Jupiter "expressively," as in the statement,
"Jupiter was a Greek god." To refer to something is, on Husserl's view,
somewhat analogous to challenging someone to a contest. If the challenge
is not taken up, one has nevertheless made a reference or referred to an
"object."

As we have just seen, it is the mental act which accounts for an expression's having a signification; thus Husserl might well quarrel with the
statement (from William Alston) that "for an expression to have a meaning
is for it to refer to something other than itself" — assuming this to mean
that the expression's referential character provides the expression with
a signification. For Husserl claims : "An expression gets a reference to an
object only because it has a signification..." (p. 49) [5] Such a dispute would
be merely verbal, however, for according to Husserl the mental act which
allegedly gives the signification necessarily refers to an intentional object.
He also says that "the act of signifying is the definite way of intending the
object" (*Ibid.*), and he explicitly cautions against the error of distinguishing

---

[5] It is the possession of a signification which distinguishes expressions from mere
signs. Husserl points out at the very beginning of the first investigation that signs, e.g.,
fossil bones "signify" or "point to" something other than themselves, but they have no
signification (pp. 23-25).

the act which signifies from the act which refers, means, or intends (p. 50). In other words, the mental act of signifying is, from a slightly different perspective, the same as the act which refers to an object.

Since Husserl analyzes expressions — perhaps better, uses of expressions — in terms of mental acts, certain parallels arise between (uses of) expressions and mental acts in general. We have remarked that an expression has reference to an object because the mental act essentially associated with the expression has reference to an object; just as every act has, in addition, a "content," so every expression has a signification. Indeed, the "content" of the act of meaning something expressively is identical with the signification of the expression used (p. 46). And just as an act's object should never be identified with its "content" (i.e. just as the object *that* is intended must be distinguished from the object *as* it is intended (p. 400)), so an expression's object should never be identified with the expression's signification. To say the former is really to say the latter. Finally, since the act's "content" is never the act itself, so the expression's signification is never the act of meaning something expressively itself. In summary : to refer to something with an expression, or expressively, is to mean (*meinen*) something; that which is meant (*das Gemeinte*, the object) is never identical with the way in which it is meant; the way of meaning something, the "mode of presentation" (in Frege's terms), is the signification of the expression; and the act of meaning something expressively, sometimes called quite understandably the "act of signifying," is distinct from both the object meant and the signification of the expression used.

What I have been sketching can be, and for the sake of clarity probably should be, related to Husserl' radical division of existence into two realms — the ideal and the real. The real is characterized "essentially" by temporality (p. 123); everything real occurs, so to speak, within time. Real existence comprises, consequently, all mental acts, physical objects, persons, and events; in short, whatever is datable. The ideal, which includes all significations as well as "species" (or universals), consists of non-temporal or timeless entities. Most important for Husserl's interest is the distinction between real mental acts and ideal significations.[6] When I utter, for example, "The three altitudes of a triangle intersect at one point," my act of judging is "a fleeting experience, originating and passing away," i.e., it is a real existent. But what I say, the proposition or *Wahrheit an sich*, "does not originate and pass away," i.e., it is an ideal existent; it is moreover

---

[6] For Gilbert Ryle's account of what I say just below, see his "The Theory of Meaning" in *Philosophy and Ordinary Language*, ed. by Charles E. Caton (Urbana, 1963), p. 149.

the signification of my statement (p. 44) or, to say the same thing, the "content" of my act of judging. Ideal existents are called "ideal unities," for they are unities in multiplicities. For instance, the signification of an expression stands to the multiple actual and possible acts of expressing that particular signification (concept or proposition) as the universal redness stands to its multiple instances, i.e., as the One stands to the Many (pp. 100, 106).[7] Husserl claims that the signification of an expression or statement is ideal, no matter whether the expression's object is real or ideal, and no matter what kind of expression is uttered.

II

One might take issue, of course, with a number of Husserl's views on ontology and the philosophy of language, but I intend to consider only two contentions both of which relate to the referential theory of meaning : one, that every expression refers to an object; two, that the signification of an expression and its object never coincide. Most current philosophers will concur with Husserl's second contention, but they will reject the first one.

It is currently quite common to distinguish between language and speech, between type and tokens, and — most relevant to the issue at hand — between linguistic units and uses or utterances of linguistic units. Earlier I mentioned that Husserl is attempting to analyze uses of expressions or, as he often puts it (p. 32), expressions in their communicative function. But, failing to observe the above distinctions, he sometimes talks as if every linguistic unit or "word" had reference to an object. That this is not (or at least should not be) his view becomes clear upon realizing what he takes an expression to be : namely, a "physical object" such as a mark on paper, a sound, etc., which someone produces with the intention of putting forth some "thought" or of communicating something to someone (p. 31). "In itself" an expression is a physical object like any other (p. 407), but in virtue of the mental act of meaning something with it or of understanding something by it, the physical "expression" becomes a genuine expression.

An articulated complex of sounds (or written marks, or the like) first becomes a spoken word or communicative speech through the fact that the speaker produces it with the intention of "expressing (*äussern*) himself about something" thereby;

---

[7] For a discussion of Husserl's ontology, see Gustav Bergmann, "The Ontology of Edmund Husserl" in the author's *Logic and Reality* (Madison, 1964), pp. 193-224.

or in other words, in certain mental acts the speaker gives to it (the complex) a sense which he wants to communicate to the hearer. (p. 32.)[8]

Spots of ink and sounds "mean" nothing until persons, in virtue of some mental activity, "mean" something with them or "understand" something by them. Husserl analyzes the act of meaning something with an "expression" (p. 74, n. 4); both are characterized by "going beyond" what is produced or what is perceived to, as he would say, what is meant.

Mental activity — if it may be called so — consists of intentional acts, and on Husserl's conception of such acts some object is necessarily intended or referred to. That every expression has an object means then that every case of expressing (i.e., *jedes Ausdrücken* rather than *jeder Ausdruck*) has reference to some object, or that every act of meaning "means" some object. Quite clearly, "object" must be understood as covering anything mentionable or referable. Whenever a person expresses himself, he expresses himself *about* something and he gives expression *to* something, e.g., a judgment, wish, command, or the like. That which he expresses himself about is the object of his expression, and that which he gives expression to (or manifests, *kundgeben*) is some mental act.[9] Advocates of the "intentionality thesis of mind" tell us that *a priori* if I judge, I judge (about) something; if I wish, I wish for something; if I ask, I ask about something; and so on. In short, Husserl regards the claim that every expression has an object as *a priori*. Consequently, there is absolutely no problem in understanding his affinity to one aspect of the referential theory of meaning : it follows rigorously from his notion of an expression and his conception of mental acts.[10]

Preferring a sympathetic interpretation to an antagonistic one, I have tried to show that Husserl's claim that every expression has an object is at least not wildly absurd. He would surely deny, for instance, that in saying "This book is red," I am executing four mental acts and referring thereby to four distinct objects. He would maintain, rather, that every "word" is used either to refer to something or else in conjunction with other words to make a reference. Even on this most charitable interpretation, his view

---

[8] Bergmann seems to agree : "Words spoken are sounds among sounds; words written, marks of chalk or ink. By themselves, they do not represent anything, don't refer to anything. We refer by means of them to what we have made them represent," "Meaning" in *ibid.*, p. 93.

[9] In cases other than mere judgment or assertion, one gives expression to or manifests more than one act; for example, in saying "I wish you luck," one manifests an act of wishing and an act of signifying.

[10] I mention this because several writers express some puzzlement over their predecessors' subscription to the referential theory of meaning, e.g., Ryle in "The Theory of Meaning," Caton, *loc. cit.*, pp. 131-132.

may be unsound, but it is not obviously unsound : one cannot refute it by simply pointing out that "or" refers to no object. It must be admitted, however, that Husserl does not follow through with the strand in his thought upon which my interpretation rests. Had he done so, and had he pursued further the multifunctionality of expressions, he would surely have arrived at a position not unlike that of several current philosophers. One need not stretch a point too extremely to see a number of similarities between Husserl's various "acts of expressing" and J. L. Austin's various "speech acts." [11]

III

J. N. Mohanty, in his recent book on *Edmund Husserl's Theory of Meaning*,[12] goes to considerable length to show that Husserl rejects the referential theory, i.e., that Husserl refuses to identify the signification and the object of an expression. No doubt Husserl does "reject" the referential theory (this we have seen), but whether he is justified in so doing is another question. It is not unimportant to take note of the following : (1) Husserl admits that cases arise in which a change in the meant object effects a change in the signification of "the same words" (pp. 79-80); (2) he insists that the act of signifying is not to be distinguished from the act of meaning or intending an object (p. 50); (3) he grants that it is impossible to describe acts of meaning (*meinende Akte*) without having recourse to the meant things (*die gemeinten Sachen*) (p. 11) — which seems to say that we cannot distinguish, e.g., the act of meaning *that chair* from the act of meaning *this book* without talking about the chair and the book; and (4) following his long discussion of expressions which fluctuate in signification from case to case, viz., "occasional" or "indexical" expressions, and of expressions which "do not possess an identical signification-content in every case of their application" (p. 88), e.g., empirical expressions like "horse," Husserl finally allows that the only expressions free from fluctuation of signification are exact expressions, i.e., those which occur in propositions of mathematics and pure logic and which allegedly refer to ideal, immutable objects and states of affairs. In light of these remarks, and others, I propose to argue that Husserl has no justification for rejecting the referential theory of meaning.

[11] J. L. Austin, *How to do things with Words* (London, 1962), lecture VIII and following.
[12] J. N. Mohanty, *Edmund Husserl's Theory of Meaning* (The Hague, 1964), especially pp. 17-23, 43, 75-76, 98.

The main arguments for distinguishing signification and object occur in Sect. 12 of the first investigation where Husserl calls attention to (1) expressions which have different significations but the same object, and (2) expressions which have different objects but the same signification (pp. 47-48).[13] In illustration of (1) he mentions the following "names": "the Victor of Jena" and "the Vanquished of Waterloo." Husserl does not say that these two expressions refer to Napoleon, though presumably he thinks that they do; and he does not argue that they have different significations, stating simply that they obviously (*offenbar*) do. If expressions "E_1" and "E_2" refer to the same object and yet have different significations, then — the argument appears to go — the signification of "E_1" (or "E_2") must be distinguished from the object of "E_1" (or "E_2"). The problem facing Husserl is pointed up by asking how he proposes to distinguish between significations. My contention is that he is unable to do so except by appeal to intentional objects, i.e., to the respective objects of the expressions in question. If S_1 can be distinguished from S_2 only by distinguishing O_1 from O_2, then there appears to be no justification for distinguishing S_1 from O_1 or S_2 from O_2.

To use an expression with sense or to understand it is, on Husserl's view, to perform an act of meaning or understanding. And such an act, like every other, has reference to an object, though the object — being an intentional object — need not actually exist. Now when we understand "the Victor of Jena" and then "the Vanquished of Waterloo," we are — Husserl seems to hold — referentially directed to one and the same object, viz., Napoleon; but we refer to it (him) in different "ways," first as the Victor of Jena and then as the Vanquished of Waterloo. Alternatively stated, the two acts of understanding have the same object but different "contents."

Notice, however, that it is solely in virtue of a fair bit of *knowledge* about French history that we are able to provide this account. Suppose someone knew practically nothing about French history. He would no doubt understand the two expressions, and he would recognize — in spite of his ignorance — that they differ in signification. By the mere understanding of these expressions, this person would be "conscious" of different significations. "Whenever we use an expression or understand it, it signifies something for us, i.e., we are actually conscious of its sense" (p. 183). But what is he "actually conscious" of in understanding the two expressions?

---

[13] Mohanty appears to accept both arguments, for he paraphrases them (p. 17) without any critical discussion.

What is he referentially directed to? Obviously, such a person is unable to give different answers to these questions, i.e., he is unable to distinguish what he is conscious of (allegedly, the senses) from what he is referentially directed to (allegedly, the object). In short, knowledge and never mere understanding of an expression allows one to distinguish the signification from the object. But Husserl holds that in merely understanding an expression one is referentially directed to an object; in fact, to be referentially directed to an object is nearly the definition of understanding an expression. Hence, when I understand, e.g., "the seventh man to climb Mt. Everest," I am referentially directed to an object; but the only object I am able to cite is the seventh man to climb Mt. Everest.

What can it mean to say, on Husserl's view, that the expression "the Victor of Jena" refers to Napoleon? Clearly not that these marks on paper "mean" (refer to) Napoleon, for until animated by a sense-giving act marks on paper "mean" nothing, until then they do not even constitute an expression. Nor can it mean that in order to understand the expression one must be referentially directed to (or "have in mind") Napoleon — or, if it did mean this, it would be false — though one must be referentially directed to some object. To even make sense of the claim, we must, so to speak, go beyond understanding the expression to a consideration of what most people know, viz., that Napoleon was the Victor of Jena. But, as I have insisted, knowing this fact is not a requisite for understanding the expression, thus for being referentially directed to some object. In fact, it is just the converse. Knowing what an expression refers to, in the sense that "the Victor of Jena" refers to Napoleon, is not even relevant to an analysis of understanding the expression. But only by bringing to the analysis the extraneous feature of knowledge is Husserl able to present the least semblance of an argument for distinguishing the signification from the object.

That one signification differs from another is said to be obvious or given (p. 183); likewise, that one "act-character" differs from another is said to be "beyond description" (p. 384). These are, I think, revealing assertions. For, first, they reveal Husserl's inability to account for sameness and difference of significations; and second, they lead us to ask "What is given in an act of understanding, or any act for that matter?" The answer is, of course, the intentional object; nothing is more evident than the object of a mental act. In understanding "the Victor of Jena," the intentional object *the Victor of Jena* is given; and in understanding "the Vanquished of Waterloo," *the Vanquished of Waterloo*. One should not forget that intentional objects can be anything. Our person ignorant of French history recognizes that the two expressions differ in signification because he recognizes that the two respective intentional objects differ. To recognize the one is to recognize the other.

Further reasons could be adduced in support of my argument, but I see no need for this. I want to turn briefly to Husserl's second "argument" for distinguishing signification and object. It is, unfortunately, hopelessly confused, for — among other things — Husserl fails to heed the difference between an expression type and expression tokens, and he begins talking about "objective reference" instead of "object." He says that "two expressions can have the same signification but a different objective reference" (p. 47); but he means that two uses of one expression can refer to different objects although the signification of the expression remains the same. Unlike most current philosophers, who use so-called "indexical expressions" to illustrate this claim, Husserl uses the expression "a horse." In the statement "Bucephalus is a horse" and then in "This old nag is a horse," the expression "a horse," says Husserl, has the same signification; but in the former statement it refers to Bucephalus while in the latter it refers to this old nag. To begin with, one wants to say that "a horse" is not a referring expression at all, or at least that it does not refer to this, then that individual horse. If anything, it refers to the universal horseness, or what Husserl calls a "species" or "essence." Secondly, if, in the first statement, "a horse" did refer to Bucephalus, then the statement would be analogous to, say, "Napoleon is the Victor of Jena." But of course it isn't. And, finally, when Husserl does deal with expressions which retain the same signification in different uses, e.g., "this" and other indexicals, he claims that they change signification with each different use, i.e., with each different object or state of affairs they are used to refer to (pp. 79-80). Hence, the second "argument" proves wholly unsuccessful.

I have attempted to show that by analyzing meaning and understanding in terms of intentional acts Husserl has no grounds for maintaining that the signification and object of an expression never coincide. Given his conception of intentional acts, Husserl may make only an analogous distinction at best — perhaps that between the direct object of an expression (which might be called the signification) and the indirect object (which might be called the object). On this view, the direct object of "the Victor of Jena" would be *the Victor of Jena*, and the indirect would be — if there is one — the person victorious at Jena. In this example, as opposed to, say, "the golden mountain," there is such an indirect object, viz., Napoleon, whether one knows it or not. But then, expressions which have no indirect object, e.g., "the golden mountain," would have — using Husserl's terminology again — no object at all; and this has been denied.

Or else, the signification of such expressions, i.e., the direct object of reference, would be identical with the only object of reference; and this too has been denied. Consequently, the suggestion that by signification and object Husserl actually means direct object and indirect object helps to preserve his views solely with regard to definite descriptions which "fit" an actually existing thing or person. But Husserl wants to extend his distinction between signification and object beyond such a limited sphere. Hence the suggestion fails to extricate him from the difficulties I have pointed up. I don't want to leave the impression, however, that Husserl has nothing of interest or importance to say about expressions, "acts," and related issues; on the contrary, I think that for anyone concerned with such issues Husserl's L.U. is *ein unentbehrliches Werk*.[14]

[14] The writing of this paper was supported by a Temple University Summer Research Award (1968) for which I express my gratitude.

THE LOGIC OF PARTS AND WHOLES
IN HUSSERL'S *INVESTIGATIONS**

by

R. Sokolowski

(Washington, D.C.)

In his preface to the second edition of the *Prolegomena* Husserl makes the
following remark about the Third of his *Logical Investigations,* which is
entitled, "Toward a Theory of Wholes and Parts." "I have the impression
that this Investigation was all too little read. It helped me a great deal, and
indeed it is an essential presupposition for full understanding of the Investigations that follow it." [1] Neglect of this Investigation could indeed prove
disastrous to understanding Husserl's thought; although it seems to treat
merely questions of logic and method and says nothing about subjectivity,
it provides a formal structure that reappears at many strategic places in
the *Investigations* and in Husserl's later work. It serves as the skeleton for
Husserl's more elaborate philosophical doctrines about subjectivity and
its world.

The logic of parts and wholes functions most visibly in what Husserl will
later call his "noematic" analysis : The descriptions of the structure of
objects constituted in consciousness. The senses that blend noematically
to structure given regions of reality are taken to be "parts" of a "whole."
The necessary rules that govern such blends are possible because parts and
wholes in general can be blended in certain ways. Thus the necessary,
a priori "evidence" that certain noematic structures manifest is based upon
formal rules that govern the relationships of parts and wholes in general.

* First published in *Philosophy and Phenomenological Research*, Vol. 28, 1967-68,
pp. 537-553: Reprinted here with permission — J.N.M.
[1] Halle, 1928, p. xv. We will refer henceforth to the first edition : *Logische Untersuchungen,* Halle, Vol. 1, 1900; vol. 2, 1901. We will give the number of the Investigation
in roman numerals, followed by the chapter number : III # 10 means Investigation III,
chapter 10. We will give chapter numbers instead of page numbers in order to make reference to the second edition possible. Usually the chapters are short enough so that such
reference is sufficient; where further precision is needed, the page number of the first
edition will be given. References will be given directly to the body of our text.

Noematic analysis studies how the logic of parts and wholes is realized in various regions of reality.

Part-whole logic is also operative in Husserl's description of subjectivity. His complex analyses of intentional acts, for instance, are simply applications of part-whole relationships to intentionality. The analysis of acts into quality, material and sensory components in the *Investigations*, and their analysis into noeses, hyletic data and noemas in the *Ideas*, are instances of the use of parts and wholes. The Third Investigation thus "helped a great deal" by serving as the formal rule guiding Husserl's phenomenological analyses.

Even more basically, the doctrine of parts and wholes at least partially justifies his philosophical language. In the *Prolegomena*, Husserl says that the first task facing phenomenology as a nascent science is the elaboration of precise concepts and terms, the articulation of a vocabulary proper to his philosophy (#67). Husserl's terms are introduced by making philosophical distinctions and, as we have already anticipated, the distinctions are made according to the pattern of part-whole structures. Thus the very meaningfulness of what he says depends on the legitimacy of part-whole logic. Another justification of Husserl's philosophical speech is given in the transcendental epoché, but this is a dimension different from the formal one treated in Investigation III. And even after the reduction is carried out, the formal structure of parts and wholes still remains operative in forming phenomenological concepts.

1. THE LOGIC OF PARTS AND WHOLES

Husserl uses parts and wholes in Investigation II as a weapon against the theory of abstraction proposed by Berkeley and Hume (II #36, #39, #40-42). Only in Investigation III are they treated for their own sake, however. Husserl begins this Investigation with a very general distinction, that between simple objects and complex objects. Simple objects are those which have no parts, complex those with parts. Complex objects are wholes with parts. No definition of parts and wholes can be given, nor can the relation between them be established or clarified by any more primitive terminology. Parts and wholes are primitive and irreducible terms as long as they are taken in an undifferentiated, general way.

The distinction that is pivotal for the logic of parts and wholes follows immediately. Husserl distinguishes between two types of parts : *moments* and *pieces*.

Moments are parts that permeate each other. They are inseparable from one another and from their wholes. I may consider a material object as a whole, composed of the parts called "extension," "surface," "color," and "brightness." These parts permeate one another in such a way that one cannot be given unless the others are also present. I cannot disengage brightness from color, I cannot consider color without locating it within a certain surface, and I cannot consider surface without seeing it as a moment of an extended thing. The necessity of blending these different parts is not due to any psychological disposition in me or in my culture, but is grounded in the sense of the parts (III #7). Each part, by virtue of what it is, contains within itself a *rule* dictating the necessary progression of supplements that it must possess, the necessary series of horizons within which it must rest : brightness entails color, color entails surface, surface entails extension. These are essentially dependent parts, moments of a whole (III #10).

Pieces are parts that do not permeate one another and hence are separable from their wholes. I can consider a tree as a whole made up of branches, trunk, leaves, roots, bark, etc. All these are parts that can be separated from the whole; I can consider a branch as an entity in itself. I can disengage it at least in imagination from its whole in a way in which I cannot disengage brightness from color or color from surface. Pieces are parts that are independent of one another and of the whole to which they belong. They can be phenomena for consciousness apart from their wholes, whereas moments cannot be phenomena without the parts and wholes upon which they depend.

The separability of pieces does not mean that they can be disengaged from *all* wholes. Even if I consider a branch apart from the tree, the branch itself must still be seen as a figure against a background. Because it is a physical thing, a branch can only be conceived as an object supplemented by a spatial horizon or background against which it appears. Thus a given object may be a piece of a whole in one respect and a moment of a whole in another respect (III #7).

Husserl articulates a network of definitions and laws governing the many relationships that follow upon the distinction of moments and pieces. He distinguishes between *founded* parts, those that require the presence of other parts (part A is founded on part B if A cannot be had without B), and *founding* ones, those that serve as the condition for dependent parts without themselves necessarily being dependent (part K founds Part L if L cannot be had without K; it is left undecided whether K needs L. If it does, then the founding relationship is reciprocal; if not, it is unilateral. Cf. III #16).

Husserl further defines a *concretum* as an object that can be taken as a whole, and an *abstractum* as one that can only be presented as a moment, as a dependent part of a whole (III #17). The term "abstract" is frequently used in Husserl's later writings and always keeps the sense it has here. It means a moment that must be completed by further dimensions. Thus in the problem of transcendental reduction, the noematic world could be called "abstract" because it must be completed by the dimension of subjectivity as that which constitutes it. Consciousness, on the other hand, is separable from the natural world and can be considered as an isolated sphere of absolute experience (*Ideas* I, #51).

Another important distinction is that between *immediate* and *mediate* parts (III #16, #18). Brightness is a mediate part of surface because it blends with surface, it forms a whole with it, only through the mediation of other parts. It must be mediated by the moment of color; the color has a certain brightness, and by virtue of the color's inherence in the surface, the surface too has brightness as a mediate part. But brightness is an immediate moment of color because the two blend without the mediation of any further parts. The distinction between mediate and immediate allows Husserl to speak about the "distance" of parts from their wholes. Color is a closer moment to a material thing than brightness is (brightness is *farther*) because color belongs to its whole through the mediation of fewer parts than brightness needs (III #19).

The definition of immediate and mediate, closer and farther parts gives Husserl the terminology to compare pieces and moments more radically. The relationships among moments are strictly determined; certain mediations are apodictically necessary because of the sense of such moments. Brightness cannot be immediately blended with surface, it must be mediated by color. There is a rigid, *a priori* rule governing the "distance" and the mediations between brightness and surface of extension; moments cannot be haphazardly blended with one another. The distance of pieces from their wholes, on the other hand, shows no such necessary structure. A finger is a piece of the hand, which in turn is a piece of the body, but there is no necessity of mediating the distance between finger and body by the hand; I can consider a finger an immediate part of the body itself. Pieces are arbitrarily called "near" or "far" parts of their wholes. They have none of the necessary hierarchical structure of mediation found in moments. Moments are subject to *a priori* rules of progression in a way in which pieces are not, unless of course, we are dealing with specially contrived wholes, such as aesthetic structures, where a certain sequence of dependences is needed (III #19, #24).

This device Husserl uses for establishing aspects of things as parts is called, even at this early stage of his thought, "variation" (III #7, esp. p. 232). It is a procedure that uses the contrast between stasis and change. If one aspect of a thing can be varied while another aspect remains unchanged, then we can legitimately distinguish between two parts of a whole, or at least between a whole and its part. If the brightness of a color can vary while the color remains the same, the two can be considered as distinct parts. If the motion of a thing can change while the thing remains the same, the motion is simply a part, a moment, of the totality called a moving thing. The use of such free variation is not startling in the case of such well established distinctions as that between color and surface, but Husserl puts it to use in formulating his structural distinctions in subjectivity. He uses it to distinguish, for example, between the quality and material of intentional acts (V #20). Several acts may contain the same "sense" and "object" as that which they intend, and yet differ in the mode in which they intend it. I can perceive the fact that the tree is green, I can hope for this fact, desire it, detest it, etc. In each case one moment remains the same, for it is the same object and sense that is intended in all these acts; and yet another moment, which Husserl calls the quality of acts, changes, because the object is intended in different ways. The part-whole structure is thus introduced into analysis of intentional acts; Husserl now has moments and aspects of acts to talk about. This is his way of fixing the fundamental and primitive concepts to be used in phenomenology.

Pieces and their relationships to wholes are not very important philosophically. Their greatest value is to serve as a foil, as a contrary, polar concept allowing the concept of moment to be established. Moments and their relationships to one another and to wholes are important philosophical tools; they allow philosophical distinctions to be made, the distinctions that leave objects intact physically but broken up phenomenologically or metaphysically. Aristotle's matter and form or substance and accidents, the Thomist essence and existence, Spinoza's substance and modes, Wittgenstein's word and word usage, would all be classed under the part-whole logic of moments. They are distinctions not between separable things, but between aspects that are "abstract" in Husserl's sense : They cannot be realized in isolation but require completion, according to rule, in a whole.

2. THE APPLICATION OF PART-WHOLE LOGIC
IN THE *LOGICAL INVESTIGATIONS*

A survey of the many uses of part-whole structures in the *Investigations* will also dispel the impression that the *Investigations* are a series of only loosely related studies. In fact, they are tightly written and follow a closely knit argument. The impression of dispersion comes from not understanding the place of Investigations III and IV, which seem to be studies of "logical" themes as opposed to the studies of subjectivity in the rest of the work. But the logical studies in these two Investigations are a key to the methodology Husserl uses in the others.

(a) The entire Fourth Investigation is an application of part-whole logic to the realm of meanings, as Husserl declares in the Introduction to this section. It discusses the nature of a pure, ideal grammar. Simple meanings, says Husserl, can be combined in certain ways to form complex meanings, but such combinations must follow certain rules in order to result in truly meaningful wholes. For example, the combination "king but or blue" is not a meaningful whole. It is not a well-formed expression and what results from it is simply a "pile of words," not a unified sense (*Worthaufen*, IV #14). On the other hand, a combination like "the house is green' is a well-formed expression and succeeds in forming a unified sense. It obeys the grammatical, syntactic rules for forming complex meanings.

Husserl says that there are certain words, syncategorematic terms, that are used only as operators in forming such complex meanings. Words like "but," "or," "and," etc. do not name any objects, but serve only to bind other words into unified wholes. Syncategorematic terms are moments of wholes. They have a meaning, but it is a meaning that demands completion according to certain rules (IV #5, #7-10). Husserl then proposes that philosophers investigate the "ideal grammar." They should list the various syncategorematic forms that are possible and compute the various combinations that result when they are permuted with one another. This will yield the sum of grammatical, syntactic rules that must be obeyed in making well-formed expressions, expressions that can exist "as meanings." Husserl considers such computation the work of mathematicians, and indeed mathematical logic has worked in this direction.[2]

---

[2] In the *Prolegomena*, #71, Husserl assigns part of the work of elaborating phenomenology to "the mathematicians." See also IV #13-14, and *Formal and Transcendental Logic*, #28-36, #52-53. For a recent example of how such purely formal computation can be applied even to syntax, see N. Chomsky, *Syntactic Structures* (The Hague, 1957).

Husserl admits, incidentally, that certain sequences of meanings may form a unified meaning and still be contradictory. "All squares are round" is a well-formed expression grammatically and *can* exist as a meaning says Husserl, even though we have evidence that such a sense could never be real, for it contradicts itself. A complex of meanings must first be well-formed grammatically before we can ask whether or not it can be real, whether or not it contradicts itself. A series of meanings that is not well formed is "meaningless' (*unsinnig*), such as the group of words, "king but or blue." But a well-formed statement may still be contradictory (*widersinnig*). Meaningfulness is a prior condition for noncontradiction (IV #12). In his general theory of an ideal grammar, Husserl's logic of parts and wholes plays an important role; the very concept of well-formed expressions takes such expressions as wholes composed of properly blended syncategorematic terms as moments.

(b) Husserl uses the part-whole relation to express the relationship between words and their meanings. He had already said in the First Investigation that word meanings are intimately fused with the words that express them. The acts that constitute meanings and the acts that constitute the physical word are unified in an act-totality (I #10). Now he can say with more precision what that totality is : in the case of verbal meaning, the physical word is founded on the meaning; it is only a moment of the whole that we call a "meaningful word." A physical word is not a word except as a moment of a greater whole. It has the dependent, founded sense of a part that cannot exist alone (V #19, p. 383; VI #7, p. 500). This application of part-whole logic prevents us from taking words to be first constituted as independent entities and then added extrinsically, like pieces, to meanings which are also preformed as independent parts.

(c) Husserl not only applies his schema of part and whole to meanings; he also uses it in describing the structure of subjectivity itself. We have already seen that he makes use of it to distinguish between the quality and material of acts (C #20, p. 391). Even more significant is his application of the logic of part and whole to the relation between acts and sensations. Intentions, he claims, are never separated from sensations. They arise only as objectivating apprehensions (*Auffassungen*) of sensations (III #22, esp. p. 270, VI #25, p. 562). Intentions are not "pieces" of the stream of consciousness that could be separated from the sensory cushion in which they are found; they are moments that must be supplemented by sensible data. (Whether the inverse is true is not answered by Husserl in this work; cf. V #15b.) Husserl's use of the part-whole logic with acts and sensations thus roots intentionality firmly in the sensibility that is part of man's conscious existence, and keeps him from talking about a free-floating "thought" disengaged from corporeality.

(d) Parts and wholes are also used in the analysis of compound acts. Husserl says that certain acts can serve as foundations for others. For example, an act of perception can be supplemented by an act of desire; in such a case, a quality of desire is added to the quality of perception originally given. But the quality of desire is not a piece or a thing added to the act; it is simply another moment which is founded upon perception and could not be realized or even conceived without an act of perception as its base (V #15a, #18).

(e) Part-whole logic is especially useful in explaining how categorial acts are founded on acts of simple perception. Categorial objects, such as relations, propositions, states of affairs, groups, etc., are constituted by categorial activities performed by subjectivity. In them, there is something more than the simple senses that consciousness accepts in immediate perception. There is a categorial form, such as the form of a proposition, group, or relation, and this form is the product of conscious action. However, the categorial acts that constitute them are founded upon acts of simple perception. Together they form a whole of which categorial acts are only moments. Categorial intentionalities are not separable, pure reason; the idea of a reason that articulates itself in independence of simple intentionalities (and of the sensibility in them) is emphatically denied by Husserl (VI #46, esp. p. 618, # 60, p. 655).

Not only categorial acts but also categorial forms must be considered as dependent parts, as moments of greater wholes. They must be supplemented by the objects that are set in relationships or collected into groups; they are always relations or groups *of* certain things. Categorial forms are not constituted before experience, as Kant's *a priori* forms are. They are articulated upon what is experienced and are functions or moments of direct experience.

(f) A concept which Husserl introduces in the *Investigations*, and which later becomes very important for his phenomenology, is that of profiles. A material object presented in consciousness is described phenomenologically as a synthesis of profiles or aspects; a desk appears as a sequence of visual and perhaps tactile profiles, all of which coalesce to constitute the single entity called "desk." No single act of perception can comprehensively grasp all the profiles of such an object. The experience of it is necessarily fluid, always anticipating further aspects and leaving behind those given in the present. The relationship between these profiles and the thing known in them is difficult to conceptualize, and there is a constant danger of making both the thing and its profiles too substantial, of considering them as "pieces" that are separable, at least in thought, from one another. This leads to the caricature of a "thing in itself" concealed behind appearances, not becoming a phenomenon itself. This misconception is the result of thinking about profiles and objects according to the schema of the logic of "pieces and wholes" instead of taking them as Husserl does, according to the logic of "moments and wholes." The series of faces that a thing presents phenomenologically is a series of moments; profiles cannot be disengaged from things. They make no sense except when we see them as aspects or appearings of things. The thing itself, of course, is not just another profile along with the rest; it is the synthesis of profiles, the whole of which profiles are moments. But it can never be spoken of phenomenologically except as such a whole : a synthesis of profiles (III #21, esp. p. 269, VI #48, esp. p. 624).

The doctrine of profiles and perception is important in Husserl since it later becomes the criterion for distinguishing between experience of worldly reality and transcendental experience of subjectivity. It is also one of Husserl's most important epistemological theories, since it strikes at the disjunction between appearances and things in themselves. Yet its force can easily be lost if the wrong logic of parts and wholes is applied to it.

(g) Correlative to the relationship between profiles and things, Husserl says that intentional acts are composed of smaller units which, in the *Investigations*, he calls partial intentions or partial acts (VI #47). In his lectures on time he interprets them as temporal profiles. Once again, if these partial acts or temporal profiles are taken to be pieces, then the whole act becomes not a synthesis but a collection, and the unity of consciousness is lost. Instead, they must be taken as moments forming a synthetic whole, as parts intelligible only as aspects of the whole. Thus when Husserl distinguishes conscious intentionality into the dimensions of acts and sensations, partial acts and complete acts, material and quality, and temporal phases, he does not break consciousness into pieces. He simply articulates moments of consciousness which must be distinguished if we are to speak of its structure scientifically, but which can never be separated, even in thought, from the whole of consciousness.

We have examined Husserl's use of moment-whole logic in seven important themes. The use of moment-whole structures is not univocal in all these cases; the way in which a profile is a moment of a thing-synthesis is different from the way in which categorial acts are founded upon simple acts. To speak with Aristotle, "moment" is analogous and said in many ways, but no matter how it may be said in a given analysis, it does forbid us to make separable pieces out of the parts we distinguish (*Metaphysics* 1035b 32-34).[3]

By way of contrast we may give an instance where Husserl's logic of pieces and wholes would apply. Consider the perception of a material thing. The fact that the thing is a synthesis of profiles is an instance of moment-whole logic, but the actual sequence of profiles that is followed in perception is a case of piece-whole logic. I can walk around and see the sides of a tree in clockwise sequence, then look up and down from a given point, then touch certain parts of the tree, etc. But I could just as well reverse the process, mix up the sequence, or only perform certain parts of it, leaving out the rest. An arbitrariness and separability are possible here that could not be found in the logic of moments and wholes. Consequently, no *a priori*, apodictic, necessary phenomenological analysis of this sequence is possible. This is one of the reasons why Husserl gives so few examples of "concrete" phenomenological analysis. Once one leaves the realm of general, formal description and enters into particular sequences of experience, one leaves the necessary logic of moments and wholes and enters the factual, contingent structure of pieces and wholes. An *a priori* is only possible for the former, never for the latter. Since Husserl wants to formulate phenomenology as a rigorous, apodictic science stating necessary truths, most of his concrete, particular analyses are simply sketched briefly as examples of how to proceed in this area; his own interests are limited to the realm of necessary *a priori* laws about subjectivity and the world.

3. PARTS AND WHOLES IN THE GENERAL PROBLEMATIC OF THE *INVESTIGATIONS*

We have discussed a series of specific applications of part-whole logic in the *Investigations*. This logic also functions in a more general way within the wider philosophical issues Husserl treats in this work. We shall discuss its role in his treatment of objectivity, evidence, and *a priori* truths. These three themes must not be isolated from one another; our discussion of part-whole logic in them will show how they are only aspects of one general problematic.

In the *Investigations*, Husserl is not concerned with describing subjectivity for its own sake. His descriptions are geared specifically to showing how

---

[3] It would be interesting to compare Husserl's doctrine with Aristotle's theory of parts in *Metaphysics* VII.

subjectivity transcends itself in knowledge. He wants to explain how objectivity can become present "in" subjectivity, how experience can transcend a given instant and grasp a meaning that is valid not only at this time for this person, but always and for everyone (*Prolegomena*, preface, vii; *Investigations*, introduction, p. 9).

Subjectivity can transcend itself and reach objectivity in different ways. First, it can possess objective meanings in acts of simple intending, empty intentionalities, in which meanings or objects are not asserted as real or perceived in any way, but simply "meant." Such acts contain meanings that transcend the individual, are objective, and may even be communicated though they may not be real. Even contradictions such as "square circle" can exist as meanings and be entertained as objectivities that transcend the subjectivity intending them.

Secondly, subjectivity can go further by verifying the meanings that it intends and thus obtain grounds for asserting them as real. A transition is made from acts of simple intending to acts of verification or authentication. The meanings and objects are not asserted in evidence; the acts of simple intending are fulfilled in real perception. Subjectivity possesses "more" objectivity now because it has evidence for the permanence and truth of what it previously simply "meant" with no claim on truth. These two forms of intentionality, "simple intending" and "assertion," are the two basic types of objectivating acts by which consciousness can become related to an object (V #38, #41).

But there are degrees of evidence, and hence degrees for the fulfillment of intentions. An object or a truth can be given "in person," and yet only vaguely and indistinctly (VI #16). The ideal of evidence is complete, vivid presentation of all the aspects of what is intended, with no profiles left as merely anticipated by intentions. Such an ideal is never realized in the case of external perception because of the spatiality inherent in such perceiving. There are always aspects of things that are merely intended and not directly given in the perception of material things (VI 37-39).

Besides direct perception, however, there is still another way to bring some intentions to evidence : by incorporating statements into the chains of deductive, explanatory propositions that make up a science. Some truths can be brought to evidence only in this indirect way. The network of propositions that comprises a science provides grounds for asserting the reality of certain meanings, and thus enables subjectivity to reach the firm basis of objectivity in another way. As Plato says in the *Meno*, when simple opinions are chained down by reasoned understanding of causes, they become permanent knowledge (98 A). The evidence that is given in the network of science is thus objectivity *par excellence*. For this reason, the *Logical Investigations* begin and end with the problem of evidence and fulfillment in the context of scientific theory. In the *Prolegomena*, when outlining the phenomenology he hopes to establish, Husserl says he will elaborate a "science of sciences," a science that will give the elements and structures basic to scientific theory (#66). And the entire work culminates in the second part of Investigation VI, where Husserl discusses how acts that mean categorial objects find their fulfillment. It is precisely such categorially formed objects that make up the structure of sciences. Scientific theory does not deal with objects given in simple perception, but with objects transformed categorially and thus introduced into a network of explanations. All of Husserl's analyses of consciousness in the *Investigations* lead teleologically to this point.

From what we have discussed, we can distill three ways in which consciousness transcends itself. (1) Consciousness goes beyond its immediate experience in simple intentionalities, when it possesses meanings that may or may not be capable of fulfillment. (2) It goes further when it possesses realizable meanings, meanings that can be and actually are verified in acts of fulfillment. (3) It can do more than realize a given meaning in an act of simple perception; it can realize it in the context of scientific explanation, and thus obtain reasoned grounds for asserting the reality of what it intends. How does the part-whole logic function in each of these forms of objectivity?

(1) In acts of simple intention, composite meanings must comprise a grammatically well-formed whole. A group of words like "the however upon still" breaks grammatical rules and does not even exist as a meaning. No objectivity is reached in it. A string of words like "the house is red," or even one like "a four-sided figure has three sides," both qualify as well-formed wholes and can exist as meanings, as something entertained in simple intentionalities. The latter example is self-contradicting, of course, and so cannot be realized in any act of fulfillment of the mere intention, but this does not disqualify it from being accepted as a meaning. Thus the "whole" that we work with here is a single proposition, and its parts are considered simply under their grammatical form. No matter what the content of the terms may be, as long as the grammatical structure is correct we have satisfied all the conditions for this level of objectivity.

(2) In the case of meanings that are to be realized in acts of fulfillment, a complex meaning must be not only grammatically well formed but also consistent with itself. "This square is round" is not self-consistent and thus could never be brought to fulfillment in an act of authentication (VI #30-31).

The "whole" we work with here is still a single proposition but now the content of the terms becomes relevant. It is no longer simply a matter of grammatical wholes and parts. If we are to reach the further objectivity of a fulfilling intention, one in which the complex meaning is not only simply intended but also assertable as real, then the content of the meaning-parts becomes a factor because self-contradiction must be excluded.

It should be mentioned that in the first edition of his *Logical Investigations* Husserl nowhere explicitly gives any conditions disqualifying such statements as "tall virtue sleeps furiously," or "color plus number equals four," in which the meaninglessness is not based upon any formal contradiction but simply upon the failure of the words to be relevant to one another. Such statements are grammatically correct and not contradictory, and yet are meaningless. Wittgenstein and the linguistic philosophers have put great emphasis on such verbal confusions, the result of mixing irreconcilable language games. Husserl does treat the subject in *Formal and Transcendental Logic* (#80).[4]

(3) In the case of intentions that are to be fulfilled in the context of scientific theory, the complex meaning must be not only well formed grammatically, not only consistent with itself, but also consistent with all the other propositions that make up the science. It must be relevant to the science in question (i.e., it must be decidable by the principles of that science) and it must not contradict any of the propositions accepted in it. The "whole" dealt with here is much larger than a single proposition. It is the entire structure of a scientific theory. The proposition we want to substantiate becomes simply a part of this greater whole, within which it must take a consistent place. If the truth of the proposition depends upon the grounds given it in the theory, then the asserted proposition becomes a "moment" of the entire scientific theory. It cannot stand by itself or be asserted on its own evidence alone; it needs completion, according to rule, by the network of propositions upon which it is founded. Just as syncategorematic words demand incorporation into larger linguistic wholes by virtue of their very meaning, so do certain propositions demand incorporation into the larger whole of a science if they are to be asserted as true. A theorem in geometry and a formula in physics cannot be brought to evidence or asserted as true except in the context of the entire science to which they belong.

The fact that a science is a unified whole is stressed by Husserl even in the *Prolegomena*, where he says that a theory is a fixed network (*festes*

---

[4] The second edition of the *Investigations* also mentions it in IV #10.

Gefüge) of interrelated propositions, some of which serve as the ground for others (#6-7, #63). Every unity, he claims, is constituted as such by means of rules, and it is precisely these rules for unification that phenomenology, as the "science of sciences, the theory of theories," must investigate. The rules in question will be those that dictate how parts of a science can be integrated into a whole; how propositions can be related to one another in a consistent and relevant way so that they comprise not just a collection of statements but a unified totality.

In the second section of Investigation VI, Husserl calls for a formal logic that will give all the rules governing part-whole structures in scientific theory (#62-63). The logic he speaks of here covers a wider scope than the "pure grammar" he discusses in Investigation IV. In the latter, he wants a computation of the various transformations a given individual proposition can undergo. He wants a list of rules describing the correctness of grammatically well-formed propositions and indicating the transformations such a proposition can undergo while remaining consistent *with itself*. Investigation VI, however, deals not with single propositions but with many propositions and their mutual compatibility. The "pure logic" discussed here deals with the formal rules that guide the interrelationships and transformations of many propositions in a single science. Since such propositions are only moments in a scientific whole, the "pure logic" states the formal rules guiding the incorporation of such moments into this type of totality.

Categorial formations are what enable an object to be incorporated into a science; when a simple object is made the subject of categorial constitution, it becomes possible to relate this object to others, to describe its characteristics, subject it to enumerations, etc. Categorial transformations make scientific analysis of an object possible. True, an object can be given in immediate perception with noncategorial evidence, but such perception is not scientific. Only when it is transformed in categorial constitution can it enter into a network of reasoned explanations that give grounds for assertions about the object.

Hence the entire *Logical Investigations* culminate in the second section of Investigation VI, where Husserl studies how categorial intentions can be brought from simple intentionalities to fulfillment. The first section deals with the difference between intentions and fulfillment in general, and the second deals specifically with the problem of categorial objects. Here Husserl reaches the farthest point in his "science of sciences." The "pure logic" he calls for in this section, the rules that guide "authentic thinking," really amount to a description of categorial forms and their interrelationships. They are the structures of "pure reason" that serve as a scaffolding, a necessary condition, for any series of propositions that would claim to be a science, with all the objectivity a science possesses. And since the pure logic is equivalent to showing how given categorial forms can be moments in a scientific whole, even this explanation of objectivity is based upon another application of the logic of wholes and parts.

(4) We have shown the place of part-whole logic in three levels of objectivity that consciousness can possess. Husserl uses parts and wholes in still another way in the *Investigations*, in a way that is connected to the problem of objectivity and evidence but does not fit simply under any of the three classes we have distinguished so far. If we take a complex meaning such as "the tree is green," we can easily distinguish between merely intending it and actually fulfilling it in perception. The issue is not so clear with a complex meaning like, "a given area cannot be simultaneously green and red." Here there is really no distinction between intention and perception. As long as we clearly intend the meaning, as long as we understand it, we perceive its truth. Such a "self-evident" proposition cannot be only "potentially" perceived, as "the tree is green" can. It can only exist as actually known, never as just potentially or hypothetically assumed. Clear intention and perception here are the same. Such statements can be called *a priori* truths because they do not stand in need of any verification independent of simply intending them.

The example we have given is a negative statement : green excludes red over the same area. Positive statements are also possible : "every color is a modification of a surface," "every sound has a certain intensity." Here also, if we clearly understand the meanings, we perceive the truth of what is said. The dimension of clarity is important, and although not explicitly discussed in the *Logical Investigations*, it is treated by Husserl in *Formal and Transcendental Logic* (#16).

All such self-evident statements, whether positive or negative, are instances of part-whole logic. In the positive ones, the objects related to one another are seen to be moments that imply one another by virtue of their very meaning. In the negative cases, the objects are moments which, when related to a certain whole, exclude one another. Husserl observes that even such exclusion is a form of unification into a certain whole, because it is only when related to specific totalities that the moments exclude one another (VI #33). For example, colors exclude one another only if they are predicated of the same area. In a statement in which the area mentioned can itself be subdivided, such as "this box is green and red," the colors do not exclude one another.

Husserl emphasizes very strongly the objectivity of such self-evident *a priori* statements. They are not merely an anthropological or cultural fact, the result of a tendency of people at a certain time to demand no justification for certain intentions. They are not merely the result of psychological dispositions or laws of human consciousness; they are rather grounded in the meanings themselves, in the senses that make up the complex meaning. We have here a case of "objectivity" and "transcendence" which is different from that of simple meaning, or of meanings fulfilled in direct perception, different even from that objectivity attained in scientific explanation. It is the objectivity of self-evidence (IV #10, #14).

The validity of such evidence is important in Husserl's philosophy because he claims that his own analyses of subjectivity result in *a priori*, self-evident statements. His assertion of the quality-material structure of acts, for example, his distinction between meaning and object meant, his statement of the dependence of categorial objects upon simple objects — all these phenomenological assertions are supposed to be *a priori* and self-evident in the way "every sound has a certain intensity" is (*Prolegomena*, #65-66). His assertions, he claims, do not stand in need of verification. We do not need to understand them first and then try to see if they are true or not; the very understanding of them is perception of their truth. Thus on the basis of part-whole logic Husserl can claim apodicticity for his phenomenological language even apart from the "Cartesian" theme of the transcendental reduction which is only implicitly present in the *Investigations*.[5]

We have examined the function of parts and wholes in the general problematic governing the *Investigations*, the study of how subjectivity can possess objectivity and otherness in knowledge. The logic of parts and wholes serves as a formal basis for each of the levels of objectivity that consciousness can reach. It should be clear from this analysis that Investigations II and IV are not excursions from the main path followed by this work, but that they fit intrinsically into its argument.

4. A COMPARISON OF HUSSERL WITH WAISMANN AND COHEN

The peculiarities of Husserl's part-whole logic, and especially of his *a priori*, self-evident statements, can be accentuated by comparing his doctrine

---

[5] On this point see the important #7 of the introduction to the *Investigations*.

with that of two contemporary thinkers who write in the tradition of linguistic philosophy. F. Waismann, in *Principles of Linguistic Philosophy* (New York, 1965, esp. pp. 57-68), and L. J. Cohen, in *The Diversity of Meaning* (London, 1962, esp. pp. 155-162), discuss similar problems and the latter explicitly takes a position against Husserl. Husserl says that the *a priori* and evident quality of such statements as "every color has a certain brightness" derives from the meanings fused together in these statements. We can give two characteristics of his position : (1) the necessity of the statements follows from the nature of the *meanings*; i.e., the meanings of the terms are constituted prior to the statements, and so the statements depend on the meanings. (2) We are not free to decide for or against the necessity of the statements. The self-evidence of the statements leaves us with no alternative but to accept them as true, provided we understand the meanings clearly.

Waismann and Cohen both would admit that the statements in question are necessarily true, but they disagree with Husserl as to what the necessity must be grounded upon. They reject Husserl's postulation of "Platonic" meanings that are determined in themselves. Instead, they say that the determination of the meanings results from a decision to use words in a certain way in a given culture. Thus against (2) above, they would claim that we are indeed free to determine the self-evidence of the statements in question. We, or the members of our linguistic community, decree that these statements are to be accepted as self-evident and necessary. We impart the necessity to them, we determine them *as a rule* that will govern the use of the terms making up the statements. Red and green do not exclude one another because of anything in themselves; rather the linguistic community legislates that "red" and "green" will be used in an exclusive sense, and does so by insisting that "red and green exclude one another over a given surface," is to be accepted as *a priori*, incapable of being falsified by experience. Such statements are linguistic prescriptions, not assertions of essential structures as they are for Husserl. Their *a priori* character comes by decree, not from the terms used in them. As regards (1), the nature of the meanings is now seen to follow from the necessity of the statements in which they are prescriptively used. The relationship of dependence is reversed. For Husserl, the statements depend on the meanings; for Waismann and Cohen the meanings, the prescribed use of the terms, depend upon a decision governing the statements. The statement itself *is* a rule for the meaning (use) of the term.

The problem of how to explain *a priori* propositions thus appears as one of the crucial points of opposition between Husserl's phenomenology and linguistic philosophy, for Waismann's doctrine is very much influenced by Wittgenstein. Although Waismann and Cohen succeed in dispelling Husserl's phenomenological Platonism, his assertion of essential structures present in meanings, they leave us with no objective grounds for the linguistic decisions that determine *a priori* propositions. Are human decisions, linguistic or otherwise, made with no motives offered "in the things themselves?". Is consciousness simply a legislator for reality, and does it never submit to the evidence of what is given? These questions are acute enough when applied to language about the world : they become even more pressing when applied to philosophical language. Are the distinctions made in philosophical speech and explanation simply linguistic prescriptions? We have seen that the most important use of Husserl's part-whole logic is its application to the philosophical distinctions he makes in phenomenology; this logic is the basis of the *a priori* self-evidence he attributes to what he says in his "science of sciences." But if necessary statements are merely prescriptive rules, then philosophy itself can never be a science and its speech must become rhetoric, the language of persuasion, instead of the language of description and assertion.

OUTLINES OF A THEORY OF
"ESSENTIALLY OCCASIONAL EXPRESSIONS"*

by

Aron Gurwitsch

(New York)

(*edited by* Lester Embree)

In describing the organization with which the perceptual world always presents itself to consciousness, whether thematically or marginally, we must use expressions such as "in front," "behind," "near," "far," etc. These terms imply a certain relativity to a referential system in the sense that an object to which one of these terms may be applied under certain circumstances, i.e. with respect to one orientation of the referential system, may no longer be designated by the same term when some change in the orientation of this system occurs. Sitting at my desk, I may designate a book which lies on my desk by saying "this is in front of me." When I turn my back, the book can no longer be designated by the term "in front," which now applies, say, to a picture hanging on the wall; but the picture was not "in front of me" before I turned my back on the book. As to the application of the terms in question to objects and the designation of the latter by the former, a certain equivocation appears insofar as the same term sometimes does and sometimes does not apply to the same object.

The terms mentioned are not the only ones exhibiting the relativity in question.[1] It also affects words like "this," "that," "here," "there,"

---

* Published for the first time with the kind permission of Mrs. Aron Gurwitsch. The manuscript has been edited by Lester Embree to whom I am grateful — J. N. M.

The present text is a section omitted from the final draft of the author's book, *The Field of Consciousness* (Duquesne University Press, Pittsburgh, Pa. : 1964). It was composed ca. 1950. In preparing it for publication I have introduced section and paragraph divisions, altered some of the footnotes, my additions are in square brackets, and smoothed the expression throughout. I thank Mrs. Aron Gurwitsch for permission to make this text available. — Lester Embree.

[1] In the case of "near" and "far," there is still another relativity. Sitting at my desk, I may say that the books on the shelves are near; living in New York, I may say that Philadelphia is near. But the "nearness" in the first example is not the same as in the latter. A relativity of this kind is also involved in words like "hot," "cool," "great," "small," "fast," "slow," etc. In the tropics, "hot" weather means something different from what it means in a moderate climate; a "fast" mode of transportation today is not what it was a hundred years ago, etc. But these words do not imply a relativity with respect to a

"now," "yesterday," "soon," "later," "I," "you," "he," "it," etc. Thus a whole class of words present the following anomaly and paradox. Whereas with regard to all other expressions, e.g. "house," "book," "to walk," "to write," etc., the relation between the word and any given object or event depends entirely and exclusively upon the nature of the object and the meaning of the word, such is not the case with regard to the words of the sort we have mentioned. As to these words, their relation to a given object cannot be determined without ambiguity solely in terms of their meanings and the nature of the object. Nonetheless, the words in question have definite meanings; they are easily understood; in no concrete case does any doubt arise as to whether a given object does or does not fall under the meaning of one of these words.

I

Bertrand Russell has studied words of this sort under the heading of "egocentric particulars." [2] He limited his discussion to the word "this," because, he thought, every other "egocentric particular" can be defined in terms of "this." Not wishing to dwell upon whether or not this reduction is possible, we take his discussion of "this" as the treatment of a paradigmatic example. [3] To which class of words, Russell asks, does "this" belong?

---

referential system. Here the reference is rather to a certain scale which is, as it were, graduated with regard to what passes in various fields of experience as the average standard. This relativity with regard to a scale derives from the fact that the average standards are not the same in all fields of experience and that, furthermore, they vary according to the general environment, both natural and cultural. (Cf. Edmund Husserl, *Erfahrung und Urteil*, edited by Ludwig Landgrebe, Prague, 1939, 46.) In what follows we will be concerned only with relativity with regard to a referential system and not with that regarding scales and average standards.

   [2] *An Inquiry into Meaning and Truth*, New York, 1940, Ch. VII.

   [3] One remark, however, concerning Russell's definition of "I" as "the biography to which this belongs" (*ibid.*, p. 134) is not out of place. His definition implies that "I" refers to the Ego as subject of a biography and contexture of experiences, unified and systematized by causal relations. This interpretation is borne out by Russell's subsequent statements :

   "The word 'I,' since it applies to something which persists throughout a certain period of time, is to be derived from 'I-now,' as that series of events which is related to 'I-now' by certain causal relations. ... 'I-now' denotes a set of occurrences, namely all those that are happening to me at the moment. 'This' denotes some of these occurrences. 'I' as opposed to 'I-now' can be defined by causal relations to 'this,' just as well as 'I-now' for I can only denote by 'this' something that I am experiencing." (*Ibid.*, pp. 141ff.)

It will appear below in III that as a first person pronoun 'I' does not refer to or even connote the Ego as a causal unity, the personality which has a biography.

Is it a proper name which designates an object without indicating any of
its attributes? One might take "this" to be a proper name like "Smith"
which is applied to many persons without connoting any property which these
persons have in common. There is, however, a constant relation between
a proper name and the person named, whereas that which is designated
by "this" changes from one occasion to another. It is true that an object
is given its name by arbitrary convention. But there is no arbitrary convention in calling some object "this" any more than there is a subsequent arbitrary convention in not calling the same object "this" when one wishes
to refer to it on a different occasion.[4] Moreover, it is impossible to consider "this" as a general predicate. General concepts have instances. Once
an object is recognized to be an instance of a general concept, it remains an
instance forever and the term in question may always be applied to the
object. But "this" sometimes may and sometimes may not be applied to the
same object. Finally, "this" cannot be regarded as a concealed description,
for the description of an object characterizes the object permanently. Were
"this" interpreted as meaning "object of the present act of attention,"
the problem would merely be transferred to the word "present," which
is also an "egocentric particular," and the same holds anyway for the tense
of a verb.

Confronted with the paradox that "this" may only be applied to one object
at a time but to different objects at different times, Russell turns to the
circumstances under which "this" is used rather than "that." In both cases
there is a verbal reaction to a stimulus, i.e. a reaction which involves the
innervation of certain muscles so that a sentence is emitted. This verbal
reaction may be immediate or delayed. If it is delayed, the effect of the
stimulus is not an immediate motor impulse and verbal response; rather
this effect is stored in "some kind of reservoir" and then subsequently
released by a new stimulus. The delayed reaction thus being produced by
a cause different from that of the immediate reaction, the effects are
different. Whereas the immediate verbal reaction begins with the words
"this is...," a delayed reaction begins with the words "that was". According
to Russell, "egocentric particulars" merely designate causal relations
between that which is stated and the stating of it. Taken in isolation,
they have no meaning at all. When two sentences differ only with respect
to an "egocentric particular" — the one containing "this" and the other

---

[4] As to both the similarity and difference between a proper and a demonstrative
pronoun, cf. Edmund Husserl, *Logische Untersuchungen*, Vol. II, Second Investigation,
pp. 20f.

containing "that" — the difference between them does not concern their meanings but merely their causations, which in one case is direct or immediate and in the other case is indirect or delayed.

To refute this theory requires a discussion of the phenomenon of meaning, i.e. of the fact that words have meanings, at greater length than may be undertaken in the present context.[5] One point, however, requires some clarification. Let us assume a physiological mechanism so to function that as an immediate reaction to a specific stimulus I stamp my right foot and as a delayed reaction to the same stimulus I stamp my left foot. On the grounds of Russell's theory, there is nothing to make this reaction incommensurable with the utterance of "this" and "that." In principle it makes little if any difference whether the reaction to a stimulus affects the leg muscles or the muscles of the vocal organs, and, in the latter case, whether this sound or a different one is emitted. In each case, there is a stimulus, a physiological mechanism set to functioning by the stimulus, and a reaction owing to the functioning of that mechanism which is provoked by the stimulus as a final effect. Stamping one's feet, emitting a sound, and saying "this" are, in Russell's theory, reactions of substantially the same kind insofar as all three are considered final effects. However, in saying "this" my reaction to the stimulus is of a specific nature in that I refer and point to the stimulus, designate and denominate it, give it a name and call it by this name, although the name is of but a momentary and transitory use. Not only do I thus experience my saying "this," but whoever hears it, provided he understands the language which I am speaking, understands the word "this" as the designation of an object.

The meaningfulness of a word consists not in its being emitted subsequent to the stimulus but also, and mainly, in the reference to and thus the denotation of the stimulus. Whereas all three reactions which we have considered may be said to be alike in that they *result from* the stimulus, the utterance of the word "this" is distinguished with respect to the other two reactions in that it *refers to* the stimulus. In Russell's theory, this difference is overlooked. He explains the causation, either immediate or delayed, of a reaction to a stimulus, but what he fails — and, on the grounds of his theory, cannot help failing — to account for is the fact that some reactions, in addition to being provoked by, also bear pointing

[5] Cf., however, Edmund Husserl, *Logische Untersuchungen*, Vol. I, First Investigation, "Ausdruck und Bedeutung," [Aron Gurwitsch, *Phenomenology and the Theory of Science*, ed. Lester Embree, Northwestern University Press, Evanston, Ill. : 1974, pp. 228ff.], and Dorion Cairns, "The Ideality of Verbal Expressions," *Philosophy and Phenomenological Research*, Vol. I (1941).

reference to, the stimulus.[6] The latter fact ought not to be disregarded in a causal explanation, either psychological or physiological. To be complete, the explanation of a phenomenon must take all aspects of this phenomenon into account; it must, therefore, also account for the distinctive character by which some reactions differ from others. The fact that in some reactions the subject experiences a reference to the object (the stimulus in the examples under discussion) is a psychological fact which must be dealt with even in a physiological explanation.[7] At any rate, meaningfulness is a fact *sui generis* and this holds for "egocentric particulars" which, paradoxical or not, are meaningful.

II

We now turn to Edmund Husserl's discussion of the same problem.[8] Since "egocentric particulars" are ambiguous in that they apply to different objects on different occasions, their ambiguity must be explicated. "Egocentric particulars" do not have the same kind of ambiguity as homonyms,

---

[6] The point at issue is obscured by Russell's most unfortunate use of machines to illustrate his theory (*loc. cit.*, pp. 138ff.). The functioning of a machine can be accounted for only in terms of physical laws and the mechanics of the machine. No other factor is involved. This is no less true when, by some ingenuity, the machine is so constructed as to emit sounds which, when uttered by a person, would be meaningful words, but since they are emitted by a machine, are final effects produced by the mechanism of the machine. Russell is perfectly right in asserting that nothing but causal chains are involved when a machine, immediately after a coin has been inserted, emits the sounds "this is a penny' and after a certain time emits the sounds "that was a penny." But by so functioning the machine does not seem to us to get any "nearer to the capacities of human speech." It is indeed hard to see how "the consideration of this ingenious toy may enable us to eliminate irrelevant problems." Russell's illustration is simply a $\mu\epsilon\tau\acute{\alpha}$-$\beta\alpha\sigma\iota\varsigma$ $\epsilon\acute{\iota}\varsigma$ $\acute{\alpha}\lambda\lambda o$ $\gamma\acute{\epsilon}\nu o\varsigma$, viz. a $\gamma\acute{\epsilon}\nu o\varsigma$ in which there are no phenomena and, therefore, no problems of meanings and from which, consequently, these problems need not be eliminated. In the *Logische Untersuchungen* (Vol. I, § 22), Husserl has shown the absurdity of interpreting logical laws and, quite generally, laws and facts concerning meaning as causal factors. Russell tries, however, to account for facts of meaning in terms of causal relationships. Either enterprise is equally hopeless, for meanings and causal relations are incommensurable. Besides these objections, Russell's "physiological" construction — "too schematic to count as actual physiology" (*loc. cit.*, p. 140) — is also open to objection from the physiological point of view. Köhler has dismissed machines as of illustrative value for physiological processes in his thorough discussion of the question in Ch. IV of *Gestalt Psychology*, New York, 1947.

[7] In a different context, this point has been stressed by Koffka in "Psychologie," in *Lehrbuch der Philosophie*, Vol. II, *Die Philosophie in ihren Einzelgebieten*, ed. M. Dessoir, Berlin, 1925, pp. 536f.

[8] For the following, Cf. Husserl, *Logische Untersuchungen*, Vol. II, First Investigation, § 26.

such as "beaver," which designates both an animal and the lower part of a helmet. The ambiguity of homonyms is accidental. Two or more meanings, between which there is no relation whatever, happen to be attached to the same sound or the same configuration of marks. Because the meanings are unrelated, the ambiguity of a homonym may be removed with an arbitrary convention. In the case of "egocentric particulars," on the contrary, the ambiguity is not due to a linguistic accident, but lies in the very meaning of the words. The word "here," for instance, applies and is meant to apply to any object whatsoever which, on any occasion when the word is used, happens to be in the immediate surroundings of the speaker. Hence while the word "here" may be applied to an indefinite number of objects, these objects are not unrelated, for each one of them, on the occasion of its being designated by the word "here," fulfills a specific condition. It appears, furthermore, that the ambiguity of "egocentric particulars" may not be removed by arbitrary convention without affecting the meanings of such words. Here the ambiguity is *essential.*

To know which object is meant in a given case by an "egocentric particular," it does not suffice that one hear and understand the word; allowance must also be made for the circumstances of the utterance of the word. This allowance is a *conditio sine qua non* for the full understanding of an "egocentric particular," i.e. for the apprehension of the particular object which on a given occasion is designated by the word in question. Husserl thus treats the words under discussion under the title of "essentially occasional expressions (*wesentlich okkasionelle Ausdrücke*)," a phrase we shall employ hereafter. A theory of such expressions must fulfill two requirements : (1) it must account for their essential ambiguity and (2) it must take the circumstances of their occurence into account. These are the necessary and sufficient conditions for the understanding of the expressions in question. In the latter respect, the theory must show how, owing to this allowance, the meaning of an essentially occasional expression in any given case of the application of this expression is actually restricted to but one object. In the practical use of these words, no doubt ever arises as to which object happens to be meant.

To see how such a theory may be established, we shall follow Husserl's discussion of the word "I." [9] The person who is presently speaking refers

---

[9] [For the author's position on the phenomenological problem of the Ego itself, cf. "Phenomenology of Thematics and of the Pure Ego : Studies of the Relation between Gestalt Theory and Phenomenology," trans. Fred Kersten, and "A Non-Egological Conception of Consciousness" in Aron Gurwitsch, *Studies in Phenomenology and Psychology*, Northwestern University Press, Evanston, Ill. : 1966.]

to himself with this word. But we cannot say that the meaning of "I" is "the presently speaking person referring to himself." Were this the meaning of the word "I," it might be substituted for "I." But the sentence "I am cheerful" obviously does not have precisely the same meaning as the sentence "The person presently speaking and referring to himself is cheerful." The assertion formulated in the second sentence extends further than that expressed in the first sentence. Nonetheless, the word "I" obviously serves to designate the person who is presently speaking as referring to himself. Similarly, the word "here" has the function of designating the immediate surroundings of the speaker; the function of the word "this" consists in expressing a reference to something in these immediate surroundings; that of the word "soon" in indicating an event as imminent in the comparatively near future with respect to the moment of the utterance of the word, etc.

With respect to essentially occasional expressions, a distinction must thus be made between the *meaning function* and the *specific meaning*, in Husserl's terminology between *anzeigende Bedeutung* (signifying meaning) and *angezeigte Bedeutung* (signified meaning). It is only the latter which varies according to the occasions on which the word is used. There is no ambiguity in the meaning function; on all occasions and under all circumstances the word "before" has the same function, namely that of indicating a moment of time previous to that of the utterance. *Meaning functions are to essentially occasional expressions what meanings are to normal words*, such as "table," "heavy," "to read," etc. That is to say, the meaning functions give meaningfulness to the expressions in question and make them differ from mere noises. Whenever we encounter an essentially occasional expression, we do not understand its *specific meaning*, i.e. we do not know the particular object which it happens to designate, unless we allow for the circumstances of its utterance. But even without allowing for these circumstances, we understand the meaning function of the word; we know that it serves to designate objects of a definite kind and we also know of which kind these objects are. The understanding of the meaning function is immediately attached to the perception of the visible or audible configuration of the word and is quite independent of all circumstances, in no way different from how this is the case with other words.

It is in the nature of a meaning function to refer to a range of variables as subsumable. These variables cannot be of any sort whatever but must fulfill a specific condition which is defined by the function; in the case of "here," for example, the condition consists in being found in the more or less vaguely circumscribed immediate surroundings of whoever uses the word. This theory of the essentially occasional expressions accounts thus for their essential ambiguity (in ascribing it to their meaning functions rather than to their meanings) and for the fact that all objects which are designated by the same essentially occasional expression have a certain character in common, namely that owing to which they are subsumable under the meaning function in question. Each one of these objects, however, exhibits this character not permanently but only on the occasion of its designation by the essentially occasional expression under consideration. From the very fact that the meaning function refers to a range of variables, it follows that the actual choice of a determinate variable in a given case, (in other words, the specification of the meaning function, its determination, and, so to speak, individuation into the specific meaning which is in question in the case under consideration), must depend upon factors extrinsic to the meaning function itself. Hence the need to allow for the circumstances of the utterance of an essentially occasional expression in order to ascertain its specific meaning in a given case. This need is not merely an accidental fact but derives rather from the very nature of these expressions as having meaning functions.

Often, though not always, the specification of a meaning function is a matter of perception.[10] Someone says "this thing here" and we know that he means to designate something in his surroundings. Looking in the appropriate direction, we perceive a book. Owing to this perception, what previously was an unspecified meaning, i.e. a mere meaning function referring to a range of variables, becomes specified. Instead of the somehow indeterminate meaning "something in the surroundings of the speaker," we now have a definite meaning "the book by X, bound in red, lying on the table, etc." By means of the perception, one meaning is thus replaced by another one. This substitution may also be brought about by representations or images rather than actual perceptions, when, for example, the surroundings of the speaker do not fall into our perceptual field but are familiar to us from previous experiences so that we may form representations or images of them. Reading in a letter from a friend "this garden is now in blossom," we know which particular garden is meant. Thus, it seems acts of perception, imagination, representation, and also of imageless thought contribute towards the meaning of essentially occasional expressions. But, according to Husserl, this contribution is strictly confined to the mentioned substitution. In other words, these acts specify and determine a meaning function, but they do not give meaning to a word which

---

[10] Cf. Husserl, *Logische Untersuchungen*, Vol. II, Sixth Investigation, § 5.

otherwise would be devoid of meaning. The meaningfulness of essentially occasional expressions, i.e. the fact that they are experienced as words, i.e. understood, and not as mere noises, does not derive from any specifying act but resides entirely in these expressions themselves as bearers of meaning functions. Perception, representation, etc. are meaning-*specifying*, not meaning-*bestowing*.

III

Husserl's account of the essentially occasional expressions is clearly satisfactory as far as their interpretation in terms of meanings is concerned. Yet there still remains the singular status of these words which, unlike all others, have meaning functions rather than meanings. Which structure of consciousness is responsible for the existence of a whole class of words of so singular a status? Husserl himself later felt that his account was incomplete and ascribed his failure to dispose of these expressions completely in the *Logische Untersuchungen* to the fact that he had at that time still not taken the phenomenon of horizonal consciousness into consideration.[11]

In characterizing the orientational aspect with which the perceptual world permanently appears in consciousness, we use essentially occasional expressions, such as "near," "far," "in front," "behind," etc. Such expressions are unavoidable. In fact, to the extent to which they have spatial denotations, "essentially occasional expressions" refer to and derive their meanings from, the orientational aspect of the perceptual world, i.e. its organization along the three spatial dimensions. The two directions along each of these dimensions, i.e. forward and backward, upward and downward, leftward and rightward, and the difference between nearness and farness in each direction refer to the place which the body happens to occupy. Each one of the essentially occasional expressions in question designates a specific orientational character or, to put it more accurately, its meaning function consists in this designation. The constancy of these meaning functions corresponds to the invariants of the organizational and orientational system.

---

[11] Cf. Edmund Husserl, *Formal and Transcendental Logic*, trans. Dorion Cairns, Martinus Nijhoff, The Hague, 1969, 80. Cf. also Edmund Husserl, *Ideen zu einer reinen Phänomenologie und phänomenologischen Philosophie*, Book I, ed. Walter Biemel, The Hague, Martinus Nijhoff, 1950, 27, 45, & 47 and Ludwig Landgrebe, "The World as a Phenomenological Problem," *Philosophy and Phenomenological Research*, Vol. I (1941), pp. 39f.

Among these invariants must also be reckoned the reference of the system to the body as center of organization. Although the orientational directions as such are invariant, the coincidence of any one of them with this or that direction in objective space is not constant but, on the contrary, dependent upon the position of the body and, therefore, varies with this position. Consequently, when applied to objects and directions in objective space, designations of orientational characters must necessarily exhibit an ambiguity which derives from the mentioned invariant reference of these characters to the body. Hence also the need of resorting to means other than the mere understanding of meaning functions in order to ascertain the object or objective direction to which the orientational character is applied under given circumstances, i.e. with respect to the position which the body happens to occupy.

The same is correspondingly true of those "essentially occasional expressions" which have temporal denotations, such as "now," "sooner," "later," etc. Here the reference is to the moment of the utterance of the expression; this moment, the present, serves as a center of orientation with regard to which the differentiation between past and future occurs. The time in question is not phenomenal but objective time, i.e. the temporality which belongs to the perceptual world as its order form, and not that which is immanent to and characteristic of the stream of consciousness. It goes without saying that the perceptual world permanently presents a temporal as well as a spatial organization. Thus the singular status of the essentially occasional expressions derives from the particular organizational aspect with which the perceptual world presents itself.

It is owing to the permanent awareness, at least in marginal form, of the perceptual world that the understanding of essentially occasional expressions never involves any difficulty and that there never arises any doubt about the specific meaning which any of these expressions happens to have in a given case. Essentially occasional expressions have their phenomenal origin, i.e. their underlying experiential basis, in the present awareness, at least in the marginal form, of the three always-present orders of existence in their mutual interrelations, namely : the stream of consciousness, embodied existence, and the perceptual world.[12]

It is with respect to this experiential basis that the word "I" must be interpreted. As already mentioned, by means of this word the person presently speaking designates himself. Used in a given case by a determinate speaker, the word "I" does not refer to the biography of the speaker or

---

[12] [Cf. *The Field of Consciousness*, pp. 382ff. and 414ff.]

to his Ego in the sense of a causal unity. Rather, it refers to that awareness which the speaker like every conscious subject permanently has of himself and upon which the evidence of the "*cogito sum*" rests, viz. the inner awareness of the present segment of the stream of consciousness with its intrinsic phenomenal temporality. To this must be added the awareness of the embodied existence, taken as it is actually given in experience, i.e. awareness of those somatic facts which at the moment happen to present themselves with their pointing reference to the more or less confused horizon of corporeity; and, finally, the awareness of that sector of the perceptual world in which the speaker experiences himself as placed. Thus the specific meaning of the word "I" varies not only from one speaker to another but also with respect to the same person, according to the occasion on which this word is uttered.[13] In this respect, also there is no substantial difference between "I" and the other essentially occasional expressions such as "to the right," "in front," etc. Each of these expressions, when uttered at the same time by two persons, has for the one a specific meaning different from that which it has for the other; and also, when used by the same person on different occasions, its specific meaning depends upon and varies also with the place in which the speaker finds himself and with the orientation of his body. *Mutatis mutandis* the same holds for essentially occasional expressions of the temporal sort.

Thus far we have considered the expressions in question from the standpoint of the speaker. As far as the hearer is concerned, the point of interest is that he takes these expressions with the specific meaning which they have for the speaker. The hearer understands the expressions under discussion with reference to the orientational system of the speaker and not to his own, rather as if he occupied the place which the speaker occupies and rather as if his body had that orientation which the body of the speaker happens to have. This fact is closely related to the apprehension of the speaker by the hearer and, quite generally, of one person by another person as an "*alter ego*." That is to say, one apprehends the other as a subject endowed with a stream of consciousness such as one experiences in himself and one apprehends the other as a subject to whom the perceptual world also presents itself in its organizational aspect but with reference to a different center of orientation, namely : that in which it would appear if one were in the place of the speaker. For a complete account of the essentially occasional expressions, the facts and problems of intersubjectivity must then be taken

---

[13] Russell's definition of the word "I" (cf. note 3, above) fails to account for the latter variation.

into consideration; but these problems lie beyond the scope of the present investigation.[14] Another pertinent fact, for the full elucidation of which one must allow for intersubjectivity, concerns the understanding of essentially occasional expressions when they are encountered in reading, e.g. books of history, in novels, etc. In this case, also, the reader takes these expressions with reference to the person who utters them and to the circumstances of the utterance : either the writer himself or the person, be he historical or fictitious, whom the writer has utter them.

To corroborate the theory just advanced and especially the interpretation of the word "I," we wish to refer to some remarks of Wilhelm von Humboldt on the personal pronoun.[15] Personal pronouns exist in languages not insofar as language incorporates thought or logic, but rather insofar as language is related to interaction between men. Personal pronouns owe their existence to actual speech and it is through actual speech that they are introduced into thought. In this sense personal pronouns are rooted in the innermost nature of language considered under the aspect of communication. Actual speech consists in one person speaking to another person. The former is the addresser and the latter is the addressee. Addresser and addressee stand in correlation to each other and, as thus correlated, both are in a relation of opposition to any third person. There is a formal system of relations realized in every case of actual speech, and this system is invariant with respect to all particular circumstances of the given case. This system consists of the addresser, the addressee, and those persons who are not included in this correlation. It is to this system that the personal pronouns refer, each one designating one member of this system with regard to and only with regard to the place which this member holds in the relational system, i.e. with regard to the functional significance of the member within the system.

One may say that personal pronouns actually designate places within the relational system and that they designate persons only insofar as these pronouns happen to occupy certain places in the system under discussion. In their pure and genuine form, personal pronouns thus prove to be rela-

---

[14] The fifth of Husserl's *Cartesian Meditations* (trans. Dorion Cairns, The Hague, Martinus Nijhoff, 1960), especially §§ 49ff., is devoted to the phenomenological problem of intersubjectivity. [For a development of Husserl's notion of essentially occasional expressions in connection with problems of intersubjective understanding, cf. Alfred Schutz, *Phenomenology of the Social World*, trans. George Walsh and Frederick Lehnert, Evanston, Ill. : Northwestern University Press, 1967, § 24.]

[15] "Ueber die Verwandschaft der Ortsadverbien mit dem Pronomen in einigen Sprachen," in *Gesammelten Schriften*, Berlin, 1907, Vol. VI, Part I.

tional concepts (*Verhältnisbegriffe*) which exist only with reference to each other within the invariant formal system.

The "I" is not the individual seen with these properties and found in these spatial relations, but rather the subject standing in consciousness over-against an other at this moment... It is the same with "you" and "he". All are hypostatized relational concepts, indeed about individual and present things, but utterly indifferent to their characteristics and only referring back to a relationship in which all three concepts are mutually contained and conditioned.[16]

From this it appears that relational concepts as expressed by personal pronouns are highly abstract. To express these abstract concepts with words conveying more intuitive meaning, i.e. derived from a domain more open to intuition, the words chosen must be of such a nature as to render the essential peculiarities of the abstract concepts.[17] Words for "I" and "you" must be applicable to every individual, for any individual may become an "I" or a "you"; the difference between the "I" and the "you" must clearly appear as a correlational difference in such a way that they stand in opposition to a possible third term. Though the words to be used should have intuitive meaning, there can be no qualitative difference.

According to von Humboldt, space is an order in which these requirements of formal structure are met. Thus he examines languages in which adverbs of place are closely related to personal pronouns and confirms his thesis, of Kantian inspiration, that the pure forms of intuition, namely space and time, are particularly fit for illustrating abstract concepts.[18] In the case under discussion, one might think that the role of space consists in more than merely providing a medium for illustrative rendering. Actual interaction takes place in perceptual space and the men engaged in this interaction are aware of each other as standing in spatial relations. On the other hand, personal pronouns, in their genuine purity, designate the relational positions which persons engaged in social interaction hold with regard to each other within the mentioned formal system, for instance as addresser or addressee. It is therefore highly plausible that an inner affinity exists between personal pronouns as designating relations of interaction

---

[16] "*Ich ist nicht das mit diesen Eigenschaften versehene, in diesen räumlichen Verhältnissen befindliche Individuum, sondern der sich in diesem Augenblick einem Andern im Bewusstsein, als ein Subjekt, gegenüberstellende... Eben so geht es mit Du und Er. Alle sind hypostasierte Verhältnisbegriffe, zwar auf individuelle, vorhandene Dinge, aber in völliger Gleichgültigkeit auf die Beschaffenheit dieser, nur in Rücksicht auf das eine Verhältnis bezogen, in welchem alle diese drei Begriffe sich nur gegenseitig durch einander halten und bestimmen.*" (*Ibid.*, 306.)

[17] *Ibid.*, pp. 310ff.

[18] *Ibid.*, p. 329.

and those words by which spatial relations between persons engaged in interaction are expressed, at least insofar as the formal structure of either class of expressions is concerned.

IV

There is still another use of the essentially occasional expressions, especially demonstratives. Instead of designating things in the perceptual world, demonstratives may be used to refer to items in a context. Thus in developing an argument one may say "from this it appears," "this proves that," after formulating a mathematical theorem, one may go on to prove it with the words "this follows from," etc. Obviously, demonstratives used in this way exhibit the same ambiguity as other essentially occasional expressions do, viz. essential and not accidental ambiguity. Consequently, here again the distinction must be made between the meaning function and the specific meaning. And here too it is only the meaning function which is constant, for the function of the demonstratives consists in indicating and pointing to items of a context which are in a certain relation to that which, at the present time, is the theme. The circumstances of the utterance, — the place in which the speaker finds himself, the orientation of his body, and the moment of objective time at which he speaks — are here immaterial and irrelevant to the specification of the meaning function. Allowance for the facts just mentioned is neither sufficient nor necessary for ascertaining the preceding theorem which is meant by "this" in a piece of mathematical reasoning, the argument for a view which is meant by "from this," the event to which "this" or "that" refers in a report or a novel, etc.

Demonstratives used to refer to a context do not designate orientational characters, they have no spatial denotations. And when they have temporal denotations, the time referred to is not the objective time of the perceptual world to the present of which the moment of utterance belongs, but rather the time of the novel or the report. Demonstratives in the use under discussion refer to items of a context to which the present theme also pertains and of which at present it appears as the center. The relations between the theme and the items of the context or the thematic field referred to by the demonstratives may well be characterized in terms of nearness and farness. But this is a rather figurative manner of speaking. Nearness and farness must not be taken in a spatial or in a temporal sense, although they sometimes have a temporal sense, i.e. when the context in question consists of a sequence of events. Nearness and farness in this case stand for immediacy and mediacy. The specific sense of immediacy and mediacy in a given case depends upon the nature of the context in question; in the case of a mathematical context, the specific sense of immediacy and mediacy is different from what it is in a musical context and it is different again in a historical context, etc. The determinate particular context in question in a given case supplies the specification of the meaning function of the demonstratives.

Demonstratives cannot be understood as to their *specific meanings* except with regard to the particular context in which they occur.[19] Hence as far as demonstratives are concerned allowance for the concrete particular context plays the same role as that which allowance for the circumstances under which they are uttered, viz. facts in the perceptual world, plays in the normal use of essentially occasional expressions. We have seen that normal essentially occasional expressions have their phenomenological origin in the permanent awareness, at least in marginal form, of the perceptual world, embodied existence, and the stream of consciousness in their mutual interrelations. Correspondingly, the basis in experience from which the demonstratives, as considered here, derive their status lies in the phenomenon of context as such, i.e. in the fact that every theme appears in a thematic field, emerging from and occupying the center of this field. In the case of demonstratives, the center of reference is obviously that which happens to be the theme at the moment of their utterance. The theme plays the same role here that the position of the speaker in perceptual space and the orientation of his body play in the case of normal essentially occasional expressions.

All these analogies are not surprising. When facts pertaining to the perceptual world, embodied existence, and the stream of consciousness are experienced in marginal form, this form concerns only the relation of these facts to the theme, i.e. their disconnection and exclusion from the systematic unity of the thematic process when, for example, in mathematical reasoning, this process happens to bear upon a subject matter which belongs to none of the mentioned three orders of existence. Though appearing in marginal form, the facts in question are not experienced as scattered data but, on the contrary, as pointing and referring to each other, and thus pertaining to a coherent order, i.e. to a context founded upon relevancy. For this very reason, marginal consciousness of the three orders of existence in question, taken to the extent to which and exactly as they actually present themselves, is conscious of them as potential thematic fields. As to the perceptual world, it reveals itself as a special case of continuity of context

[19] Cf. Husserl, *Logische Untersuchungen*, First Investigation, p. 84.

based upon relevancy. The same holds evidently both for the stream of consciousness and embodied existence. Either order exhibits coherence due to and derived from the intrinsic material relations which exist among the contents pertaining to the order in question.

To a more penetrating analysis, what we have called normal essentially occasional expressions appear as special cases, while the demonstratives, as we have considered them, seem to lead us nearer to the experiential basis of words which have meaning functions rather than meanings. The existence of words of such a status derives from the phenomenon of context considered in its widest generality, i.e. as to its purely formal structure, regardless of every specification; but every specific context proves a special case of this formal structure. In other words, the expressions under discussion owe their existence to that structure of consciousness on account of which whatever is given as a theme appears as pertaining to a certain order or realm of existence. It is this structure that underlies the possibility of words whose function consists in referring to items of the order in question according to the relations of immediacy and mediacy between the items referred to and the theme. The formal structure of the phenomenon of context does not depend upon the specific nature of any particular context, but is an invariant of consciousness. This structure consists in the way a thematic field is organized with respect to a center which stands in relations of greater or lesser immediacy to the items of the field. It is because of their invariance that the meaning functions of words which derive from this phenomenon have constancy, i.e. do not vary from one specific context to another. Hence these words, as to their meaning function, may be applied to every context; and, when so applied, the specification of their meaning function is, in every given case, drawn from the specific nature of the context in question. An example of an incipient, although by no means accomplished, specification is offered by what we have called essentially occasional expressions. The particularity of the latter, viz. their spatial and temporal denotations with regard to objective space and time, depends upon the particular nature of the specific context to which they refer.

HUSSERL'S CONCEPTION OF
A PURELY LOGICAL GRAMMAR*

by

YEHOSHUA BAR-HILLEL

(Jerusalem)

The assumption that there exists a common grammatical core which is valid for all languages and which can be determined by *a priori* insight is an old and venerable speculation of both linguists and philosophers. This assumption is not fashionable any more, and the old arguments adduced for it could not withstand the onslaught on the empirical evidence provided by the study of "exotic" languages. Nevertheless, in a certain sense, to be more closely determined later on, it has been taken up by no less a man than Rudolf Carnap, one of the leading logicians and anti-speculative philosophers of our time.

It should therefore be of more than purely historical interest to investigate into what one of the most influential philosophers of this century, Edmund Husserl, had to say on this topic. Carnap studied some time with Husserl and it is not impossible that at least part of the impact that led him later on to write his *Logical Syntax of Language* [1] originated at that time.

I intend to deal almost exclusively with the fourth chapter of the first part of the second volume of Husserl's *Logische Untersuchungen*, in the revised version of the second edition of 1913. Husserl himself insists in the preface to this edition that he did not change his point of view relative to the first edition of 1900. He improved the text in a few respects and added a few points that were to be elaborated in later publications. The major changes seem to be due to the impact of Anton Marty's criticisms of the text of the first edition in his *Untersuchungen zur Grundlegung der allgemeinen Grammatik und Sprachphilosophie*, Halle a.S., 1908.

---

  * Reprinted from *Philosophy and Phenomenological Research*, 17, 1956-1957 with permission. — J. N. M.
  [1] R. Carnap, *Logical Syntax of Language* (New York and London, 1937). This is an enlarged and revised translation of *Die Logische Syntax der Sprache* (Vienna, 1934).

I

I have no idea who was the first man to ponder about the fact that certain sequences of words in a given (natural) language make sense, whereas other sequences of these very same words do not make sense. This is not as silly as it sounds. As a matter of fact, it has been taken up again recently by very sophisticated people within the framework of a new science, the Theory of Communication, and has found there an interesting and rather surprising explanation which is, however, irrelevant for our purposes.[2] Husserl, at any rate, who ponders about this very fact (327), claims that, though a very considerable part of the restrictions on the significance of word sequences is due to accidental linguistic habits, there is another part which is rather due to the fact that within the realm of meanings there are *a priori* laws of connection and change, of which the grammatical incompatibilities, that exist in every developed language, are only the more or less articulated manifestations.

Now, this is certainly not a very novel doctrine. As a matter of fact, it is hardly more than common sense, if the technical jargon of its formulation is discounted. Aristotle would have doubtless said that the word sequence 'Grammar is winged' does not make sense, since being-winged is not a possible characteristic of a science. He did not say so in so many words, because the distinction between significant and non-significant word sequences was not made at this time, at least not in these terms. He did say, however, that 'winged' is not predicable of 'grammar,'[3] for the reason stated above. This grammatical incompatibility has its roots in the ontological circumstance that the differentiae of different genera that do not stand in the relation of subordination are *toto coelo* different.

I do not think that Aristotle ever considered the question how he came to know this ontological circumstance. Returning to Husserl and asking this question of him, we get the answer : through *apodictic evidence*. "The incompatibility of the connection is an essential (*wesensgesetzlich*) one, i.e., not merely subjective, and it is not due merely to a factual inability (by forces of our "mental organization") that we are unable to perform the unity (*die Einheit vollziehen*). In those cases which we have here before our eyes, the impossibility is rather objective, ideal, based in the "nature," in

---

[2] See, e.g., G. A. Miller, *Language and Communication* (New York, 1951), especially chapter 5.

[3] Aristotle deals with this topic in chapter 3 of *Categoriae*. For a critique of Aristotle's treatment, see my doctoral thesis *Theory of Syntactical Categories* (in Hebrew) (Jerusalem, 1947), pp. 4-5.

the pure essence of the realm of meanings, and may be grasped as such through apodictic evidence." (318) That's it. Those of us who are not much impressed by an appeal to "apodictic evidence" will be put on their guard by this appeal and will perhaps become even more suspicious than they were before towards the attempt of explaining grammatical incompatibilities through incompatibilities in the realm of meanings, or in the realm of (non-linguistic) entities, respectively. These two realms should by no means be confounded : there may be an incompatibility in the realm of entities when there is none in the realm of meanings. The expressions 'wooden iron' and 'round quadrilateral' are significant, their meanings exist, though there exist no corresponding entities, nor could they possibly exist. The sentence 'all quadrilaterals have 5 vertices' is an honest-to-God significant sentence, though it does not denote a possible state-of-affairs. (327) Husserl is certainly more sophisticated than Aristotle in the treatment of significance, but this is not sufficient to persuade us to accept his appeal to apodictic evidence as a good answer to a good question.

Let us now see in greater detail what Husserl did grasp with the help of his apodictic evidence. The word sequence "this careless is green' makes no unitary sense. Though each word by itself is significant, the combination of their meanings in the order indicated by the sequence is not — this much tells us our apodictic evidence. The non-significance of 'this careless is green' is of a different type from that of, say, 'this blum is a green' which lacks significance because one of its constituent words lacks significance. But — and now comes an insight of Husserl's which, though not spectacularly deep and revolutionary, may well have been expressed here for the first time, with a tolerable degree of clarity — having convinced himself of the non-significance of the sequence 'this careless is green,' one is immediately sure also that any other sequence *of the same form* is non-significant : non-significant are also 'this hot is green,' 'this green is hot,' etc. All these sequences have the same form since (a) the meanings of their constituent words, insofar as their meanings are *forms* (*Formen*), i.e., meanings of formative expressions like 'this,' 'is,' 'if,' 'and,' etc., are the same, and (b) the meanings of their constituent words, insofar as these meanings are matters (*Materien*), *belong to the same categories*. Since 'hot' and 'careless' belong to the same meaning category, the replacement of one of these words by the other within a given expression will leave this expression significant if it was so before and leave it non-significant if it was so before. Replacing a word within a given significant expression by a word belonging to a different meaning category will *always* turn this expression into a non-significant one. The significant 'this tree is green' turns non-significant, if 'tree' is replaced by 'careless,' by 'slowly,' by 'goes,' or by 'and.' (This need not be the case the other way round, of course. Replacing 'green' in 'this careless is green' by a word belonging to a different category will not always turn this non-significant expression into a significant one, as the reader will readily verify for himself.)

Let us not discuss here the question how to distinguish between words signifying forms and words signifying materials. This is a notoriously difficult question and still under discussion. Hence one should perhaps not take Husserl to task for his optimism in assuming this distinction to be clearer than it is. Let us only note in passing that 'this' is regarded by Husserl as a formative word. (319) [4] But we must certainly ask ourselves what Husserl's meaning categories are supposed to be. And here an unpleasant surprise is awaiting us : these categories turn out to be nothing else but the objective counterparts of the grammatical categories that were regarded as standard in Husserl's time (at least for Indo-European languages)! "Where a nominal matter stands, there may stand any arbitrary nominal matter, but not an adjectival or a relational or a whole propositional (*ganze propositionale*) matter." (319) It follows that in order to decide which words (or expressions) can significantly replace a given word in a given context we have just to determine its grammatical category — the whole detour through the realm of meanings is at the best completely superfluous and at the worst positively damaging by misleading the inquirer into a labyrinth from which he might not find his way out again.

There can be no doubt that Husserl's apodictic evidence is, in our context, nothing but a certain kind of grammatical intuition. If Husserl's intuition in this field were sound, we would still have gained with its help certain insights, in spite of their misleading formulation. Unfortunately, Husserl's insight was not sound and has been found lacking in at least two respects. I shall state these respects somewhat dogmatically here, as I already discussed this question at some length elsewhere.[5] First, it is simply not the case, at least not *prima facie* so, that an adjectival matter appearing in a significant text can never be replaced by a nominal matter, yielding again a significant text. It is beyond doubt that 'this tree is a plant' is significant and still is obtainable from 'this tree is green' by just such a replacement. Now I think that this objection can be met by a sufficient number of additional *ad hoc* grammatical rules, but Husserl does not discuss

---

[4] It is almost unbelievable in how many different ways the functioning of the particle 'this' and of the other demonstratives, has been misunderstood by philosophers. Bertrand Russel regarded 'this' at one time as the only logically proper name.

[5] In my thesis mentioned in note 3.

such rules. Nor is it clear that the overall system resulting from these additions will be a sufficiently simple one. Second, it can at least be doubted whether most speakers of English would regard 'this algebraic number is green' as a significant sentence at all. It seems hardly to be even a matter that could be settled simply by statistical investigations. The terms 'sentence,' 'significant,' 'silly,' and 'ridiculous' are not sufficiently univocal to attach much significance to the results of a questionnaire in which the testees will have to tell whether according to their intuition the word-sequence 'this algebraic number is green' is a sentence and, if so, whether it is non-significant or significant but silly or ridiculous. Husserl's assertion that "through the free replacement of matters within their category there may result false, silly, or ridiculous meanings (whole sentences or possible sentence-parts), but still necessarily unitary meanings...," as a factual statement, is therefore of doubtful validity. However, if understood as a proposal for the syntactical categorization of the expressions of German (and Husserl's examples are always taken from that language), i.e., for the erection of a language-system, closely connected with ordinary German, it has to be judged by its intrinsic merits. And here it should be stressed that, in spite of all the shortcomings in the details, Husserl has got hold of a basic insight into the techniques of language investigation. He may well have been the first to see clearly the fundamental role played in linguistic analysis by what modern linguists call *commutation*.

In summing up the first part of our critique, we may say that Husserl was one of the initiators of the technique of commutation in logico-linguistic analysis but failed in two respects : first, he did not realize that the traditional parts of speech were not useful syntactical categories beyond a first crude approximation; second, by leaving unnecessarily the linguistic level, he misled himself and others into believing that something can be achieved by exploring the realm of meanings with the help of an apodictic evidence. No support for this belief is supplied by Husserl, and the few positive theses he formulates in this field are hopelessly wrong.

II

Just as Husserl's treatment of meaning categories is an important though not always adequate anticipation of the modern theories of syntactic (or semantic) categories, so there is to be found in his distinction between *nonsense* (*Unsinn*) and *countersense* (*Widersinn*) an interesting anticipation of the modern conceptions of *rules of formation* and *rules of transformation*.

To be more exact, there seems to exist a far-reaching parallelism between Carnap's conception of these two major kinds of semantic [6] rules of a language-system — a conception now almost universally accepted — and Husserl's conception of the major kinds of laws of meaning : *the laws of avoiding nonsense* (*Gesetze des zu vermeidenden Unsinns*) and *the laws of avoiding formal countersense* (*Gesetze des zu vermeidenden formalen Widersinns*). (334-335)

Nowadays, the L-emptiness of the predicate 'is-a-round-quadrangle,' i.e., the fact that, for logical reasons, there can be no entity that is a round quadrangle, will be confused only by few philosophers with the non-significance of the word-sequence 'is-a-round-or,' [7] i.e., with the fact that this word-sequence is not well-formed. In other words : hardly anyone will now treat on a par the L-falsity of the sentence 'G is a round quadrangle,' i.e., the fact that, according to the rules of transformation of (a certain formalized counterpart of) English, this sentence cannot be true, with the non-sententiality of the word-sequence 'G is a round or,' i.e., with the fact that, according to the rules of formation of (this formalized counterpart of) English, this word-sequence does not form a sentence. It was otherwise fifty-five years ago. At that time, the distinction between these two types of meaninglessness (*Sinnlosen*) seems not to have been the philosophical commonplace it is today, and Husserl goes to great lengths in stressing its importance. It is not implausible that the present conception of this distinction is to a large measure due to Husserl's efforts though perhaps mainly through indirect channels.

However, Husserl does not formulate his distinction in the clear-cut way it is done by Carnap, for instance, nor should we expect this thirty-five years before Carnap's relevant publication. Again he makes the fatal transition from the straightforward formulation in terms of the well-formedness of certain sequences of signs to the formulation in terms of compatibility, complication, and modification of meanings. If we are ready to forget Husserl's detour through the realm of meanings and "translate" his insights into the purely syntactical idiom, we shall not hesitate to accept

---

[6] In *Logical Syntax*, only syntactical language-systems (non-interpreted calculi) were treated, and these rules therefore were regarded as syntactic. Later, however, as is well-known, Carnap began to study also semantical (interpreted) language-systems. For such systems, he now prefers the terms 'rules of truth' or 'rules of ranges' to 'rules of transformation.' See *Introduction to Semantics* (Harvard University Press, 1946).

[7] The full stop belongs essentially to the word sequence : Without it, our remark would be in need of many qualifications in order to remain valid. If well-formedness were simply understood as being part of a sentence, then 'is a round or' would be well-formed, since 'This is a round or elliptical table.' is certainly a sentence.

his evaluation that the rules of avoiding nonsense are logically prior to the
rules of avoiding countersense, that the statement of the rules of formation
of a certain language-system has to precede the statement of its rules of
transformation. This should not have been a very deep insight since it is
only trivial that the definition of the consequence relation between sentences
— the major point of the transformation rules — should be based upon
the definition of sentence itself — the major point of the formation rules.

I think that Husserl was right in his claim that the basic role played
by the rules of formation in the construction (or description) of any language had not been clearly realized by other logicians and that the classical
theory of terms and judgments that used to be presented in preparation for
the treatment of inference was entirely inadequate. (329, 331, 342) And I
think that he was right when he stressed the legitimacy of the idea of a *universal grammar*, as conceived by the rationalists of the 17th and 18th centuries.
(336) But not before Carnap's investigations into General (Logical) Syntax
has this idea been realized to any appreciable degree of adequacy, and
certainly not by Husserl himself. Though Husserl stresses the distinction
between the "prescientific private conceptions of the grammarians about
the meaning forms" and "the empirically distorted ideas that historical
grammar, say of Latin, presents him," on the one hand, and "the pure
system of forms that is scientifically determinate and theoretically coherent,"
i.e., Husserl's own theory of meaning forms (339), on the other hand, no
real indication whatsoever is given where and how to draw this distinction.
Husserl regards it as an *a priori* property of all languages to have forms for
the plural, for instance, thereby justifying the significance of the question,
how "the" plural is expressed in German, Latin, or Chinese. But it seems
that he would regard it as illicit to ask a similar question with respect to,
say, the ablative. I do not deny that there seems to exist some distinction
between these two features, that we somehow have the feeling that all
languages should contain some simple means of expressing "the" plural
but do not feel the same with respect to "the" ablative. Modern psychologically trained linguists are, I think, in a position to explain this difference
of attitude on behalf of the linguistically innocent speakers of Indo-European
languages. But this does not justify by any means Husserl's distinction.

There is only one way of arriving at the common ideal grammatical
framework of all empirical languages, namely by departing from the very
definition of language. Nothing belongs to that framework that does not
follow from this definition. The justification for an *a priori* statement that
all languages contain, say, words and sentences can only be that this must
be so by definition. But whether all languages contain nouns, or negation-

signs, or modal expressions, after a general definition of noun etc. has been given if this definition forms no part of the definition of language, can only be established by empirical investigation. Pure Syntax, in Carnap's sense, is a formal science whose statements, if true, are analytically so. Though Carnap defines in a general way [8] when a symbol of any given language is, say, a negation-symbol, it is, of course, quite possible that a certain language should contain no negation-symbol. (As a matter of fact, certain language-systems, well-known to formal logicians, contain no such symbol.) But it is still a theorem of General Syntax that if a language contains, say, a (proper) negation-expression and a (proper) disjunction-expression, then it contains also a (proper) conjunction-*expression*, though it is of course quite possible for a language to contain a negation-symbol and a disjunction-symbol without containing a conjunction-symbol. Just as it is a theorem of General Syntax that for each language containing proper negation, disjunction, and conjunction, the principles of traditional logic such as those of excluded middle and of contradiction are valid. [9]

The *a priori* fundaments of language which linguistics has to become conscious of, according to Husserl's challenge (338), are nothing but analytic consequences of the definition (or conception) of language. Husserl was right when he defended the non-psychological character of his purely logical syntax — as well as of logic proper — against Marty's psychologistic arguments (341), and many variants of such a syntax such as combinatorial, arithmetized, and structural syntax, have proved their value. However, the last word about the exact relationship between logical syntax and the empirical sciences such as psychology and sociology, has not been said yet.

There seems to be one point in which Husserl was not radical enough. He concedes (341) that the "upper" part of logic which — in Carnap's terms — is based upon the rules of transformation is irrelevant for (descriptive) grammar. He is satisfied with having shown that the "lower" part of logic — the rules of formation — is theoretically relevant for grammar though of little practical value. We have tried to show elsewhere, [10] in elaboration of the basic insights of Carnap, that rules of transformation are no less relevant for linguistics than rules of formation, thereby counterbalancing Husserl's stress on the relevance of the formation rules for logic. Therefore, I shall say no more here on this topic.

---

[8] *Logical Syntax*, p. 202.
[9] *Logical Syntax*, p. 203.
[10] "Logical Syntax and Semantics," *Language* (1954), pp. 30, 230-237.

In conclusion, we may say that Husserl's conception of a purely logical grammar has to be regarded, in a very essential and pregnant sense, as a forerunner of Carnap's conception of a general logical syntax. One has "only" to omit the detour through the realm of meanings and the reliance upon an apodictic evidence and to add a mastery in modern symbolic logic and its philosophy in order to perform the transition from Husserl to Carnap. These three steps seem to me essential improvements, but I shall not try here to justify this opinion.

HUSSERL'S CONCEPTION OF
"THE GRAMMATICAL"
AND CONTEMPORARY LINGUISTICS *

by

JAMES M. EDIE

(Evanston, Illinois)

Since the Middle Ages philosophers have periodically made proposals for a universal *a priori* grammar, frequently suggesting that such a grammar be considered as a branch or an application of formal logic. These researches have never progressed very far, not even during the period when grammarians were themselves primarily logicians. In the modern period, since scientific linguistics has vindicated its own independence of logic and philosophy, philosophical proposals of this kind have fallen into "scientific" disrepute. Thus, Edmund Husserl's project for a "pure logical grammar" — which is probably the most recent full-scale proposal in this area from the side of philosophy — has fallen upon deaf ears. But now, within the past decade, Noam Chomsky has begun to propose, from the side of linguistics itself, a program for the study of grammar which, if it were to succeed, might seem to justify the earlier intuitions of rationalistic philosophy and to give a new grounding to its ancient quest. Might it not be, after all, that what was needed was a more sophisticated development of grammatical studies themselves before such a proposal could be sufficiently clarified to be prosecuted with any confidence?

However that may be, we are concerned here, first of all, with Husserl, who not only neglects scientific linguistics but even the philosophical tradition. It is true that he mentions Von Humboldt [1] and Scotus (Thomas of Erfurt) [2] and refers in a general way to the seventeenth-century French grammarians, but he attempts to restate the problem completely independently of tradition, starting once again from the beginning, *de novo*. He is

---

* Reprinted from Lester E. Embree (ed.), *Life-World and Consciousness*, Evanston : Northwestern University Press, 1972, with permission. — J. N. M.

[1] Edmund Husserl, *Logische Untersuchungen* (Tübingen, 1968), II, i, 342. (Cited hereafter as "LU". All references are to Volume II.)

[2] Edmund Husserl, *Formal and Transcendental Logic*, trans. Dorion Cairns (The Hague, 1969), p. 49. (Cited herafter as "FTL.")

interested in establishing the basis for an eidetics of language within his
general phenomenological reflection on our experience of speaking a
language.[3] Such an approach will not provide a complete or a totalitarian
account of language; in fact it will be limited to an examination of certain
a priori characteristics of languages which might, at first glance, seem
to be no more than the enumeration of a series of trivialities [4] which

---

[3] The word "pure" in Husserl's terminology seems to be a synonym for "formal."
In the first edition of *Logische Untersuchungen* he spoke simply of "pure grammar";
but since he later recognizes that there are other aprioris than the logical ones he is concerned with, which govern the study of grammar, in the second edition he speaks of
"pure logical grammar" (LU, p. 340).

[4] One of the few studies of Husserl's notion of a pure logical grammar which has
been published up to now suffers, it seems to me, from some serious confusions and an
inordinate amount of Carnapian bluster. Yehoshua Bar-Hillel ("Husserl's Conception of
a Purely Logical Grammar," *Philosophy and Phenomenological Research*, XVII (1957),
362-369) states a number of points "somewhat dogmatically" (p. 365) because they had
previously been argued in his doctoral dissertation on the *Theory of Syntactical Categories*
(Jerusalem, 1947), in Hebrew. I am not competent to read Hebrew and thus do not know
if Bar-Hillel there took account of Husserl's more developed conception of pure logical
grammar as it is found in *Formal and Transcendental Logic*; but in this article he seems to
be mesmerized by Husserl's somewhat naive vocabulary (his talk of "parts of speech"
etc., as if these were properly refined grammatical categories) and by the material examples
given in the Fourth Investigation. He also believes, like others, that Husserl was misled
in taking the surface structures of Indo-European languages as ultimate grammatical
categories; and, of course, his mind boggles at notions like "apodictic evidence," though
he does not mention this last. We cannot discuss this confused article in detail and must
limit ourselves to making a few corrective remarks. We concede that Husserl's vocabulary
is linguistically unsophisticated at some points in the Fourth Investigation. As Suzanne
Bachelard has pointed out (*A Study of Husserl's "Formal and Transcendental Logic*,"
trans. Lester E. Embree (Evanston, 1968), pp. 6-7), Husserl's choice of examples in the
Fourth Investigation can easily mislead the unwary because they are of material (or synthetic) countersense and have not been properly formalized; it is only in *Formal and
Transcendental Logic* that he more completely formalized his expressions. This is because
the "investigations" were introductory and directed to his contemporaries; they were
meant to "stimulate thinking" and were not meant to be definitive; by using examples
which were easier to understand, we are told, Husserl hoped to initiate his readers to
certain distinctions, and he feared to impose on his readers a completely abstract form
of exposition, a fear nowhere present in *Formal and Transcendental Logic*. Bar-Hillel
is thus able to argue that, since the form S is p can be rendered materially not only by
"This tree is green" but also by "This tree is a plant," Husserl's "intuition" that only
"adjectives" could take the place of p in the *Urform* is shown to be unsound. But Husserl's
point properly concerns predicates (whatever their "nonsyntactical form" may be) and
not just the "adjective" as a "part of speech" in ordinary German grammar. Even in
ordinary school grammar we do distinguish between predicate nouns and predicate
adjectives; but the important point is that only *predicates*, syntactically formed as such,
can be predicated of a substantive, and this is a question not of the surface grammar
of Indo-European languages but of categories of signification or meaning. Since Bar-
Hillel apparently thinks the move from grammatical categories to meaning-categories
is illegitimate, he can, on that basis, effortlessly make nonsense of most of what Husserl
says; but this seems to me to miss the real point Husserl is making. Another critical victory

— in their abstract generality — may seem to emasculate the phenomenon of language by reducing its enormous and known complexities and rich resources for expression to some unreal and emaciated "essence." [5]

But if it should be the case that natural languages obey certain *a priori* laws and manifest an "ideal framework" which is "absolutely stable," in spite of the empirical and accidental differences proper to each particular language, then the neglect of this aspect of linguistic reality would render the linguist ultimately unable to account rationally for his science. And Husserl firmly believes this to be the case :

Language has not only physiological, psychological and cultural-historical, but also *a priori* foundations. These last concern the essential meaning-forms and the

---

is claimed by showing that "the full stop belongs essentially to the word sequence" (Bar-Hillel, p. 366) because such a sequence as "is a round or" is perfectly well formed if it is taken as a part of a sentence like "This is a round or elliptical table." But this is merely to throw sand into the eyes of the reader, at least of the reader who takes Bar-Hillel's account of Husserl's theory, even as it appears in the Fourth Investigation, as a faithful account. The "full stop" does not belong essentially to just any word sequence but only to sentences; and "is a round or" may be a "piece" of the sentence given for it, but it is not a "member" of such (or any other) sentence. Husserl has clearly met Bar-Hillel's "full stop" requirement for sentences because a sentence is an independent unit of meaning. The word sequence "is a round or" is *unsinnig* precisely because it is not a unit of meaning and is not a well-formed expression; it is not an independent unit of meaning, and it is not even a dependent "member" of the complete sentence which Bar-Hillel constructs for it. It is neither a dependent nor an independent unit of meaning, though in a unified sentence, such as "This is a round or elliptical table," elements in this string help constitute the dependent syntactical categories that function properly within the sentence. I believe that Bar-Hillel's hypercritical and unsympathetic reading of Husserl comes from his Carnapian enthusiasm exclusively. In an earlier article ("Logical Syntax and Semantics," *Language*, XXXI (1954), 230-237), Bar-Hillel credits Carnap with both distinguishing and then fusing together grammar and logic, "with grammar treating approximately the formational part of syntax and logic its transformational part." "The relation of *commutability* may be sufficient," he writes, "for formational analysis, but other relations, such as that of formal *consequence*, must be added for transformational analysis" (pp. 236-237). But this is surely part of the point Husserl was making in the Fourth Investigation, and Bar-Hillel grudgingly admits this in his 1957 article (pp. 366ff.). These two articles by Bar-Hillel should, in my opinion, not be read except in conjunction with the reply to the 1954 article by Noam Chomsky ("Logical Syntax and Semantics, Their Linguistic Relevance," *Language*, XXX (1955), 36-45) and Bar-Hillel's own uncharacteristically temperate remarks in "Remarks on Carnap's Logical Syntax of Language" in The Philosophy of Rudolf Carnap, ed. P. A. Schilpp (La Salle, Ill., 1963), pp. 519-543. For a different kind of "rejoinder" to Bar-Hillel's attack on Husserl see J. N. Mohanty, *Edmund Husserl's theory of Meaning* (The Hague, 1964), pp. 104-115.

[5] As Bar-Hillel has shown with filial devotion, Husserl's work can be read as a flawed precursor of Carnap's, but we should keep in mind the essential difference that, from the beginning to the end, Husserl was concerned, not with artificially constructed "ideal" languages or the use of algorithms to define some independent mathematical system which could, in some extended sense, be called "language," but with *natural language itself*.

a priori laws of their combinations and modifications, and no language is thinkable which would not be essentially determined by this a priori. Every linguist, whether or not he is clearly aware of the fact, operates with concepts coming from this domain.[6]

The very fact that one can meaningfully ask such questions as : How do German, Latin, Chinese, etc., express "the "plural, "the" categorical proposition, "the" hypothetical premise, "the" modes of possibility and probability, "the" negative, etc., shows the conceptual validity of such an inquiry into the aprioris of grammar.[7] Against his contemporaries, among whom the sense of the *a priori* had "threatened, almost, to atrophy," Husserl asks philosophers to "learn by heart" that, wherever philosophical interests are involved, "it is of the greatest importance sharply to separate the *a priori*." [8] We must not ignore "the great intuition of Kant." It does not become philosophers, who are almost the sole guardians of "pure theory" among us, to let themselves be guided merely by questions of practical and empirical utility and, in the case of grammar, to allow this study to be simply parceled out among a number of ill-defined empirical sciences, since it is also governed by a framework of unified *a priori* laws which define its true "scientific" boundaries.

Husserl's study of grammar locates this discipline as the first or lowest level of formal logic and states that a phenomenological approach to logic must "be guided" by language. He means by this, not that the empirical, psychological, physiological, historical, and cultural bases of language be incorporated into philosophy nor that logic is dependent on any given natural language, but rather that the study of "the grammatical" (not a given, empirical "grammar") is the *first level* of logical reflection. The two primordial types of intentional experience, according to Husserl, are (1) the experience of the world and (2) the experience of language. The theoretical elaboration of the first is logically posterior to the theoretical investigation of the second, namely, language.[9]

To consider language in itself is to operate an implicit phenomenological reduction, i.e., to turn from the *Lebenswelt* of factual experience in which meanings are instantiated in factual situations to the separated meanings themselves, as they are experienced in their ideality, independently of any

---

[6] *LU*, p. 338.

[7] *LU*, p. 339.

[8] *LU*, p. 337. Cf. Bachelard, *A Study of Husserl's "Formal and Transcendental Logic,"* pp. 10-11.

[9] See André de Muralt, *L'Idée de la phénoménologie* (Paris, 1958), pp. 115ff., and Bachelard, *A Study*, pp. 18ff., 33ff.

possible factual reference.[10] The experience of language is the experience of meaning par excellence; it is our route of access to the realm of "the meant," of "sense" and "signification." If one distinguishes the realm of significations (what Husserl calls "categories of signification" as opposed to the "categories of the object") from the realm of objects signified *through* language, one isolates within formal logic the territory of "apophantic analytics" or the purely formal study of the structures of judgment.[11]

Now, the *first level* of the implicit phenomenological reduction (if we can call it that) which is operated by the "linguistic turn" away from the world toward language itself is that of the discovery and analysis of *the grammatical*. Husserl calls this the study of the "pure morphology of significations" (*reine Formenlehre der Bedeutungen*) or "pure *a priori* (logical) grammar." Such a study is strictly *a priori* and purely logical, a study of "the grammatical" as opposed to the empirical and historical investigation of comparative grammars; it constitutes the first level of "apophantic analytics," to be followed by the second (the logic of noncontradiction) and the third (the logic of truth) levels of the formal analysis of signification.

No philosopher can escape the *a priori* rules which prescribe the conditions under which a linguistic utterance can have unified, intelligible sense. The study of grammar, in this sense, is necessarily philosophical. Pure logical grammar (or apophantic morphology) is, according to Husserl, that first branch of formal logic which establishes the formal grammatical rules necessary for any statement to be meaningful at all; it is prior to and independent of all questions of the formal validity and the truth value of statements. Every judgment must, for instance, respect the *a priori* grammatical rule that in a well-formed sentence a substantive must take the place of S (in the "primitive form" S is p) and a predicate must be substituted for p. If this rule is violated, nonsense (*Unsinn*) results. We get strings of words like "King but where seems and," This frivolous is green," "Red is world," "A man is and," etc., which are devoid of any unified meaning; the words individually may have meaning, but, when they are arranged ungrammatically, they have none. It is the purpose of pure logical grammar to derive from the originary form of judgment (S is p) the laws which govern the formation of potentially meaningful affirmative, negative, universal, particular, hypothetical, causal, conjunctive, disjunctive, etc., forms. It is in this sense that *das Grammatische selbst* founds the second and third levels of formal logic and establishes rules which are always already taken

---

[10] De Muralt, *L'Idée de la phénoménologie*, pp. 124-125.

[11] *LU, Prolegomena*, Chapter Eleven, the Fourth Investigation; and Bachelard, *A Study*, p. 3.

for granted in the logic of noncontradiction and truth. These purely formal grammatical laws are wholly independent of the truth or falsity of the statements which they rule and guarantee only that the statements formed in accord with them will be free of *Unsinn* (nonsense). They have no relevance to the material contradiction (*Widersinn*) involved in such well-formed sentences as "Squares are round" or "This algebraic number is green," etc. The laws of logical grammar save us from *formal nonsense* only; it is the other levels of logic which save us from contradiction and countersense.

However, thus to vindicate the value of pure grammatical aprioris is not to assert that logic is based on ordinary language or empirical linguistics. Husserl insists on this : logic is grounded not on grammar but on "the grammatical" :

It is ... not without reason that people often say that formal logic has let itself be guided by grammar. In the case of the theory of forms, however, this is not a reproach but a necessity — provided that, for guided by grammar (a word intended to bring to mind *de facto* historical languages and their grammatical description), guidance by the grammatical itself be substituted.[12]

This is grammar raised to the level of the analysis of the formal conditions of thought. It is here that Husserl joins the seventeenth-century proponents of a *grammaire générale et raisonnée* in conscious opposition to the accepted views of his historicist and psychologistic contemporaries. The task of logical grammar is to study and furnish the *a priori* rules which govern the structural coherence of "parts of speech" with one another in sentences. Such grammatical rules are not just historical accidents or conventions but necessary conditions of meaningfulness and for the avoidance of nonsense; they are not, without the higher levels of formal logic built upon them, sufficient conditions for the avoidance of contradiction and error :

Nothing else has so greatly confused discussion of the question of the correct relationship between logic and grammar as the continual confounding of the two logical spheres that we have distinguished sharply as the lower and the upper and have characterized by means of their negative counterparts : the sphere of nonsense and the sphere of countersense.[13]

Husserl, thus, vindicates the place of grammar (*rein-logische Grammatik*), as a theory in its own right, within his phenomenological hierarchy of

---

[12] *FTL*, p. 70.

[13] *LU*, p. 341. There is also an important discussion of this distinction in Aron Gurwitsch, *The Field of Consciousness* (Pittsburgh, 1964), pp. 331ff., on "Philosophical Problems of Logic."

"sciences." But it is, so to speak, the emptiest and the most formal of all. Its rules provide the barest minimal conditions necessary to avoid nonsense in forming linguistic statements. They exclude only the purest nonsense, which it would never occur to anyone to utter. Pure grammar establishes rules which are always subunderstood and already taken for granted in all the formal systems which study and establish the sufficient conditions for meaningful expressions. But the fact that the uncovering of these conditions has no "practical" value and even seems to make a science of what is trivially obvious is no reason to despise it. Its theoretical value for philosophy, Husserl tells us, is "all the greater." Husserl takes pride in this discovery; he even glories in the fact that only philosophers are concerned with the *a priori*, with the discovery of truths so fundamental that all the other sciences taken them for granted. It is, he believes, precisely such "obvious" trivialities as those expressed by the rules of pure grammar that mask the deepest philosophical problems, and he sees that, in a profound, if paradoxical, sense, philosophy is the science of trivialities.[14] The clear distinction which he was able to establish between pure grammar and the "higher" levels of formal analytics seemed to him to be a theoretical discovery of the first magnitude and a necessary point of departure for the elaboration of a phenomenological theory of consciousness.

PURE LOGICAL GRAMMAR

We can best give a general outline of what Husserl means by pure logical grammar by taking his earliest discussion of this problem in the Fourth of the *Logical Investigations* together with his more developed discussions of the *Formal and Transcendental Logic*. These discussions, in turn, are but one application of the "logic of wholes and parts" of the Third Investigation. A grammatical unit is, indeed, one of the best illustrations of Husserl's doctrine of wholes and parts.

If we enquire into the reasons why certain combinations are permitted and certain others prohibited in our language, we shall be, in a very great measure, referred to accidental linguistic habits and, in general, to facts of linguistic development that are different with different linguistic communities. But, in another part, we meet with the essential distinction between independent and dependent meanings, as also with the *a priori* laws — essentially connected with that distinction — of combinations of meanings and of meaning modifications : laws that must more or less clearly exhibit themselves in the theory of grammatical forms and in a

---

[14] *LU*, p. 342.

corresponding class of grammatical incompatibilities in every developed language.[15]

A linguistic expression, whether dependent (like a word which functions as a syntactical category within a sentence) or independent (a sentence or proposition), is a string of sounds whose unity is founded in its "meaning." Any string of sounds devoid of a unified sense (or meaning) is just that : a string of noises. What makes a string of sounds a linguistic expression is its unified meaning. A "nominal" (substantival) or an "adjectival" (predicate) expression is an example of dependent meanings; only a fully propositional meaning, which joins such dependent parts into a unified whole, is independent. The first task of logical grammar is to establish the "pure categories of meaning" as they can be related in this dependent-independent relationship.[16] (It is not necessary here to follow Husserl into his detailed discussions of simple and compound meanings in relationship to simple and compound expressions and the relations of these to simple and compound objects or "referents," though this would be necessary in any complete account of his thought.)

What is important is that any linguistic expression is a "whole" composed of "parts" which are *members* (or "moments") of the constituted whole rather than merely *pieces* (discrete elements) only incidentally and *de facto* attached to one another; a *member* of a whole obeys laws which are distinctive of the role it plays within this unified system and which are not the same as it would exercise were it, *per impossibile*, detached from the whole of which it is an integral part. The members of a whole interpenetrate and codetermine one another and, as such, are inseparable from one another and from the whole of which they are parts. Mere "pieces," on the contrary, would be just what they are even if separated from the whole of which they are, by analysis, found to be parts. An example of parts which codetermine one another as members of a whole would be the "extension," "surface," "color," and "brightness" of a physical, perceptual object. One is not present without the other; there cannot be brightness without color, or color without surface, or surface without extension. As did Plato before him,[17] Husserl considers color and surface to be related according to an *a priori* law (which is "synthetic" or "material" rather than "analytical" since the idea of color is not analytically contained in the idea of surface or extension) given in perception.[18] Such an *a priori* law is not the result of my

[15] *LU*, pp. 327-328.
[16] *LU*, p. 330.
[17] *Meno* 75B.
[18] *LU*, pp. 252-253.

personal or cultural conditioning; it is not an empirical psychological fact
about my experience, nor is it based on some statistical probability. It is
a law founded in the very *meaning* of color and extension; what I mean by
color and what I mean by extension require that every instance of one be
an instance of the other; and, once I understand this, every experience which
illustrates the one will illustrate the other, an I can know this without any
appeal to future experience. That brightness entails color, color entails
surface, surface entails extension is an *a priori* law of the constitution of
perceptual objects, and no act of perception will or can contradict such a
law because it is part of what is *meant* by a physical perceptual object.
Another way of stating this is to say that a physical perceptual object is
a "whole" which consists of parts which are integrated into the whole as
constituent members of this unified object.[19]

We can apply this notion to grammar immediately by noting that an
independent meaning, namely, a proposition, is a formal structural whole
which consists of at least a minimal number of constituent parts which are
related to one another by *a priori* laws which govern their meaning-functions
within the one unified whole which is a complete, meaningful sentence.
In other words, what one means by a complete, unified, independent linguistic expression (S is p) is that its parts be related to one another by
a priori laws of composition which we call "syntax." [20] Dependent terms
also have a unified kernel of meaning, but this meaning requires that it be
completed according to certain rules if it is to function within the meaningful
complex which is a whole sentence. In short, a sentence will be grammatically
well-formed, and hence potentially meaningful, if and only if certain
a priori rules for the correct integration of partial meanings into a whole
meaning are observed. These rules are the laws of pure logical grammar;
they are laws which govern the potential meaningfulness of sentences
and are independent of and prior to the laws which govern internal consistency and possible truth. Meaningfulness is a prior condition for non-
contradiction. The string "King but or blue" is meaningless (*unsinnig*),

---

[19] See the excellent article by Robert Sokolowski, "The Logic of Parts and Wholes
in Husserl's *Investigations*," *Philosophy and Phenomenological Research*, XXVIII (1968),
537-553, esp. pp. 538ff. and 542ff., 548ff. [included in this volume. — J. N. M.] Note also
that I must neglect many fundamental aspects and applications of Husserl's general theory
in this brief reference to it. Sokolowski gives a good outline of the various other applications of this general theory in Husserl's later phenomenology. See also Gurwitsch, *The
Field of Consciousness*, pp. 194-197.

[20] "The proposition as a whole has forms appertaining to wholeness; and, by their
means, it has a unitary relation to the meant as a whole, to what is categorially formed
thus and so....; each member is *formed as entering into the whole*" (*FTL*, pp. 298-299).

whereas the string "There are some squares which are round" is inconsistent or contradictory (*widersinnig*); the former, but not the latter, violates *a priori* and purely formal "grammatical" rules. The rules of grammar are sufficient only to guarantee grammatical coherence; they are not sufficient, though they are necessary, to guarantee logical consistency in the full sense. Pure logical grammar classifies meaning-forms and is concerned with "the *mere possibility of judgments as judgments,* without inquiry whether they are true or false, or contradictory." [21] Truth and falsity according to Husserl, pertain not to propositions as such but to the laws of the *assertion* of propositions and thus belong to a higher level of logic.

The second step in the elaboration of a pure logical grammar (after establishing the "pure" or formal categories of meaning such as S, p, S is p, etc.) concerns the laws of the *composition* of partial meanings into well-formed wholes or sentences.[22] At the limit, no word can be taken and defined without relation to its possible grammatical functions within a complete, unified meaning-whole; the grammatical distinctions ("parts of speech," etc.) given in dictionaries bear testimony to this fact. Wherever there is found some grammatical distinction (or "marker") attached to a word, this is the mark of a certain incompleteness of meaning: and thus grammatical distinctions are guides to essential meaning-distinctions within sentences.[23] Sentences, unlike words, have no such "markers."

We begin with the analysis of the pure syntactical categories. When words are combined to form sentences, they are necessarily given a syntactical "form" which permits their integration as partial or dependent meanings into a complete or independent expression. This requires that there be a restricted number of primitive connecting forms, such as the predicative, attributive, conjunctive, disjunctive, hypothetical, etc., and that there be pure syntactical forms, such as the substantive, the predicative, the propositional, etc. This is the basis for the fundamental distinction between *syntactical forms* and *syntactical stuffs* and for the recognition that the propositional form presupposes the subject form and the predicate form. Whether I take a given word as the "subject" of a sentence ("This paper is white") or as the "object" ("I am writing on this paper"), the word — as a "term" — bears the core of meaning (and reference) which remains identical though its syntactical form varies in each case. The

[21] *FTL*, p. 50.
[22] *LU*, p. 336. Husserl here gives his own list of the tasks of pure logical grammar.
[23] Husserl does not use the current term "marker" (*LU*, p. 317). See Marvin Farber, *The Foundation of Phenomenology* (New York, 1962), p. 317.
[24] *FTL*, p. 305.

specific meaning and referentiality of the proposition (to a "state of affairs") is mediated through the meaning and referentiality of its constituent terms. That is to say that the proposition is a higher categorial unity "founded" on the meaning of its constituents through its giving them the syntactical form necessary to produce a unified and complete sense. Now, it can be readily seen that the number of syntactical stuffs can be infinite while the number of syntactical forms is limited and capable of complete formal definition.

Husserl calls a given unity of syntactical stuff and form the *syntagma*. All the members (i.e., constituent parts) of a proposition are *syntagmas* (and we can here neglect the analysis of the infrasyntagmatic elements or "pieces" of words and sentences which belongs to phonology), and the proposition as a whole is also a *syntagma* of a higher order (i.e., "self-sufficient predicational whole..., a unity of syntactical stuff in a syntactical form").[24] Different members of a proposition can have the same form and different stuffs and, conversely, can have different forms but the same stuff; and these forms can be fitted into hierarchies in which what is syntactically formed on one level becomes the "stuff" of a higher form, e.g., when the proposition itself (S is p) is formed, and when it is modified modally (Is S p?, S may be p, If S is p, Then S is p, S must be p, etc.), these more complex modal forms are constructed on the basis of the Urform (S is p), which is itself composed of the infrapropositional syntagmas S (substantive), is (copular unity-form), and p (predicate).[25]

We must note, of course, that, when a word actually occurs in a sentence, it has already been modified according to its proper syntactical form (and this form retrospectively dictates the manner in which it is defined in dictionaries under its proper "parts of speech"), since a "pure nonsyntactical stuff" is only a limit concept which can nowhere be found in actual, meaningful language (all of which is already always syntactically formed) :

The forming, of course, is not an activity that was, or could have been, executed on stuffs given in advance : That would presuppose the countersense, that one could have stuffs beforehand — as though they were concrete objects, instead of being abstract moments in significations.[26]

All the members of a proposition are "non-self-sufficient" under all circumstances; they are only what they are in the whole. I can reach the "pure stuff" of an expression only by an ideal analysis. For instance, if I

---

[25] The "copular unity-form" is a specification of more general "conjunctive" forms (*FTL*, pp. 300, 308).

[26] *FTL*, p. 298.

examine the "syntactical stuffs" given in the sentence "This tree is green," I am left with such words as "tree" and "green," etc. These can be considered as "unformed stuffs," but they are not completely unformed and thus should be called "nonsyntactical forms." For instance if I freely vary in imagination words like "green," "greenness," or "similar," "similarity," etc., as they can appear in different syntactical forms, I reach a kernel of nonsyntactical meaning (*Kernform*) which remains essentially the same in its various syntactical formations; such a meaning-form "animates" a pure *Kernstoff*, which is essentially prelinguistic — the very stuff of prepredicative experience itself. Nonsyntactical stuff (*Kernstoff*) and nonsyntactical form (*Kernform*) constitute the *syntactical stuff* which is "formed" by the pure laws of syntax (*Kerngebilde*). Nonsyntactical matter and form are only abstractions from experience; they are nonindependent constituent parts of the lowest meaningful unit, namely, the "syntactical matter" of a sentence, or what we might call the "word." [27]

Now it is clear that "syntactical form" is something much more general and "formal" than syntactical stuff. If we vary different material terms like "paper," "man," "humanity," "sincerity," etc., we find that, in spite of their differences in meaning and referentiality, they possess in common an identical "form," namely, that of "the substantive." The same is true of "the adjectival" (which Husserl divides into "attributes" and "properties") [28] and the other basic syntactical forms.

The third and final task of pure logical grammar is, then, the construction of a closed system of basic syntactical forms and a "minimum number of independent elementary laws" for their combinations. Husserl here introduces the notion of grammatical "operation" according to which sentences can be generated. There are two interrelated tasks here which can be distinguished.

1. The fundamental forms of judgments establish laws according to which subordinate forms can be generated by derivation from the most fundamental (and, in this case, most general and abstract) forms. This is possible because the most general forms dominate the whole of pure logical grammar : the formation of a given sentence is an "operation" according to an abstract and formal rule which carries with it the law of its possible reiteration :

This moreover, should be emphasized expressly : *Every operative fashioning of one form out of others has its law*; and this law, in the case of operations proper, is of

---

[27] *FTL*, pp. 308-309.
[28] *FTL*, p. 303.

such a nature that the generated form can itself be submitted to a repetition of the same operation. *Every law of operation thus bears within itself a law of reiteration.* Conformity to this law of *reiterable operation* extends throughout the whole province of judgments, and makes it possible to construct reiteratively (by means of fundamental forms and fundamental operations, which can be laid down) the infinity of possible forms of judgments.[29]

Thus the form S is p is more original than the form Sp is q, which is an operational transformation of it by the "operation" of converting a predicate into an attribute. These are operations which Husserls calls "nominalization" [30] by which predicates can be transformed into substantives and also by which whole sentences can become substantives in later, derived judgments; these manifest a hierarchy of possible derivations. "This paper is white" (S is p) — "This white paper is before me" (Sp is q) — "This white paper before me is wrinkled" ((Sp)q is r) etc.[31]

2. The second manner in which the "primitive" form of judgment (S is p) can be transformed is through modal operations upon it. The form S is p is originary with respect to its further "doxic" modifications of the type *If S is p, So S is p, Because S is p, S may be p, Let S be p*, etc. Through the process of *modalization* the fundamental structure of the judgment (*doxische Ursetzung*) [32] is not essentially changed; it is merely modified by special "doxic" qualities (the hypothetical, the optative, the causal, etc.), and this holds also of the more complex forms derived from the *Urform* (thus, *If Sp is q* is a modalization of *Sp is q*, etc.).[33] It is the task of pure

---

[29] *FTL*, pp. 52-53. Cf. *LU*, pp. 328ff.

[30] *FTL*, p. 311. Cf. *LU*, pp. 324-325.

[31] *FTL*, p. 310. Let us note in passing that derivations of this kind involve us in the essential distinction between "naming" and "judging." A *proper* judgment, that is, an original, experienced, and asserted judgment, consists of material terms through which things in the world (a "state of affairs") are *named* and then *determined* (S is p); it is through its material terms that the judgment, thanks to the categorial form given these terms in the judgment, refers to the world and asserts something about it. When a proposition (S *is* p) is then taken as a unit and "nominalized" (as in Sp *is* q), the original proposition is no longer asserted; but the state of affairs to which it referred is only named, and something further is asserted of it as a new determination. The logical functions of naming and of judging are, according to Husserl, not only eidetically distinct, but the logical function of "naming" is prior to predicative thought as such. J. N. Mohanty, *Edmund Husserl's Theory of Meaning* (The Hague, 1964), pp. 99-101, gives a discussion of this distinction with reference to recent logical literature on this subject.

[32] *Ideen I* (*Husserliana* III (The Hague, 1950)), p. 327; *FTL*, p. 52.

[33] "When we penetrate more deeply, it becomes apparent that syntactical forms are separated according to levels : *Certain forms* — for example : those of the subject and the predicate — make their appearance at all levels of compositeness. Thus a whole proposition can function as a subject just as well as a simple "substantive" can. *Other forms*, however, such as those of the hypothetical antecedent and consequent, *demand stuffs that are already syntactically articulated in themselves*" (*FTL*, p. 307); cf. J. N. Mohanty,

logical grammar to discover the basic, minimal number of laws of the *derivations* and *modalizations* of the primitive *apophansis* (S is p) which will account for all the possible forms of judgment which can make sense Grammar thus is lifted up to the level of the philosophical study of language in general and becomes a part of the logical study of the formal conditions of thought :

> It gives us the primary and ideal structure of the expression of human thought in general, the ideal type of human language. This ideal structure (*ideales Gerüst*) is an *exemplar* or an *a priori* norm which defines the proper sphere of the "grammatical" (*das Grammatische selbst*), that is the formal law of expressions having meaning.[34]

TRANSFORMATIONAL GENERATIVE GRAMMAR

Husserl, thus, limits himself to giving a kind of outline of what a pure logical grammar would be if it were to be worked out within his general phenomenological architectonic of interrelated and properly subordinated "sciences." But this is sufficient to relate his project to the contemporary aprioristic approach to grammar adopted by Chomsky and his school. We cannot recapitulate the whole theory of transformational generative grammar here, but we can perhaps outline its most fundamental presuppositions.

For Husserl apophantic morphology (pure logical grammar) is the science (or "theory") which delimits (i.e., describes and defines) the whole infinite set of possible well-formed sentences thanks to a finite system of *a priori* laws which state the necessary (but not always sufficient) conditions of meaningfulness. Stated in this general way, there is an obvious similarity between what Husserl claimed could be done in the analysis of grammar and what Chomsky is in fact trying to do. They both believe that the study of grammar will illustrate certain basic laws of thought and that the "universals of grammar" are not merely the result of empirical coincidence or statistical regularities based on cross-cultural borrowing, linguistic analogies, etc., but ideal necessities of all human thought as such. For his part Husserl explicitly recognizes that there may very well be strictly empirical universals, in grammar as elsewhere, which are due to universal traits of human nature, to the contingent, historical life of the race, and that

---

Edmund Husserl's Theory of Meaning, pp. 106ff. Mohanty gives an account of Husserl's conception of pure logical grammar which differs in some respects from mine.

[34] André de Muralt, *L'Idée de la phénoménologie*, p. 142. Cf. *LU*, p. 333.

there is much in particular grammars which depends on the history of a people and even on an individual's life-experience, but the *a priori* aspect of grammar (the "ideal form" of language) is independent of such empirical facts about men and culture.[35] There is a slight, and perhaps important, difference from Chomsky here, inasmuch as Chomsky wants to account not only for "formal" but also for what he calls "substantive" universals, whereas Husserl does not expect to build up a universal grammar in all its breadth but only a pure grammar which can serve as the basis for logic. Thus he admits that his apophantic morphology does not contain the totality of all the aprioris which would be relevant to universal grammar.[36] In short, Husserl does not discuss the possible "material" aprioris which might be found in a phenomenological study of language; he leaves this door open.

There are more important and fundamental differences. Like Plato and Descartes, Chomsky seems to feel that from the very fact that it is possible to locate and describe certain *a priori* (and therefore universal) features of languages, these aprioris must be treated as "innate" ideas or even as "biological" constituents of the human organism. Husserl would certainly never draw such a conclusion, because it would involve him in the kind of "psychologism" which he spent the first half of his philosophical life learning to avoid. Chomsky, on the other hand, is unafraid of psychologism and mentalism and freely illustrates his work (as does, for instance, Merleau-Ponty from a different perspective) with what is known about the psychological processes involved in the acquisition of language; he concludes that these facts point toward the existence in the human mind of a categorial structure ("linguistic competence," *innere Sprachform*) which would be unlearned, innate, and temporally as well as logically prior to experience. But if his notion of "linguistic competence" can be divorced from the Cartesian theory of "innate ideas," as I think it can be (though I cannot argue all this here), we need not tarry over this difference from Husserl.[37] If it is possible, in short, to interpret the "formal universals"

---

[35] *LU*, pp. 336-337.

[36] *LU*, pp. 337ff.; cf. Bachelard, *A Study*, p. 10.

[37] In *FTL*, p. 30, Husserl recognizes that what Plato and Descartes envisaged in terms of "innate ideas" involved an insight which "tended blindly in the same direction" as his own investigations into the formal *a priori* structures of thought (and therefore of judgment, and therefore of language). Husserl, however, takes the *a priori* in a sense which is closer to Kant than to Descartes, namely, as those conditions necessary and sufficient for a given structure of experience to be formally determinable as such. Reason is capable of accomplishing a complete investigation of *its own sense*, not only as *de facto* ability, but in its essentially necessary structural forms; and it is in the elaboration of these necessary structural forms that it discovers the ultimate "formal *a priori* in the most

of language which constitute the *base rules* of deep grammar as aprioris in Husserl's sense, then we can easily separate the essence of Chomsky's work from the Cartesian folklore in which it is imbedded in his own writings.

In fact the notion of "linguistic competence" which Chomsky is attempting to elaborate is based on the very straightforward linguistic fact that native speakers and hearers of a language can produce and recognize on the proper occasions an infinitely varied number of appropriate and new sentences for which their empirical linguistic habits and experience up to any given point can have prepared them only in the most abstract and schematic manner. Moreover, most speakers of a language, i.e., those who know how to speak grammatically and how to distinguish grammatical from ungrammatical sentences in their language, are not aware on the level of conscious reflection just which grammatical rules enable them to give definite interpretations to ambiguous sentences, nor can they in general explicitly state the rules which enable them to formulate and distinguish well-formed from deviant utterances. Most speakers thus operate according to a complex system of hierarchically ordered linguistic rules (which must be applied in series) without explicit awareness of just what these rules are; these rules must therefore be a subconscious possession of the speaker of a language (and in fact we know that the grammar of no natural language has been completely and explicitly codified up to now.)

Chomsky's great originality has been the elaboration of a theory about the *deep structure* common to all languages and the transformational rules by which this deep structure is converted into the phonological *surface structure* of given, natural languages. "The central idea of transformational grammar," he writes, "is not only that the surface structure of a language is *distinct* from deep structure but that 'surface structure is determined by repeated application of certain formal operations called 'gram-

---

fundamental sense" (*FTL*, p. 30), namely, the formal *a priori* of reason itself. The means for the elaboration of the ultimate structures of reason are found noematically in the structures of judgment and, thus, of language. But there is here no investigation into some transempirical *source* of experience or *ability* conceived as being temporally prior to experience; it is rather the present, logical explication of what this experience essentially means. For Husserl's relation to Kant in this regard see Gurwitsch, *The Field of Consciousness*, p. 197. See also Bachelard, *A Study*, pp. lvii–lix. In short, rather than take "*a priori*" to mean, as Chomsky presupposes, some physiological or psychological (he has called it both "biological" and "mentalistic") mechanism hidden deep in the human organism, it may be possible to give the aprioris of language a "transcendental" explanation. That Chomsky himself would not accept this transformation of the "innate" into the "transcendental" is unimportant so long as it can be theoretically justified. And that is what we believe to be not only possible but necessary.

matical transformations' to objects of a more elementary sort." [38] In short, a given sentence can be studied either from the point of view of its physical shape as a string of sounds or morphemes or from the point of view of how it expresses a unit of thought, and the latter is not adequately accounted for by the surface arrangement and phrasing of its component parts. Sentences with very similar surface structures can be seen to require very different grammatical interpretations (as, for instance, "I persuaded John to leave" and "I expected John to leave").[39] We are not interested just here in the intricacies of Chomsky's analyses, and philosophers will probably grant him more readily than structural linguists will that the deeper "logical form" of sentences is frequently belied by their surface grammatical forms. This kind of distinction between surface and deep grammar is exactly what Husserl was aiming at when he distinguished "the grammatical" from empirical grammars,[40] though he nowhere anticipated the spectacular developments in linguistic theory which Chomsky has initiated without him.

We must limit ourselves here to a brief account of the nature and structure of deep grammar as Chomsky postulates it. In order to account for the full range of infinitely variable "new" sentences which we are capable of producing and recognizing on the surface level there must be a highly restricted and hierarchically ordered system of recursive rules (what Husserl called "reiterable operations") which constitute, in fact, the deep structure of language, and, then, a set of transformational rules which can account for the productions of the surface level. The transformational rules differ for each natural language; but what Chomsky calls base rules (which establish the basic grammatical categories and subcategories and the rules of their combinations) are "formal universals" common to all languages. They are

---

[38] Noam Chomsky, *Aspects of the Theory of Syntax* (Cambridge, Mass., 1965), pp. 16-17.

[39] Noam Chomsky, *Current Issues in Linguistic Theory* (The Hague, 1967), p. 9, and *Language and Mind* (New York, 1968), p. 32.

[40] "The inability of surface structure to indicate semantically significant grammatical relations i.e., to serve as a deep structure) is one fundamental fact that motivated the development of transformational generative grammar, in both its classical and modern varieties" (Noam Chomsky, "Topics in the Theory of Generative Grammar," in *Current Trends in Linguistics*, ed. Thomas A. Sebeok (The Hague, 1966), III, 8). Bertrand Russell has of course distinguished logical form from grammatical form within "philosophical grammar" ("The Philosophy of Logical Atomism," in *Logic and Knowledge, Essays 1901-1950*, ed. R. Marsh (London, 1956), pp. 175-282), and Wittgenstein distinguished "deep grammar" from "surface grammar" (Philosophical Investigations, (Oxford, 1953), p. 168) as structures of natural language — not, therefore, in the sense of Carnap. Whether these can be properly related to the sense in which Husserl and Chomsky make this distinction requires much more thorough study.

"the universal conditions that prescribe the form of human language...;
they provide the organizing principles that make language learning possible." [41] But to say in this way "that all languages are cut to the same
pattern" [42] is not necessarily "to imply that there is any point-by-point
correspondence between particular languages" :

> To say that formal properties of the base will provide the framework for the charac-
> terization of universal categories is to assume that much of the base is common to
> all languages... Insofar as aspects of the base structure are not specific to a par-
> ticular language, they need not be stated in the grammar of this language. Instead,
> they are to be stated only in general linguistic theory, as part of the definition of
> the notion "human language" itself.[43]

Thus there can be no language which violates such basic universal rules,
but not all of these rules need be explicitly incorporated into every natural
language; we are dealing with formal, *a priori* conditions only. Of course,
one must ask how these rules are discovered and elaborated, and the answer
can only be by reflection on some one or several known languages. Though
Chomsky does not say so explicitly, the method he employs would seem to
be a variant of the method which Husserl called "eidetic intuition," namely,
argument on the basis of examples chosen from empirical experience : a
free variation and comparison of a number of examples sufficient to give
one an eidetic insight into the essential structure of what is being examined
in this case, linguistic behavior. We cannot directly inspect "linguistic competence," Chomsky admits; and the very existence of the deep structures
by which "competence" is described and defined must be "theoretical."
But it is not necessary to know whether the details of Chomsky's theory
are true in order to understand what it means and how it is to be elaborated
as a "working hypothesis" which, at the limit, would account for the phenomenon of language in all its generality.

Here there are parallels with Husserl's approach which are striking.
Whether we attempt to explain the "linguistic competence" of a native
speaker-hearer or attempt to thematize the deep structure which is this
competence, there are apparently no "inductive procedures of any known
sort" which we can follow.[44] Certainly a speaker's "internalized grammar...
goes far beyond the presented primary linguistic data and is in no sense an
'inductive generalization' from these data" : [45]

---

[41] Noam Chomsky, *Cartesian Linguistics* (New York, 1966), pp. 59-60.
[42] Chomsky, *Aspects of the Theory of Syntax*, p. 30.
[43] *Ibid.*, p. 117.
[44] *Ibid.*, p. 18.
[45] *Ibid.*, p. 33.

It seems plain that language acquisition is based on the child's discovery of what from a formal point of view is a deep and abstract theory — a generative grammar of his language — many of the concepts and principles of which are only remotely related to experience by long and intricate chains of unconscious quasi-inferential steps... In short, the structure of particular languages may very well be largely determined by factors over which the individual has no conscious control and concerning which society may have little choice or freedom. On the basis of the best information now available, it seems reasonable to suppose that a child cannot help constructing a particular sort of transformational grammar to account for the data presented to him any more than he can control his perception of solid objects or his attention to line and angle. Thus it may well be that the general features of language structure reflect, not so much the course of one's experience, but rather the general character of one's capacity to acquire knowledge.[46]

Even if one hesitates to jump to Chomsky's conclusion that such considerations as these necessitate the postulating of "innate ideas," one might well be tempted to give them the weaker Husserlian framework. According to Husserl, fact and "essence" are inseparable in experience. Every fact, in order to be understood, must be brought under an eidetic law which defines its essential meaning-structure,[47] and thus linguistic facts must exemplify essential and necessary *a priori* structures no less than perceptual facts. It would seem that nothing essential is lost to Chomsky's theory if its "universals" are understood as eidetic aprioris of the kind discussed by Husserl.

There is a further point. If there *are* eidetic or *a priori* structures of language *as such*, it ought to be possible, at least theoretically, to establish such structures on the basis of even one well-selected example, a single instance of the *a priori* law in question, since no instance of the phenomenon in question could fail to illustrate its essential and necessary structure.[48] And we find that Chomsky makes a claim for his theory similar to this well-known Husserlian axiom. He writes :

Study of a wide range of languages is only one of the ways to evaluate the hypothesis that some formal condition is a linguistic universal. Paradoxical as this may seem at first glance, considerations internal to a single language may provide significant support for the conclusion that some formal property should be

---

[46] *Ibid.*, pp. 58-59.

[47] *Ideen I*, Chapter One.

[48] Cf. Maurice Merleau-Ponty, "Phenomenology and the Sciences of Man," in *The Primacy of Perception and Other Essays*, ed. James M. Edie (Evanston, 1964), pp. 51ff., 56ff., and 66-73. This seems to me to be one of the best and most suggestive discussions of the method of eidetic intuition and its relation to "inductive procedures" which has yet been written. Merleau-Ponty points out that even in the empirical sciences, insofar as they formulate general laws, one instance is frequently sufficient to demonstrate the law. See also Gurwitsch, *The Field of Consciousness*, pp. 194-197.

attributed not to the theory of the particular language in question (its grammar) but rather to the general linguistic theory on which the particular grammar is based.[49]

And also, like Husserl, Chomsky believes that the aprioris of grammar ("the grammatical") reveal the structures of thought itself :

The central doctrine of Cartesian linguistics is that the general features of grammatical structure are common to all language and reflect certain fundamental properties of the mind... There are, then, certain language universals that set limits to the variety of human language. Such universal conditions are not learned; rather they provide the organizing principles that make language learning possible, that must exist if data is to lead to knowledge.[50]

If we were able to examine the claims of transformational generative grammar in greater detail than we can permit ourselves here, we would be able to bring out a number of theoretical claims which appear to be just as Husserlian as we should expect on the basis of these general methodological statements. Let us limit ourselves here to the parallel discussions of "nominalization" which we find in Husserl and Chomsky. Various kinds of nominalizations are Husserl's most frequent and sustained examples of the fundamental kinds of *operations* which can be applied to judgments and judgment forms. There is a whole hierarchy of such possible operations. There is, first of all, the "operational transformation... of converting a predicate into an attribute" [51] through which what had been a predicate in a proper judgment becomes absorbed into the substantive as a determining characteristic which is no longer affirmed but simply presupposed as the basis for further predication. Furthermore, any predicate (any "adjectival") form can be nominalized and become the subject of further judgments itself (e.g., "The quality p is appropriate to S," "The green of this tree is beautiful," and so on).[52] Finally, and more importantly, the proposition itself (and through it the state of affairs to which it refers) can be nominalized and thus become the substrate for a new judgment ("The fact that S is p" becomes the subject of a further predication). This is possible because, in the most fundamental sense, the primitive form of all judging (S is p) is itself "an operation : the operation of determining a determinable substrate" [53] and, as such, can always be *reiterated* and thus generate higher and more complex forms having the same (though

---

[49] Chomsky, *Aspects of the Theory of Syntax*, p. 209.
[50] Chomsky, *Cartesian Linguistics*, pp. 59-60.
[51] *FTL*, p. 52.
[52] *FTL*, p. 79, and Suzanne Bachelard, *A Study*, pp. 34 and 77.
[53] *FTL*, p. 53.

now hidden) formal structure. In this way the primal form can generate the infinite set of possible sentences. If we attend only to the *form* of propositions, we leave aside whatever complexities might be discovered by a material analysis of the terms of an actual judgment and grasp the subject (S) of the judgmental operation as a "simple object," ultimately just as "something" or "one" (*Etwas überhaupt*), as subject to determination in general (without specifying the particular kind or appropriateness or validity of any particular determination other than to say that any given determination, whatever it may be, must be compatible with the sense of the subject).[54] It is on the basis of these considerations that Husserl affirms within pure logical grammar the "pre-eminence of the substantival category." [55] Adjectives (predicates, whether relations or attributes) can always be substantivized, Husserl shows, whereas the converse is not the case. The proposition, as the operation of determining a determinable substrate, is necessarily ordered in terms of its substantival member, and an analysis of the manner in which a predicate can be chosen as a determination of a given subject form must be established on each level of apophantic analytics, i.e., on the level of analytical noncontradiction, and on the level of possible referential truth. The "pre-eminence of the substantive" thus expresses an absolutely fundamental structure of the logic of discourse.[56]

Now, if we turn to the claims of transformational grammar, what do we find? Chomsky believes that the Port Royal grammarians were the first to discover the distinction between deep structure and surface structure as well as some transformational rules for converting semantically significant structures of the base (deep structure) into the more derived surface structures in which their true, underlying form is obscured. In their analysis of the derivations of relative clauses and noun phrases which

---

[54] We here touch on a point of great importance for Husserl's phenomenology as a whole : it is through the intermediary of the operation of nominalization that we can establish the interrelation between apophantics (which studies the categories of signification) and formal ontology (which studies the categories of objects), or, we might say, between "logic" and "metaphysics." See Suzanne Bachelard, *A Study*, p. 34. In *Ideen I*, p. 249, Husserl writes : "Thought of as determined exclusively by the pure forms, the concepts that have originated from "nominalization" are formal categorial variants of the idea of any objectivity whatever and furnish the fundamental conceptual material of formal ontology... This ... is decisively important for the understanding of the relationship between formal logic, as a logic of the apophansis, and the all-embracing formal ontology" (*FTL*, p. 79).

[55] *FTL*, p. 310.

[56] See De Muralt, *L'Idée*, p. 136, and Mohanty, *Edmund Husserl's Theory of Meaning*, pp. 112-113.

contain attributive adjectives, the Port Royal grammarians postulate a recursive ("operational") rule in the base such that each relative clause and each modified noun phrase is derived from a propositional structure which is essentially the same as Husserl's most abstract form (S is p). "The invisible God created the visible world" is, on the surface level, an implicit way of saying that "God, who is invisible, created the world, which is visible"; and this structure in turn implies a series of propositions such as : "God is invisible," "The world is visible," "God created the world," and so on. The most abstract underlying structure (S is p) is what determines the semantic interpretation of the surface structure, and each relative clause and each modified noun phrase (which is but a further derivation in the same line) has a proposition at its base :

The principal form of thought ... is the judgment, in which something is affirmed of something else. Its linguistic expression is the proposition, the two terms of which are the "sujet..." and the "attribut..." In the case of ... the sentences just discussed, the deep structure consists of a system of propositions. ... To form an actual sentence from such an underlying system of elementary propositions, we apply certain rules (in modern terms, grammatical transformations)... It is the deep structure underlying the actual utterance, a structure that is purely mental, that conveys the semantic content of the sentence. This deep structure is, nevertheless, related to actual sentences in that each of its component abstract propositions ... could be directly realized as a simple propositional judgment.[57]

Thus we see that what Husserl discussed in terms of "nominalizations" receives an interpretation in terms of the transformational rules which derive surface structures from the more universal structures of the base. But, there is at least one more claim on the part of transformational theory which goes quite a bit beyond this one. Chomsky argues that, in deep structure, noun phrases which are subjects logically precede verb phrases and that verb phrases are subject to selectional rules determined by the nouns. Though verbs can be "nominalized," nominalization is a transformational process of mapping deep structure onto surface structure and does not affect the essential and necessary distinction between the class of nouns and the class of verbs. Like Husserl, Chomsky requires that every sentence have a subject and a predicate and that the former logically determine the selection of the latter. Nouns thus enjoy logical priority over verbs; and no language, it is asserted is thinkable which would not contain nouns and which would not give nouns logical priority over verbs in such wise that one cannot select verbs prior to the selection of the nouns which they must modify. There

---

[57] Chomsky, *Cartesian Linguistics*, pp. 33-35. See also *Language and Mind*, pp. 25ff., where Chomsky discusses the same structures, giving them a more formal presentation.

is thus some kind of ontological structure to language, in its possible relation to its own referential use, which parallels in some way the necessary perception of the world in terms of "objects." Moreover, there are strict context-free subcategorization rules operative on the selection of nouns themselves. These are rules of the base and therefore have some universal validity and coerciveness, according to transformational theory. A noun can be either a count or a noncount noun; only if it is a count noun can it be animate or inanimate; only if it is an animate noun can it be human or nonhuman; only if it is not a count noun can it be abstract, etc. :

There is a binary choice at each stage, and the derivation is hierarchial because the rules impose an ordered set of restrictions on the syntactic features which can be associated with the nouns and limit the classification of nouns to the possibilities enumerable by the rules. As a decision in linguistic research this implies that the optimum representation of the grammar of any language contains these rules. They identify an aspect of the mechanism of language use which is fundamental.[58]

Thus we see that transformational grammar has discovered a way of making explicit the kind of universal conditions on grammar which a philosophy of language affirming the "pre-eminence of the substantival" might expect.[59] At the present state of linguistic research it would be most hazardous to draw the parallel any further.

CONCLUSION

In conclusion we cannot consider all the arguments which have been or might be brought against this unified conception of *a priori* grammar; but, granting ourselves that the unity of purpose we have discerned behind the grammatical projects of Husserl and Chomsky is acceptable, we can, per-

---

[58] G. Benjamin Oliver, "The Ontological Structure of Linguistic Theory," *The Monist*, LIII (1969), 270. The principal reference to Chomsky is *Aspects of the Theory of Syntax*, pp. 106ff. I would like also to express here my indebtedness to Oliver's unpublished dissertation, "The Relevance of Linguistic Theory to Philosophy : A Study of Transformational Theory," Northwestern University, 1967, pp. 24ff.

[59] One might well qualify this sentence by saying : "perhaps even too explicit." Professor Oliver (*loc. cit.*) has developed some serious criticisms of this aspect of transformational theory based on the "ontological" claims which it apparently makes and which, he argues, cannot be properly substantiated. I limit myself here to calling attention to the kind of conditions on sentences which transformational grammar might be able to justify; I certainly do not mean to endorse, at this stage of contemporary linguistic theory, any of the details of that theory. The general point I am making would remain valid if it can be shown that there is necessarily some categorial relativity of verb phrases to noun phrases, whatever the precise rules of categorization and subcategorization which govern this relationship may turn out to be.

haps, touch on one typical argument which we find in the writings of
Merleau-Ponty vis-à-vis Husserl [60] and in the writings of "structural linguists" like Hockett vis-à-vis Chomsky.[61] This argument is based on the
diachronic development of languages through time, an evolutionary
development which subjects languages to all the vicissitudes of cultural
history. The vast proliferation of historical human languages and their
known diachronic changes, it is argued, renders highly dubious the claim
that there is some fixed universal, nonhistorical structure of language independent of the surface structures of the natural historical languages which
I speak and which I learn. It is not only that there are gradual but never
ceasing changes in sound structure and phonology, but the very forms
and senses of words also change; and, if we compare languages over a long
period of time, we can see fundamental changes in (surface) syntax as well.
(English syntax is no longer what it was in the days of King Alfred or
Chaucer; French and Italian do not have the syntax of Latin, etc.) Are
not such fundamental and apparently all-pervasive historical changes
— to which all natural languages are subject — sufficient to cause us to
reject the rationalistic hypothesis of a universal logical grammar? The fact
that many languages, like Chinese and Bantu, seem to lack the subject-
predicate structure of the Indo-European languages studied by Husserl and
Chomsky has led some linguists to argue that these languages have a "grammar and logic" different from that of the Indo-European languages and
even that they escape the logical categories of Aristotle and Leibniz alto-
gether.[62]

To this challenge, we can give here no more than a schematic answer
but one which, if true, is sufficient to meet it. If we restrict ourselves, for the

[60] Maurice Merleau-Ponty, "On the Phenomenology of Language," *Signs*, trans.
Richard C. McCleary (Evanston, 1964), pp. 83ff. Merleau-Ponty's criticism of the
notion of pure logical grammar goes far beyond reflections on the diachronic development of language, and this is only a small part of his own theory; I intend to deal with
Merleau-Ponty's criticism of Husserl in complete detail elsewhere.

[61] Charles F. Hockett, *The State of the Art* (The Hague, 1968), pp. 60ff. As for Merleau-
Ponty against Husserl, this argument against Chomsky on the part of Hockett is only
a part of a much broader discussion. For almost ten years the structural linguists have
been more or less silent in the face of Chomsky's onslaught; they will again be able to take
heart behind Hockett's well-articulated counterattack, and it is to be hoped that the debate
which is now opening within linguistics will be of great interest and instruction to philosophers concerned with the nature and structure of language.

[62] One excellent example of this kind of argument is provided by Johannes Lohmann,
"M. Heideggers 'Ontologische Differenz' und die Sprache," *Lexis*, I (1948), 49-106.
This will shortly appear in a volume edited by Joseph J. Kockelmans on Heidegger's
philosophy of language, to be published by Northwestern University Press. Lohmann
argues explicitly that the "grammar and logic" of Chinese is different from the "grammar
and logic" of the Indo-European languages.

purposes of this paper, to the fundamental Husserlian distinction between empirical grammars and "the grammatical itself," I believe Husserl would (and Chomsky could) point to at least one structure of language which would resist the thrust of this "empiricist" observation. There are certain linguistic facts — such as the translatability of all natural languages into one another, the recognition that every natural language is sufficient for all purposes of human expression and that none is privileged, that anything which can be said in any language can, in principle, be said equally well in any other — which point in the rationalistic direction. It is not necessary that there be *no* loss of meaning in the movement of translation from one language to another (clearly the levels of meaning tied directly to phonological systems and even to morphophonemics are only incompletely translatable) but only that some categorial level of identifiable *sameness* of *meaning* be reproducible in any natural language. This, Husserl would say, is primarily the unit of meaning carried by the syntactically well-formed sentence. A sentence which is formed in accord with the fundamental *a priori* laws of signification *must necessarily have a sense*, and this sense must necessarily be *one*. This is the *apriorisches Bedeutungsgesetz* which normatively determines and guarantees the possibility and the unity of a given independent meaning in his sense.[63] There can be no language, he would argue, which is not formed on the basis of units of meaning (i.e., sentences as "wholes" composed of syntactically formed "members"), because this is what *is meant* by language. It is these units of meaning which are — in the primary sense — translatable from one language to another and, in principle, expressible in any. Certainly the manners in which the Bantu, the Chinese, the Semitic, and the Indo-European languages, for instance, express the various kinds of propositions differ as to their morphology, and there will be some languages whose morphology will explicitly incorporate forms for the expression of meaning that other languages must express in some other (perhaps nonmorphological) manner. But would we call a language a human language if it had no means of expressing the units of independent and unified meaning which can be thematized in logical propositions? If we answer this question negatively, we will have recognized the *fundamental form* of linguistic meaning from which all other possible forms *can* be derived; and this recognition will not be based on statistical probabilities or on an appeal to future experience but will be a conceptual or "eidetic" claim about the nature of language and thought *as such*.

---

[63] *LU*, pp. 319-320. Cf. André de Muralt, *L'Idée*, p. 138.

ON HUSSERL'S APPROACH
TO NECESSARY TRUTH *

by

C H A U N C E Y   D O W N E S

(New York)

The aim of this paper is to investigate some aspects of what Husserl means by *"A priori"* in the light of recent considerations concerning the nature of necessary truth. I shall first discuss some of the results of the dispute between Carnap and Quine about analytic sentences. These results bring to the fore linguistic aspects of the problem of necessary truth. It can be shown, I believe, that Husserl's position is substantially in accord with the basic agreements issuing from the Carnap-Quine controversy. In Husserl's view this clarification of the analytic-synthetic distinction opens up a whole new area of investigation, an area in which phenomenology would be able to locate important necessities and universalities. I have selected an instance of the explication of such an essential necessity, and I shall relate this explication to current views of necessary truth. My position will be that Husserl is in general agreement with contemporary linguistic philosophy as regards the *area* toward which philosophical attention should be directed, but that Husserl fails to provide a *method* for such investigation. The appropriate method is that of the linguistic philosophers, and I shall close with a few comments on the way in which Husserl's phenomenology may be construed as implicitly linguistic.

I

In his *From a Logical Point of View* [1] Quine makes a distinction between two types of sentences : "No unmarried man is married." and "No bachelor is married." The first sentence can be recognized as true without knowing the meaning of 'married'; one need know only the meanings of 'No,' 'is'

---

* Reprinted from *The Monist*, with permission. — J. N. M.

[1] (Cambridge, Mass. : Harvard University Press, 1953), pp. 22-23. Hereafter cited as *LPV*.

and 'un-,' and that 'married' is an adjective and 'man' is a noun. Thus, aside from the meanings of the logical constants, one need know only the syntactical facts about the substantives. Quine calls this type of sentence "logically true." [2] In the case of the second sentence, however, we need to know the meanings of 'bachelor' and 'unmarried'; mere syntax will not suffice. Both sentences are analytic in a broad sense; let us here, with Quine, reserve the term 'analytic' for sentences which are analytic in the broad sense, but not logically true.

Now let us look at these observations from the point of view of a system of formal logic. I think it is fairly clear what is needed to establish a logical truth, although various accounts would be required according as we deal with more or less formalized systems. An adequate definition for present purposes is the following : a *logical truth* is a deductive consequence of the syntactical rules of a language, assuming the meanings of the logical constants to be understood. Thus the meanings of the substantives appearing in a logical truth need not be known. However one formulates the notion of logical truth, the major point is that more is required to determine the truth of an analytic statement; the 'more' is the meaning of the substantives. To put it another way : suppose we begin with an uninterpreted system and start to relate it to a natural language; the only relations we need to establish with the natural language in order to determine logical truth are (i) the meaning postulates that relate the logical constants to the natural language, and (ii) the ranges of the variables. In order to determine analyticity we need further meaning postulates that relate the nonlogical (i.e., individual or predicate) constants to meaningful natural language words. (The term 'meaning postulates' is taken from Carnap.) On this view the statement about bachelors could be made into a logical truth by adopting the meaning postulate : 'bachelor' if and only if 'unmarried.' If this postulate is adopted, 'No bachelor is married,' becomes a logical truth.

Now how much of this procedure belongs to the province of logic? It seems to me that the relevant notion here of logic is intimately related to the notion of deductive consequence; the province of logic is the determination of whether or not a given statement is or is not a deductive consequence of other given statements. Hence if the given statements include, in addition to the usual formal logical apparatus, the statement 'bachelor' if and only if 'unmarried,' then the statement about bachelors is a logical truth since it will be a deductive consequence of the given statements. This much is surely logic. But equally surely no one regards

[2] *Ibid.*

" 'bachelor' if and only if 'unmarried' " " as part of any standard logical system. This definition, or postulate, was added to our given statements because it was necessary if the statement about bachelors was to be a logical truth. But why did we want to show that "No bachelor is married" is a *logical* truth? Certainly because we believe that statement to be *true*; we also thought it was hardly synthetic; so we tried to determine its truth by logic. But if logic is to guarantee the *truth* of a statement, the statement must be a deductive consequence of *true* given statements. This requires the truth of " 'bachelor' if and only if 'unmarried' ". So we are in the position of using the truth of " 'bachelor' if and only if 'unmarried' " in order to guarantee the truth of 'No bachelor is married.' Obviously this gets us nowhere. The role of logic in this procedure is confined to the determination of whether or not 'No bachelor is married' does or does not follow from the given statements, including the meaning postulate. Logic has nothing whatever to do with the choice of the meaning postulate, except to rule out postulates which will not provide a basis for the deduction of the statement about bachelors.[3]

Now if this account is correct, logic can provide us only with a necessary condition for the choice of meaning postulates. But logic furnishes a necessary condition, not only for theories of all kinds, but also for rational discourse in general. Hence there is no distinctive use of logic here and it follows that the choice of meaning postulates is an extralogical decision. What then are we to say of analyticity as distinguished from logical truth? Here is where Quine and Carnap disagree, and here is where Husserl, in my opinion, becomes relevant. One approach might be to claim that 'analytic' is an intuitively understood predicate that is true of a class of sentences which are nevertheless not logical truths. In addition to the negative feature of not being logical truths, these sentences would have two further features : (i) we are convinced of their truth, and (ii) we do not see how any possible experience could ever show them to be false. But obviously both these latter features are quite subjective, and Quine doubts that one can ever give an adequate explication of 'analyticity.'

Quine even considers sentences which it would be widely agreed meet both (i) and (ii) and are not logically true.[4] Consider 'Everything green is extended.' He argues that he knows perfectly well what 'green' and 'extended' mean, but he does not know if the sentence is analytic. He then proceeds

[3] R. Carnap, "Meaning Postulates," hereafter cited as "Mean. Post." reprinted in *Meaning and Necessity* (2nd ed.; Chicago : The University of Chicago Press, 1956); hereafter cited as MN.

[4] *LPV*, p. 32ff.

to argue that the explications given by Carnap for 'analytic' in an artificial language all presuppose an understanding of 'analytic' when it is just such an understanding that is lacking. Carnap and Benson Mates reply that they are expliciting an intuitively understood notion; 'analytic-in-L,' where L is an artificial language, will approximate 'analytic' as L approximates the natural language.[5]

Now we shall be concerned with the details of Husserl's position below; but it surely is clear that he believes there is an *a priori* 'structure' to our experience in some sense or other. And I think we can already see some points of agreement with Carnap. For one thing both Carnap and Husserl agree that an intension is objective. Carnap claims that there is a sufficiently clear explicandum in natural languages with which one may begin the explication of 'analyticity.'[6] In the paper "Meaning and Synonymy in Natural Languages" he outlines what he calls a "... behavioristic, operational procedure..." for clarifying "... the nature of the pragmatical concept of intension in natural languages..."[7] Carnap also mentions favorably the work of Arne Naess in trying to obtain empirical evidence concerning intensions via his questionnaire method. It is clear then that the views of Husserl and Carnap have something in common; they are both trying to clarify intensions (senses) by giving an explication. (It will be noticed that I am taking 'sense' and 'intension' as equivalent. I think this equivalence is acceptable in connection with natural languages; Carnap's explication of 'intension' is another matter. Sense is, of course, Husserl's *Sinn*.)

Now whatever Husserl may mean by '*A priori*' (this neologism appears many times in the *Cartesian Meditations*) he is surely convinced of its significance; and since he is concerned to begin with the natural standpoint, the relevant language is the natural language. Also, as I shall argue below, Husserl's *A priori* is intended to consist not of logical truths, but rather of statements I have been calling analytic. Quine seems to feel that the investigation of this domain of the *A priori* is hopeless; the notions are too vague. Carnap is, however, willing to commit himself to the acceptance of something like a natural language *A priori*. As we can see from the above account of Carnap's position, this domain is certainly not precise; but it is roughly discernible. It is the analogue in the natural language of those logical truths in L (our artificial language) which are certifiable as logical truths

---

[5] "Meaning and Synonymy in Natural Languages," reprinted in *MN*. B. Mates, "Analytic Sentences," *Philosophical Review*, 1951.

[6] "Mean. Post.," p. 22 of *MN*.

[7] *MN*, p. 235.

in virtue of meaning postulates explicitly adopted in L. Thus, logical truths in L which arise from rules other than meaning postulates are excluded from this analogy. From this we see, as explicitly claimed by Carnap and Mates (see above), that L is intended as an approximation to the natural language. Hence there must be, in the natural language, analogues of the meaning postulates in L. But of course the 'postulates' in a natural language are not often explicit (and of course they are not *postulates*); the relation between 'bachelor' and 'unmarried' is fairly explicit according to the dictionary, the relation between 'green' and 'extended' is certainly less explicit. Nevertheless, on Carnap's view the natural language postulates are 'there.' How large, how significant, this natural language *A priori* may be is another question.

In this brief recapitulation of a current controversy I have been especially concerned to bring out two points : (i) the distinction between logical truth and analyticity (I shall continue to use 'analytic' to exclude logical truth) and (ii) the problem of the 'locus' of these analytic truths. But even assuming that we can roughly locate these truths the question remains as to how we are to go about explicating them. There seem to be three suggested approaches : (i) Quine : the problem is hopeless, 'analytic' is too vague : (ii) Carnap : analytic truths are to be located in natural languages by essentially empirical means, i.e., by empirically testing the successive approximations of some artificial language to the natural language; and (iii) analytic truths are to be located by a reflective analysis of concepts and expressions in ordinary use. I have not associated names with position (iii) since that is the major problem of this paper. I hope to be able to show that at least in certain respects both Husserl and linguistic analysts are approaching various ranges of philosophical problems via position (iii). But before addressing myself directly to that question, let me try to throw some light on what Husserl means by '*A priori*.'

II

It is my suggestion that Husserl, with his *A priori*, is aiming at the range of propositions that Quine calls analytic. In this section I shal offer some evidence for this and indicate a few of the consequences of accepting such a suggestion. I am thus, for the purpose of this paper, assuming that Husserl's position is, in some broad sense, logical rather than empirical. Of course, this assumption may be contested; Husserl has often been charged with engaging in empirical psychology from his armchair.[8] I believe this charge to be false, but I shall not argue the point here. My discussion should, however, indicate in passing why some of Husserl's claims may have the appearance of being empirical.

Let me again make use of Carnap and his well known distinction between the formal mode of speech and the material mode. While in the formal mode we talk about the words themselves, in the material mode we use the words to talk about the 'world.' In this latter case we are concerned with what the words are about. But as Frege and others have noted,[9] the meaning of a word is sometimes its sense (*Sinn*) and sometimes its reference (*Bedeutung*). Perhaps in most cases we use the word to refer; but we do so via or through its sense. However, the two are so closely bound up that it takes some reflection, and perhaps an example, to make clear the distinction. Now if there are two aspects to the meaning of a word it follows that there are two aspects to the material mode of speech. I suggest, therefore, that many of Husserl's remarks concerning the *A priori*, essential necessity, etc., can be best understood if they are considered as a material mode of speech about *senses*. For example, consider the sentence, 'The Morning Star is not the Evening Star.' This is clearly in the material mode. Is the sentence true or false? I do not see how we can tell until we distinguish senses from references. If we stipulate that our problematic sentences, although in the material mode, are to be read as about senses, then the sentence quoted above is clearly true. Notice that if we read the sentence as about the *references* of the expression 'Morning Star' and 'Evening Star,' the question as to the truth of the sentence is only to be settled by empirical investigation. But if it is read as about senses, we can determine the truth of the sentence by an analysis of what the expressions *mean* to us here and now, even in our armchairs.

If this suggestion is followed, several features of Husserl's phenomenology become clearer, at least in many contexts. His exclusion of all questions concerning the physical or physiological follows quite naturally; no treatise on fruit growing can have any relevance to my present understanding of the sense of the word 'apple.' As a matter of fact, if I read a treatise on fruit growing, I shall *change* my understanding of the sense of the word 'apple' rather than *explicate* it. I think it can also be argued that Husserl's doctrine of constitution is about how senses come to be constituted, not about the

<hr/>

[8] For a recent example of this see Part V of V. J. McGill's "On Establishing Necessary Human Abilities and Disabilities," *Philosophy of Science*, 29 (October, 1962), 393-405.

[9] Husserl himself discusses this distinction on pp. 52-57 of his *Logische Untersuchungen*, II (Halle a. d. S. : Max Niemeyer, 1928).

origin of things. Most important for our present purposes, however, is the light cast upon Husserl's theory of the *A priori*. If my interpretation is sound we should be able to see that in each case of Husserl' asserting an *a priori* connection between, say A and B, what is in question is that the sense of A cannot be grasped unless we understand the sense of B. Where are we to go in order to obtain these senses? "... phenomenological explication does nothing but *explicate the sense this world has for us all, prior to any philosophizing*, and obviously gets solely from our experience — *a sense which philosophy can uncover but never alter* — ..." [10] Compare this with Wittgenstein's dictum : "Philosophy may in no way interfere with the actual use of language; it can in the end only describe it." [11] Wittgenstein refers explicitly to language; Husserl does not. Surely words have senses; but are there senses without words? This will be discussed below.

In defense of this interpretation of Husserl I shall first try to show that it is consistent with his explicit views on the nature of necessary truth. The position taken by Husserl severely restricts the scope of formal or purely logical truth, thereby leaving a vast number of necessary truths which are nonformal. It is with the study of truths of this latter kind that his work is concerned. I shall then present an illustration of the procedure Husserl uses in attempting to clarify the nature of nonformal necessary truths.

In the Third of his *Logical Investigations* Husserl has a section devoted to a discussion of analytic and synthetic propositions, where he says :

The concept of an *a priori synthetic law* and of *synthetic a priori necessity* is now really determined. Every pure law that includes material concepts in a manner that does not permit a formalization of these concepts *salva veritate* (in other words, every such law that is not an analytic necessity) is an *a priori* synthetic law. Particularizations of such laws are synthetic necessities; and this also includes empirical particularizations, such as e.g., *This red is different from this green.*[12]

Husserl's view of 'analytic necessity' is what we would now call syntactical or formal validity, and what Quine calls logical truth. Hermann Weyl quotes Husserl's definition of analytic necessity as in agreement with "... the precise concept of formal validity in mathematical logic..." [13] Husserl's definition, as quoted by Weyl, is as follows :

---

[10] *Cartesian Meditations* : *An Introduction to Phenomenology*, trans. Dorion Cairns (The Hague : Martinus Nijhoff, 1960), p. 151, hereafter cited as *CM*.

[11] *Philosophical Investigations* (New York : The Macmillan Company), 124.

[12] *The Foundation of Phenomenology*, trans. Marvin Farber (Cambridge, Mass. : Harvard University Press, 1943), p. 295. *Logische Untersuchungen*, II, p. 256.

[13] H. Weyl, *Philosophy of Mathematics and Natural Science* (Princeton : Princeton University Press, 1949), p. 18.

Analytic laws are unconditionally universal propositions containing no concepts other than formal. As opposed to the analytic laws we have their particular instances, which arise through the introduction of material concepts or of ideas positing individual existence. And as particular cases of laws always yield necessities, so particular cases of analytic laws yield analytic necessities.[14]

From all this I think it is clear that at the time of the *Logische Untersuchungen* Husserl would have regarded a sentence such as 'No bachelor is married' as a synthetic *a priori* necessity. For if we formalize we get 'No A is B,' which is not analytic for Husserl or for anybody else. But the sentence as unformalized is clearly and necessarily true; hence for Husserl it must be a synthetic *a priori* truth. Now the sentence about bachelors is certainly not an empirical truth. Many would say today that its truth follows from the meaning of the words; precisely how useful this claim may be I shall discuss below. The sentence is analytic in a semantical sense, although not in a formal or syntactical sense. Or, with Quine, it is analytic, although not a logical truth.

Notice that Husserl's distinction between analytic and synthetic *a priori* statements is radically unKantian. Kant's account is, roughly, that in analytic judgments there is an identity between the meanings of subject and predicate terms. As he put it the predicate concept is contained in the subject concept. But Kant's own illustration of such a judgment, All bodies are extended, does not meet Husserl's test of formalizability, *salva veritate*. Husserl has very substantially narrowed the range of the analytic, and thereby extended the scope of the synthetic. What he has called, in the *Logische Untersuchungen*, synthetic *a priori* laws covers statements that Kant would surely have thought analytic. Indeed Husserl's continual claim that he is engaged in the *explication* of senses seems quite inconsistent with his use of 'synthetic' if this term is taken in the Kantian sense. For Kant has expressly stated that it is analytic judgments that are explicative (*Erläuterungs-Urteile*) while synthetic judgments extend beyond the meaning of the subject term (*Erweiterungs-Urteile*). Hence for Kant, if the truth of a statement can be determined by explication, the statement is analytic. In short, what Husserl has in mind is not based on the Kantian tradition but is rather in accord with Quine and Carnap, which is not surprising if one remembers Husserl's mathematical training.

Since Husserl is clearly not interested in formal truths, I think we may assume that when he speaks of the *A priori*, essential necessity, etc., he means what he called above an '*a priori* synthetic law.' The above argument

<hr />

[14] *Ibid.* Weyl's translation makes an insignificant omission from the text of the *Logische Untersuchungen*, II, p. 254.

is intended to show that this concept is identical in substance with the contemporary concept of a necessary truth which is not a logical truth. We must now notice a shift in the meaning of 'logic'. What has hitherto been called 'logic' now becomes 'formal logic,' and the term 'logic' is used to refer to studies in necessary, but nonformal truth. In this sense of 'logic' then Husserl is investigating the same domain as contemporary analytic philosophers, philosophy is 'logic' : the logic of science, the logic of moral discourse, the logic of talk about art, and even the logic of color words.

Two problems, at least, must be noted. First, does Husserl adhere consistently to this view of the *a priori* in his other writings? On the basis of the writings with which I am familiar, I am prepared to argue that he does. But I have not examined all of Husserl's work; nor is it always obvious what he has in mind since he seems usually to omit qualifying '*a priori*' with either 'analytic' or 'synthetic.' Second, even if Husserl is aiming at the same domain as these other philosophers, can we say that his method is at all similar? What with the famous (or infamous) *Wesensschau*, may we not be faced with a totally different technique for eliciting and grounding these essential insights? Let us postpone this question until we have before us an illustration of Husserl's procedure.

III

I have selected a passage from Husserl's *Cartesian Meditations* that is relevant to the claim I am making from two points of view. First, Husserl claims that the procedure about to be illustrated is fundamental to the whole phenomenological method. Second, the results claimed by Husserl as essential and universal seem to be so because they are instances of propositions which are analytic in the sense of Quine. If this is so it would appear to follow that phenomenology is a method for analyzing concepts by tracing the analytically necessary links between senses.

That Husserl believes that the procedure is basic to phenomenology is shown by the following quotation : "At last we must bring to bear a fundamental methodological insight, which, once it is grasped, pervades the whole phenomenological method (and likewise, in the natural realm, the method of a genuine and pure internal psychology)." [15] This method is, however, not empirical : "*The method of eidetic description,* however, signifies a transfer of all empirical descriptions into a new and fundamental

---

[15] *CM,* p. 69.

dimension, ..."[16] As an illustration of how we attain a "pure *eidos*" Husserl takes perception :

Starting from this table-perception as an example, we vary the perceptual object, table, with a completely free optionalness, yet in such a manner that we keep perception fixed as perception of something, no matter what. Perhaps we begin by fictively changing the shape or the color of the object quite arbitrarily, keeping identical only its perceptual appearing. In other words : Abstaining from acceptance of its being, we change the fact of this perception into a pure possibility, one among other quite 'optional' pure possibilities — but possibilities that are possible perceptions.[17]

Husserl notes that since we are dealing with a "... realm of the as-if ...",[18] we might have taken some phantasy for our object instead of a perception. Hence :

Perception, the universal type thus acquired, floats in the air, so to speak — in the atmosphere of pure phantasiableness. Thus removed from all factualness, it has become the pure *eidos* perception, whose '*ideal*' extension is made up of all ideally possible perceptions, as purely phantasiable processes. Analyses of perception are then '*essential*' or '*eidetic*' analyses. All that we have set forth concerning syntheses belonging to the type, perception, concerning horizons of potentiality, and so forth, holds good, as can easily be seen, '*essentially*' for everything formable in this free variation, accordingly for all imaginable perceptions without exception, in other words : with absolute '*essential universality*' and with '*essential necessity*' for every particular case selected, hence for every de facto perception, since every *fact can be thought of merely as exemplifying a pure possibility.*[19]

Now there are enough uses of 'essential' here to lead us to think some radical claim is being made. Yet the upshot of this quotation seems almost trivial. We first vary a perception in any imaginable manner, yet retaining those features, whatever they may be, that enable us to call the object we are considering a perceptual object. Thus we attain a general notion of perception. Now since this is the widest possible notion of perception, anything we say about it will of course be true of any particular perception, necessarily, indeed logically. For example, if we can say that whatever is perceived as colored is also perceived as extended, then we can say of this perception of a colored table top that it is also a perception of an extended table top. By restating Husserl's argument in the formal mode, as opposed to his material mode of speech, the 'essential necessity' and the 'essential universality' can be reduced to formal, logical necessity and formal, logical universality.

[16] *Ibid.*
[17] *Ibid.*
[18] *Ibid.*
[19] *Ibid.*

Putting this in the language used in Section II above, we may say that Husserl is showing that if we can delineate certain meaning postulates about 'perception,' then we shall be able to show the necessary nature of many allegedly factual judgments. Indeed, every factual judgment will have many necessary aspects. If it is true that " 'extended' if and only if 'colored' ", then it is necessarily true that if X is colored then X is extended. (Extension is here, of course, visual extension.) So we can see how the postulates involve us in necessary truths; and since these postulates are not formalizable *salva veritate*, we can see how Husserl could think of them as synthetic *a priori*.

But notice that the necessity of the passage is hypothetical. It is not the eidos itself that is necessary. Once we have acquired the eidos, whatever falls under it will, necessarily, have the features essential to the eidos. But whence do we get the pure eidos? We are not told. The 'fictively changing' might imply a kind of armchair empiricism. But even if " 'extended' if and only if 'colored' " is an empirical generalization, the relation between it and 'If A is extended then A is colored' is an entailment, and hence necessary. But surely Husserl means more than this. In any event, I have excluded from this paper the question of Husserl's alleged empiricism. So let us consider the 'postulates' themselves as necessary. It will be recalled that they have the two features pointed out above as requisite for analyticity, viz., they are not logical truths, and it does not seem possible to conceive of any experience that would render them false. (Incidentally, notice that I have had to supply features of the content of the pure eidos perception, since Husserl does not furnish us with any content.)

Let me discuss this point a bit, because it bears upon something I am not trying to do in this paper. I am not trying to show that Husserl's *A priori* is 'merely verbal,' whatever that might mean. In the later sections of this paper I am going to suggest that access to the kinds of truths philosophers are interested in may best be achieved through attention to language. But I wish to leave entirely open the question as to what precisely is the status of these truths. So I am perfectly willing to agree that Husserl could respond to my comments about the triviality of the passage quoted above. I think the claims about essential necessity and essential universality are indeed trivial as they appear in the passage. All that is really asserted is that instantiation is an entailment, and I do not think that is at all controversial. But what about the status of the feature of the eidos itself? Since we have been talking about perception, let us continue with " 'extended' if and only if 'colored' ". Is this a verbal truth? I think Husserl's reply would certainly be negative. These 'analytic' statements are necessary because it is true that everything extended is colored and conversely. So one party to the dispute claims that analytic necessity results from the meaning of the words, and the other party to the dispute claims that analytic necessity (or, as they would perhaps prefer to say, *a priori* necessity) results from what the words mean always being the case. And this is a dispute that I do not know how to adjudicate.

All that I have attempted to show, both from the definition given in the *Logische Untersuchungen* and the illustration given in the *Cartesian Meditations*, is that Husserl too is concerned with those numerous truths and necessities that follow from the interconnections among senses. And it is trivially true that once we settle upon definitions of such terms as 'perception' much will follow necessarily. The problem of course is how to settle upon a definition, or, how to explicate a sense.

My analysis of this passage from Husserl is, of course, meant to be generalizable to all his claims about the *A priori*. Whether this is so is a matter for detailed investigation and is beyond this compass of a brief paper. There are, however, some matters of methodology in which the differences between Husserl's investigations of senses and the linguistic philosopher's attention to the uses of words is connected with the problem of necessary truth. In the next section of this paper I shall discuss a few aspects of these differences.

IV

By turning to the formal mode, explicitly talking about words, we were able to see the basis for Husserl's use of 'necessity.' But Husserl rarely talks about words; he is concerned with senses and the acts that intend them. And of course a word cannot intend anything insofar as it is a mark on paper or a sound. If we do speak of the word 'perception' intending the essence perception, we mean that someone is using the word knowingly or understandingly. For Husserl it is the act of meaning and its object, the essence, that are primary; the eidos "... is *prior to all 'concepts,'* in the sense of verbal significations; indeed, as pure concepts, these must be made to fit the eidos." [20] And there indeed seem to be cases, at least in which this is so. We speak of "groping for words," and translators must frequently strain for words in another language that will convey the meanings and concepts of the original. But if Husserl's approach to the *A priori* is to be regarded as useful and important, it remains to be shown that there are cases

---

[20] *Ibid.*, p. 71.

in which the analysis makes use of senses that are not obviously senses of words. Before turning to this question, let us consider generally what many would call Husserl's hypostatization of meanings.

What arguments can be offered in defense of Husserl's approach? First of all, we might ask if it is indeed hypostatization? Are not meanings there? Certainly phonograph records and parrots do not mean or intend anything. Perhaps we might agree that there is a need for meanings, but we are not required to convert them into objects. All we need to know are the rules of use of the sounds or marks; we then know what they 'mean.' Let us try this tack with Husserl's illustration of the development of the pure eidos perception. As I have noted, this development is singularly devoid of indications as to how we are to tell what we may freely vary and what not without losing the object's 'perceptual appearing.' We must of course know what perceiving is in order to get at the essence perception. But this is perfectly all right; a discussion of essences does not give us new information, it merely organizes our present knowledge into the categories of our epistemological theory. Suppose then we try, as a substitute for 'grasping the pure eidos perception,' the phrase "understanding the use of the word 'perception'". The pure *eidos* or essence then becomes what we know when we know how to use the word 'perception.' This translation certainly renders Husserl's 'object' language innocuous; it also renders it superfluous. Is there any virtue to retaining Husserl's approach?

There seems to me to be one perhaps valuable feature gained by speaking of meanings as objects, by freeing them from an exclusive attachment to words. Words are, so to speak, the common coin of language; but it may be worth exploring the view that there are preverbal, unarticulated, or as Husserl says in *Erfahrung und Urteil*, prepredicative meanings. Now surely if we are told that a meaning cannot be articulated, we may well be skeptical. But there are certainly many meanings that are unarticulated; thinking is more than subvocal speech. Without elaborating this in any merely speculative fashion, I want to deal with two questions : first, can we, on the narrowest possible basis, make the objectification of meanings (senses) useful in this direction? Second, what effect will this have on our view of necessary truth?

I think we can agree that we learn in a variety of ways. Sometimes, of course, by verbal communication; but probably more often by observing behavior, imitation, contextual implication, etc. If this is so, if we have meanings so to speak 'built into us' by our experiences, then the verbally expressed, articulated meaning of some sentence may or may not coincide with the prepredicative, unarticulated meaning. Note two things : one, since both mean the same thing, the coincidence is, in an extended sense, analytic; but, two, some sort of investigation is necessary in order to find this out, at least in cases of deeply buried meanings.

R. M. Hare has given an illustration of the sort of investigation I have in mind.[21] His examples involve a group of people at a dinner party discussing a dance they all performed in their youth. None of them can remember, i.e., give a verbal account of, a key step in the dance. So after dinner they dance it, and at the key point they spontaneously carry out a step. This step is recognized by them to be correct. Consider now the sentence : 'Step A is performed at point X in the eightsome reel. By dancing the eightsome reel the group came to see that the sentence was true. Since a complete description of what is meant by the expression 'eightsome reel' would include the sentence, 'Step A is performed at point X,' we see that the sentence above is analytic. But this had to be found out; indeed, there may never have been a complete description of the eightsome reel formulated. Is this the same kind of investigation as going to the dictionary to look up a word you are unsure of? I think not; the group knew how to dance this reel, they were not in need of dancing lessons. And when they danced the step properly they recognized it; they did not learn it. Hence we can argue that there were prepredicative meanings of 'eightsome reel' and 'Step A is performed at point X,' prepredicative in that these persons knew how to deal with these expressions through actions. But they did not know that (i.e., predicatively) the two were connected. Thus the investigation consisted in finding out, predicatively, what they knew all along prepredicatively.

Perhaps it may be possible to find other cases in which some form of behavior would clarify to us something that we knew prepredicatively all along. We would then find it useful to pursue meanings as part of nonverbal behavior. Note that it would have to be nonverbal in order to justify 'objectification,' for verbal behavior would take us back to the uses of words again. Now this whole area of investigation seems to me quite important. Insofar as using language is a form of behavior it should be relatable to other, nonlinguistic, forms of behavior. Indeed this may throw some light on the motive behind the correspondence theory of truth. But even if this direction did seem fruitful, it would hardly supply grounds for philosophizing in the manner of Husserl, in spite of his suggestion concerning prepredicative knowledge. For he recommends no form of overt behavior; rather he asks us fictively to vary the content of our concepts.

---

[21] "Philosophical Discoveries," *Mind*, 69 (1960).

This variation of content will enable us to delimit the scope of the concept. But we do not do anything; we merely imagine. And what we can imagine we can describe; and what we can describe is predicative, not prepredicative. This is not to say that there may not be prepredicative meanings; it is merely to say that there is no reason to believe that fictive variation will render them predicative.

Indeed the whole notion of fictive variation seems introspective and even 'reactionary'. Husserl's own procedure, as well as his general aim, seem to cry out for attention to language. The passage I quoted on perception is, at the key point, empty. Certainly once the concept has been explicated many analytic sentences can be deduced by stating the explication in the form of a meaning postulate. We can then go on to show the logical truth of particular sentences that follow from the concept. But all this play with what will follow once we explicate the concept is beside the point; we want to know how to explicate the concept. And here Husserl gives us no concrete procedures. It even seems that Husserl succumbed to a temptation pointed out by Miss Anscombe in her discussion of intentions :

All this conspires to make us think that if we want to know a man's intentions it is into the contents of his mind, and only into these that we must inquire; and hence, that if we wish to understand what intention is, we must be investigating something whose existence is purely in the sphere of the mind; and that although intention issues in actions, and the way this happens also presents interesting questions, still what physically takes place, i.e., what a man actually does, is the very last thing we need consider in our inquiry. Whereas I wish to say that it is the first.[22]

And this point of view surely places Husserl and linguistic philosophy at odds methodologically, whatever agreement may exist about the locus of philosophical activity.

V

Husserl's claims are large. He feels he has uncovered the area with which genuine philosophy should occupy itself. This is the domain of necessary, but nonformal truth, where investigation is to be carried out by explicating the necessary connections between objective senses. And I think that, thus far, he is right. But he makes an additional claim : the proper method for this is phenomenology. Now the problem is what are we to understand by 'phenomenological' analysis? Insofar as it is a method of explicating concepts it is, programmatically, appropriate. In the course of this paper

---

[22] G. E. M. Anscombe, *Intention* (Oxford, 1958), p. 9.

I have mentioned three suggestions for the explication of concepts. First that of Carnap; concepts are to be explicated by the construction of artificial languages with tentative meaning postulates. The validation of the choice of the postulates would be empirical, and the artificial language would, hopefully, approximate more and more closely to the natural language. Second, the suggestion made by Hare (and Husserl with his notion of prepredicative knowledge) that meanings may be found to 'fit' behavior in certain cases; hence, we become aware of the scope of a concept, not by really learning anything new, but by bringing to the level of articulation what we knew, in one sense, all along. Third, Husserl's notion of fictive variation, in which we try to phantasy all possible applications of the concept thereby gaining the greatest generality from which all particulars will follow 'essentially'.

There is of course a fourth suggestion, which I have not illustrated but which has been in the background throughout, viz., the method of linguistic analysis. Linguistic analysis is not empirical in Carnap's sense, although in what sense it is related to matters of fact is a very interesting question. It is however, in a way, concerned with fictive variation; not with the fictive variation of images or ideas, but with the variation in the uses of words. This is seen at perhaps its sharpest in the work of Austin, where shades of meaning are brought out by continual use of illustrations of the way in which we do talk.

A main theme of this paper is that there is an extremely close parallel between Husserl and linguistic philosophy. In Husserl's phenomenology we use the method of fictive variation to obtain necessary connections between senses. In linguistic analysis we use the method of variation in the uses of words to obtain rules governing the connections between words. But of course the words are not being studied philologically, whatever critics of linguistic philosophy may say. Rather they are to be used as an avenue to the conceptual analysis of philosophical problems. And here, it seems to me, Husserl with his concern for the objectivity of senses, and linguistic analysis with its concern for the uses of language are both trying to delimit the proper locus fo philosophical research, i.e., to elucidate the very concept of philosophical analysis.[23]

I have argued, however, that Husserl fails at the crucial point; procedures

---

[23] An interesting intermediate position is adopted by C. I. Lewis in his *An Analysis of Knowledge and Valuation* (La Salle, Illinois : Open Court Publishing Co., 1946). Lewis' notion of "consistently thinkable" would seem to require something like Husserl's fictive changing and free variation. This comparison was called to my attention by my friend and colleague Raziel Abelson.

for the explication of concepts are lacking. Husserl and linguistic philosophers are indeed doing the same thing; but linguistic philosophers have been doing it very much better. I have not argued this point by examining instances of linguistic philosophy; there are many such notable analyses. Rather I have argued negatively by trying to show that in his own terms Husserl's method of explication is incurably introspective and unreliable. Nevertheless his emphasis on objective senses and their interconnections is valuable as a corrective against overemphasis on the linguistic aspects of philosophical analysis. Indeed since some critics have overemphasized the linguistic aspects of linguistics philosophy, it may be appropriate to close with a warning from Austin himself:

In view of the prevalence of the slogan 'ordinary language,' and of such names as 'linguistic' or 'analytic' philosophy or 'the analysis of language,' one thing needs specially emphasizing to counter misunderstandings. When we examine what we should say when, what words we should use in what situations, we are looking again not merely at words (or 'meanings', whatever they may be) but also at the realities we use the words to talk about; we are using a sharpened awareness of words to sharpen our perception of, though not as a final arbiter of, the phenomena. For this reason I think it might be better to use, for this way of doing philosophy, some less misleading name than those given above — for instance 'linguistic phenomenology,' only that is rather a mouthful.[24]

---

[24] J. L. Austin, "A Plea for Excuses," in his *Philosophical Papers*, eds. J. O. Urmston and G. J. Warnock (Oxford : 1961).

HUSSERL ON TRUTH AND EVIDENCE *

by

GÜNTHER PATZIG

(Göttingen)

1. A relation of identity between evident and true sentences, and between evidence and truth in general, can only be established either by reducing evidence to truth or by founding truth on evidence in the sense that one can speak meaningfully of truth only where there is evidence. It is a permissible and perhaps useful simplification to say, that Husserl's theory of evidence in the *Logical Investigations* is determined by the attempt to work out the first mode of connection, while his so-called 'turn' towards idealism which takes place in the *Ideas* — certainly anticipated through corresponding trends of thought in the *Logical Investigations* — can be characterised, briefly but appropriately, as the attempt to reduce truth to evidence.

One could say that in the relevant passages of the *Logical Investigations* [1] it is Husserl's intention to show that a judgment that is not true cannot also be evident; in the *Ideas*,[2] we find instead the attempt to show that an evident judgment as such is true. To be sure, the intended distinction does not let itself be retained in this manner. For the two judgments "A not-true judgment is not evident" and "An evident judgment is true," being derivable from each other by contraposition, are naturally equivalent. The difference between the two sentences becomes clear if one adds that in the *Logical Investigations* Husserl looks upon truth as something primary and wants to develop the disputed essence of evidence from that of truth, while according to the *Ideas* the evidence as a phenomenal character is immediately experienced and so can be the basis on which something like

* E. Tr. by J. N. Mohanty. Reprinted and translated, with permission, from *Neue Hefte für Philosophie*, Heft 1 : Phänomenologie und Sprachanalyse. Göttingen : Vandenhoeck & Ruprecht, 1973, pp. 12-32.

[1] E. Husserl, *Logical Investigations* (E. Tr. by J. N. Findlay), Vol. I, pp. 187-196; and Vol. II, pp. 760-770. On this theme, compare E. Tugendhat, *Der Wahrheitsbegriff bei Husserl und Heidegger*, Berlin, 1970, esp. I. 1.

[2] E. Husserl, *Ideas to a Pure Phenomenology and phenomenological Philosophy* (E. Tr. Boyce Gibson), § 21 (pp. 78f.), § 24 (pp. 83f.), § 69 (pp. 180f.), §§ 137-145 (pp. 353-372).

truth (the 'Idea of truth') could be comprehended. The meaning of the two equivalent sentences is quite different, for in the first case it is evidence, while in the second case it is truth, that functions as the explicandum.

For Husserl of the *Logical Investigations*, a discussion of the peculiar nature of evidence was indispensable because he himself had made generous use of the truth-warranting power of evidence in his own attempt to provide a foundation for the assertion of ideal objects. It appeared to him favorable that he could develop this clarification of the concept of 'evidence' through a critical confrontation with an actual, and in his time, influential philosophical opinion. This doctrine may briefly be characterised as follows : Logic is concerned with such propositions as have evidence or are of the sort that all propositions which could have evidence allow themselves to be reduced to these laws of logic. For the foundation, let us say, of the laws of contradiction, excluded middle or identity, no other consideration can be advanced save that they are evident, and it is the task of logic "to exhibit the laws on which it depends that from certain premises a certain judgment can be derived with evidence." [3] In this sentence from the Logic of Höfler and Meinong we find a formulation, indications of which Husserl found suggested in John Stuart Mill, occasionally in the logics of Sigwart and Wundt, but worked out in its full definiteness and in respect of its defining importance for logic as science first in this book. The consequent formulation of logic as "Theory of evidence" is called by Husserl, in the first volume of the *Logical Investigations*, already in the title of § 49, "the third prejudice." The first prejudice of which Husserl speaks is the view of the psychologists that logic must be, if not the technology of thinking, then certainly empirical science of it. The second prejudice is the view that concepts such as 'judgment,' 'inference' could be, as expressions, meaningfully applied only to mental acts of thinking, not to the contents of those acts. To these two prejudices is now added, as the third — and certainly also psychologistic prejudice — the assertion that logic must be a theory of evidence. It would follow from this point of view that logic can undertake only psychological investigations in order to enquire into the factors which are necessary for the coming into being of "feelings of evidence" or "experiences of evidence."

Husserl counters this view with an argument which he frequently uses in various different situations : he agrees that the laws of logic can be transformed into equivalent propositions in which the expression "evidence" appears. The modus Barbara is equivalent to the proposition : "The evidence of the necessary truth of a proposition of the form 'All As are C' (or, more

---

[3] A. Höfler and A. Meinong, *Logik*, 1890, p. 18ff.

correctly expressed, evidence of its truth as a necessary consequence) can appear in an act of inference whose premises have the form "All As are B" and "All Bs are C." (The peculiarity of the locutions "necessarily following truth of a proposition" and "premises of an act of inference" need not be discussed here, since Husserl wants to talk about a theory which is rejected by him.) In the domain of logic, according to Husserl, to every proposition of the form "A is true" there must be an equivalent proposition of the form "It is possible, that any one judges with evidence that A." However, the possibility of evidence which is being asserted in these equivalent transformations of logical laws is not — Husserl's criticism of the third prejudice begins with this — a real possibility which could be investigated and established by psychology. It is rather a matter of essential possibility which need not at all take into consideration the limitations of human powers of understanding. Thus certainly there is a very large number of true propositions, but it is impossible that by presentifying these propositions men experience evidence. However this does not exclude the fact that even in these cases evidence is a 'possible' experience in the sense of ideal-possibility. Psychology can explain the natural conditions of the factual non-appearance or appearance of the ideally possible experiences of evidence. But it cannot say anything about the genuine evidence itself, namely the ideally possible experience of evidence. The evidence of which psychology speaks has a special relationship to the mental constitution of individual men; evidence in the logical sense, whose ideal possibility is asserted by the equivalent transformations of the logical laws, is an experience of pure consciousness in general. Its laws are valid for every possible consciousness. The tenor of this argument is Kantian, and it is not an accident that Kant is explicitly named.[4]

Before I go into Husserl's theses in § 51 ("The decisive points in this dispute"), I would like to add some remarks in connection with the philosophical usage of the word 'evidence.' Husserl was also influenced by this usage. Already the thought that the logical laws as such must be evident can show, how little the philosophical usage was obliged to follow the sensible and rational linguistic usage of everyday language, and how little one had reflected upon the historical origin of the concept of evidence.

Neither the everyday linguistic usage of the word 'evidence' nor the tradition of the history of philosophy permits us the assumption that the laws of logic are 'evident.' To be sure, it is correct that some propositions which one takes to be laws of logic are constantly given as especially striking

---

[4] *Logical Investigations* I, p. 191.

examples of evident propositions. However, along with these other propositions also are cited which do not belong to logic; and one often distinguishes within logic itself those that are evident (the axioms) from those that are not. It is therefore unjustified to hold that evidence could be made a mark of the logical laws as such. This was obviously the intention of Höfler and Meinong. In the context of his dispute with them, Husserl has agreed with them that to every logical law it is possible to produce an equivalent transformation in which the word 'evidence' occurs.

Although we are accustomed to use 'evidence' as a strong expression for 'true,' yet the evidence of a proposition is originally not the evidence of its *truth*. This is supported by colloquial usage as much as by appeal to the history of philosophy : we say, for example, that it is evident from the medical bulletin about the condition of a patient that the doctors have little hope of his recovery. Here 'evident' means 'appearing,' and what here appears is not the truth of the proposition that the doctors have hardly any hope, but rather the fact itself which is not spoken out in the report but becomes, so to say, visible "between the lines." Also in the history of logic, 'evidence' is not used originally in the sense of evidence of the truth of a proposition, but in a comparable sense that a proposition appears forth, i.e. follows from certain other propositions. Aristotle calls the first figure syllogisms perfect because in their case the necessity of the consequence is not only present but also at the same time obvious. The Aristotelian emphasis on evidence of some syllogisms stands at the beginning of a process of development at whose other end is the view that logical laws as such should be evident.

Also influential for Husserl's view is the well-known thesis of Descartes according to which there is a connection between truth and evidence such that given the evidence of a proposition one can infer its truth. 'Clearness' and 'distinctness,' also for Descartes, are not in themselves a *sigilum veri*. The *cogito* is indubitable not because of its evidence, but because it would still remain true even when I deceive myself — because my self-deception would itself be a *cogitatio*. But Descartes also needs, in order to justify his belief in the truth of evident propositions, that disputable chain of thought which assures us of the goodness of God, which on its part does not allow the possibility of something untrue being evident for us. Descartes's example is appropriate for the characterisation of what Husserl undertakes to do for two reasons : first, it can be shown how also in the case of Descartes there is a problematic concept of evidence; secondly, the return to Descartes makes it possible for us better to understand what exactly Husserl sought to achieve. In accordance with his presuppositions, he had to give nothing less than an evidence theory of truth without that Cartesian appeal to the benevolence of God as a guarantee of truth.

2. Husserl develops his early theory of evidence in § 51 of the first volume of the *Logical Investigations* under the title "The decisive points in this dispute," namely in the dispute between Höfler-Meinong and himself. Husserl points out that one needs first to have the right concepts of truth and evidence in order to understand the true relationship between them. Socrates could also say the same thing. However, this condition is not satisfied for 'evidence' : one speaks of evidence "as if it is an accidental feeling which appears in the case of certain judgments and is lacking in the case of others... Every normal person feels, under certain normal circumstances, the evidence in the case of the proposition "$2+1 = 1+2$" exactly as he feels pain when he gets burnt." [5] Husserl considers this formulation to be totally false : "Evidence is not an accessory feeling which is added to certain judgments either contingently or in accordance with natural laws. It is not at all a psychic character which may simply be attached to any judgment whatsoever belonging to a certain class (i.e. the so-called 'true' judgments), so that the phenomenological content of the judgment concerned, considered in itself, would remain identically the same, whether it is accompanied with this character or not." [6]

Husserl is here arguing against the view that an evident judgment is in the first place a judgment like any other judgment, and only then an evident judgment. Just as one can speak of a greedy lion, that it is in the first place a lion and then one which is not easily to be satisfied. What Husserl seeks to express only negatively is the philosophically important fact that there are predicates which do not leave untouched the meanings of the subject terms to which they are attached. Such predicates are called by Husserl "modifying predicates" and he distinguishes them from "determining predicates." [7] Husserl is obviously of the view that the predicate 'evident,' when applied to judgments, is a modifying predicate. Evident judgments and non-evident judgments are, according to him — one may very well say — not only different judgments, but are as judgments different. As contrasted with this, it would be non-sensical to say that an expensive table is different as a table from an inexpensive one, or that a greedy lion is, as a lion, different from a contented one.

---

[5] *Logical Investigations*, I, p. 194.
[6] *Ibid.*, I, pp. 194ff.
[7] *Logical Investigations*, II, pp. 514ff. This distinction was originally made by Franz Brentano. See Josef König, *Sein und Denken*, 1937, pp. 1-6 and 219-222.

In this sense, evidence is not a character that is annexed to a judgment that is already completed. Evidence is not at all a feeling whose appearance gives us the right, in an inexplicable manner, to take the judgment in connection with which it appears, to be true : "Evidence is rather nothing other than the 'experience of truth.'" [8] Husserl explains the word 'experience' (*Erlebnis*) thus : "Truth is experienced naturally in no other sense than that in which in general an ideal entity can be experienced in a real act. In other words, truth is an idea whose particular case is an actual experience in the evident judgment." Since Husserl is trying to explain evidence, a somewhat altered formulation would perhaps have been more appropriate for his purpose : the self-evident judgment, as an actual experience, is a particular case of the idea of truth. This statement of Husserl, which is bold and in many respects provocative, shall now be, in accordance with our insight, interpreted and more closely comprehended. One is speaking here of an Idea in Plato's rather than Kant's sense, and so also of its particular cases. But the theme is not, contrary to what one may at first think, the mere relation of a universal to its particular cases. In this harmless sense, the intelligent remarks that some one makes may be taken as concrete cases in relation to intelligence in general. For if it were meant in that sense, then true judgment would be the type of particular cases which represent the idea of truth. If one were talking here of evident judgment as a particular case in this sense, then obviously it is self-evidence, not truth, which would have been the general idea which is realised in a self-evident judgment. And in that case, this is what Husserl would have said : "Self-evidence is an Idea whose particular case is an actual experience in a self-evident judgment." This proposition would have been unproblematic, and we could agree with it without any misgivings. But it would have been obviously trivial and without philosophical significance. Husserl's proposition owes its inner tension to the fact that it brings to clarity a philosophical locution which does not merely make the true judgment a particular case of truth in general and the evident judgment a particular case of evidence in general. Rather we have here a sort of cross-connection between truth and evidence, namely through the assertion that an evident judgment as such is the actual experience of the idea of truth and quâ such an experience it is a particular case of that which is experienced in it, therefore of the idea of 'truth.' What makes Husserl's proposition difficult to understand and at the same time philosophically interesting is the fact that it speaks of a relation between a universal and a particular, which shall at the same time be

---

[8] *Logical Investigations*, I, p. 194.

understood as the relation between an x which is experienced and an experience of this x.

Now there is no doubt that these two relations are fundamentally different relations at the first sight, but not merely at the first sight. No one would think that a particular case must be as such also the experience of something. An experience as such is also a particular case, but it is not the experience of that of which it is a particular case. This sounds so abstract and perhaps misleading, that it would be useful to make use of an example. Everyone knows what is, generally speaking, a sunset. We need not be concerned here with the exact astronomical definition of 'sunset.' The following characterization may suffice for our purposes : the sunset, for a place on the surface of the earth, is the transition of the place, as a result of the rotation of the earth, in that half of the globe which is not now being illuminated by the sun. The sunset which occurs now in Göttingen at 21 : 15 hour is a particular case of the class of events called "sunset." One may also call this class, if one so desires, the "Idea of sunset." The particular case occurring today is as such not an experience, but a straightforward event which itself does not need to be experienced — for example, in the case of the sun being covered up by a cloud. Every sunset, occurring in a place in accordance with law, is a particular case of sunset in general, but there is no question of its being an experience.

On the other hand, one can naturally say that someone can experience a sunset. But would one ever say that the experience of this sunset is a particular case of the universal "sunset?" And yet Husserl says that the evident judgment as experience of truth is a particular case of the idea of truth. This illustration may be supplemented by many others. We wanted only to convince ourselves that in most cases there is no factual cross-connection between the two totally different relations : that of a particular case to its universal and that of an experience to its object. Now that we have determined this, we should ask ourselves whether there are not at all cases which allow themselves to be interpreted in the light of Husserl's case? Are there also examples of what Husserl finds with regard to the relation between evidence and truth? Are there cases in which experience of an object is also at the same time a particular case of that object? One may be tempted to think that Husserl, as well as we, in our search for such cases, are after a will-o'-the-wisp. However I believe that the twofold interlocking that Husserl posits between evident judgment and truth, i.e. the interlocking of the relations of a particular case to its universal and of an experience to its object, is in fact exhibited in a whole series of cases.

If we look at our sunset example, Husserl's throwing together of these different relations seems just a matter of confusion. But I suppose that Husserl was looking at other examples when he developed his idea of a cross-connection between truth and self-evidence. His theory would make at least some sense when looked at in the light of other examples than sunsets. Let us imagine someone who has travelled widely and has never experienced nostalgia. He may have heard that some people are prone to this kind of feeling. He knows by hearsay what nostalgia is like, but does not know it by experience. Let us imagine that this hardy traveller is in a foreign country, in which political disturbances make his return impossible. To add to his troubles, a sudden illness may cut short his various activities. Let us imagine that under these circumstances he remembers sadly the peaceful life back home and that he feels an intense wish to return immediately, knowing well that this is out of the question. Now in this imagined case, we would say that this particular case of nostalgia is at the same time an experience of it. We might apply Husserl's thesis and say that this particular case of nostalgia is at the same time an experience of it. We might apply Husserl's thesis and say : "Nostalgia is an idea, whose particular case is an actual experience of the longing for an impossible return home." Although this manner of speaking sounds somewhat forced, there is no philosophical problem hindering its actual understanding. Why is it that a thesis which is formally identical with Husserl's is in this case so unproblematic whereas it appeared so positively objectionable in the case of Husserl's own meditations? Obviously, the thesis about nostalgia appears so unproblematic only because in this case the 'Idea' whose particular case is the actual experience is itself the idea of an experience.

In the case of the expression 'experience' ('*Erlebnis*'), besides many other, to us, unimportant differences in meaning, two essentially different cases may be distinguished. We experience events and occurrences, but also our own states. We may experience the premiere of a play, an earthquake, the house-warming of a home (in such cases, one may also speak of 'co-experiencing'). But we may also be said to experience nostalgia, joy in success, disappointment or a feeling of admiration for Husserl. Using the problematic locution of 'outer' and 'inner' experience, one may say that experiences in the first sense relate to outer objects and events, experiences in the second sense relate to inner events and states. It seems to me much less problematic to say, that in those cases where one could speak of 'experiencing' or 'co-experiencing' in the first sense, that which is experienced is, or at least, 'could be' what it is without being experienced, while in the other cases what is experienced can be what it essentially is only as the content of an experience.

We would be saying the same thing, only differently paraphrased, if we said that the verb 'to experience' takes on, in the first case, an outer (*'affiziertes'*) object, while in the second case an inner (*'effiziertes'*) object. It is essential for the nostalgia which some one experiences that it is experienced, while it is contingent for a sunset that someone observes it and in that sense 'experiences' it.

According to Husserl's leading thesis, the evident judgment is at the same time a particular case and the experience of the idea of 'truth.' We have seen that, generally, the particular case is not an experience of the corresponding universal. It is also as little the case that an experience of something is as such also a particular case of that which is experienced. The experience of a sunset is not itself a sunset; a sunset itself is not the experience of the idea of 'sunset.' It is true that in certain cases a formulation analogous to Husserl's mode of speaking may be in conformity with facts. One may, in fact, say that a particular case of nostalgia, or an actual experience, is an experience of the idea of 'nostalgia.' A situation corresponding to Husserl's manner of speaking can obtain only where the universal, the idea whose particular case is at the same time its experience, is itself the idea of a special sort of experience. Husserl's thesis can be valid if and only if truth, which is actual experience in the self-evident judgment, is the *inner object* of that experience. From this it would follow that there can be truth only in so far as and as long as it is experienced in an evident judgment. Truth in that case cannot be compared to a picture which is at the same time illuminated by evident judgment and is then evident, but otherwise continues to exist, as it were, in darkness. On the contrary, if at all truth is to be compared to a picture, then it must be a picture which is projected on a wall by a ray of light. Perhaps it would be useful to pursue this analogy further. One could then say that even if truth be the inner object of experience of an evident judgment, the two — experience and truth — need not coincide, as little as the projected picture is identified in our analogy with its projection on the wall. In any case it holds good that the picture is bound up, in its existence, to the ray of light along with which it appears and dissolves. Likewise truth would not be the same as the experience (the evident judgment), but simply nothing other than the content of the evident judgment precisely as an evident one.

It would be expedient to break off this line of thought at this point. It has been shown that from Husserl's thesis, or in any case from the formulation of his thesis, certain consequences may be drawn which lead us away from a correct understanding of the relation between truth and evidence. We turn now to another aspect of Husserl's theory of evidence.

3. Right after the passage we have been considering, Husserl draws an analogy between two relations which, to immediate consciousness, appear as radically different. The difference between an evident judgment and a judgment not evident, he says, corresponds to the difference between perception and mere representation. This analogy is then immediately thereafter subjected to a certain restriction, though not explicitly; but the analogy, along with this restriction, is so important for his phenomenology that we should better keep it as clearly before us as possible.

To be sure, Husserl does not mean that there is an analogy between perceptions and representations on the one side and evident and non-evident judgments on the other, *as* they are understood ordinarily or by other philosophers. The analogy holds good only if one understands the two relations after Husserl. It is not the case that Husserl wants to make the difficult relation between evident and non-evident judgment intelligible by relating it to the difference between perception and mere representations, so commonplace for everyone or even for the philosophical tradition. The case is rather otherwise : Husserl establishes a parallelism between a theory which he himself developed and another theory which was developed equally well by him. A side-glance at David Hume may instruct us that this is so. For Hume, both perceptions and representations (in Husserl's manner of speaking) are 'perceptions.' We may assume that for Hume perceptions would fall in the category of those perceptions that he calls 'impressions,' while 'representations' are called by him, as is well known, 'ideas.' The difference between 'impressions' and 'ideas' — according to Hume's well-known thesis — is a difference in liveliness and force, consequently a difference in degree which, in certain limiting cases, reaches a minimum — although Hume thinks (following more the facts than his theory) it possible to set up an unbridgeable gap between the two classes. This side-glance suffices to show that the difference between perception and representation as interpreted by Hume cannot be made analogous to the difference between evident and non-evident judgment as Husserl determines it. For if Husserl sets himself up against any view, then it is the interpretation that evidence could be a matter of degree. The peculiar connection, through identity, of evidence and truth would not permit such a gradation of evidence; for a proposition is either true or false, there is no third possibility, and therefore also no graduated variation between the true and the false. (The ordinary locution pointing in this direction is misleading, but obviously an abridgement. Ordinarily one may regard the sentence "Nine comedies of Aristophanes are extant" as false, but 'more true' than the sentence "Ninety comedies of Aristophanes are extant." But that can only mean that the number nine is nearer the actual number of Aristophanes's extant comedies which is eleven, than the number ninety.)

Now Husserl's own interpretation of the relation of perception to representation can afford the basis for the analogy constructed, and Husserl's theory of perception is, along with his theory of ideal meanings, possibly the most influential chapter of early phenomenology. The difference between perceptions and representations that are not perceptions, according to Husserl, lies not in the fact that perceptions can, without a break, fit into the interconnection of experience, not in the physiological conditions of their genesis, as little in their intensity (which are the main types of explanations prevalent in Husserl's time), but only in the fact that in perception the 'bodily presence' of the perceived object is experienced. Phenomenologically, there is no question of there being a difference of degree from which one could infer that the case under consideration is a perception. As little do we experience, in perception, a consciousness of the question whether the perceived fits into our experience without a break or not. Finally, we do not also *see* any sensation and its origination from the operations of external stimuli on our nervous system : we see, hear etc. the thing itself. This naivity in the phenomenon of perception that Husserl has discovered exposed the constructive nature of an entire series of theories of perception. At the same time, it has moved philosophical theories to a level where philosophically innocent phenomena are sought to be made the source of ontological theses. How embarrassing such an ontological misuse of Husserl's analysis of the phenomenon of perception can be, has been shown by H. U. Asemissen in his book *Strukturanalytische Probleme der Wahrnehmung in der Phänomenologie Husserls.*[9]

For our purpose, it suffices to say that Husserl distinguishes perception from all mere representations such as phantasy, memory, expectation, through the fact that only in perception an entity is apprehended as bodily present, as "originally giving itself." Husserl's thesis is that, exactly analogously a non-evident judgment remains a mere intending, a mere supposing (*Vermeinen*), whereas an evident judgment is a bodily apprehension of the state of affairs so that evident and non-evident judgments are different exactly as perception (as described by Husserl) differs from mere representations. In view of this thesis, we now understand better the emphasis with which Husserl asserts the fact that 'evident' is a predicate that changes the character of the judgment. But we do not as yet understand clearly enough, how precisely this analogy between evident judgment and

[9] *Kant-Studien*, Erg.-Hefte 73, 1957, esp. pp. 77-97.

perception in which the thing itself is given, should be interpreted. According to Husserl the following holds good : if, e.g. I judge with evidence '2+2=4,' then I grasp an ideal state of affairs which I express in this judgment, and at the same time experience the agreement between my meaning and the self-present state of affairs that is intended. "Evidence is the experience of the agreement and the Idea of this agreement is Truth." [10]

Now closer examination reveals several difficulties in this thesis. To begin with, let us compare this thesis to the one we have already examined. Do the two say the same thing? Or is there a certain divergence between them? It can be shown that the two theses could not be equivalent. The thesis that was first considered was to the effect that the idea of truth is an idea whose particular case is the actual experience in evident judgment. Here the particular case is an experience i.e. the act of judging with evidence. But in the sentence presently being considered ("Evidence is the experience of the agreement, and the Idea of this agreement is Truth."), the particular case of the Idea of Truth is not the experience of agreement but the agreement itself between the opinion and the self-given state of affairs. In the second formulation, the particular case of the Idea of Truth is not an experience but a state of affairs, namely the agreement between opinion and fact. So far the second formulation seems to be essentially weaker. It appears to be more in conformity with the philosophical tradition. That truth is agreement between opinion and fact belongs to that tradition. Husserl's second thesis may be interpreted as a bare triviality, if one takes him to mean only this : it happens that an opinion actually agrees with the state of affairs that it intends. This agreement can also, in a suitable case, be experienced. We call this experience evidence, and such an agreement, generally speaking, is called truth. One is naturally led to think that Husserl could not have, after all, meant exactly this, for then his first thesis would only be an unfortunate formulation of this position. If in accordance with such an interpretation, we replace the words "is actual experience" (in the sentence "Truth is an Idea whose particular case is actual experience in evident judgment") by the words "is actually experienced," then the discrepancy between the two, the original thesis and the second one as interpreted by us, would appear to be completely harmless. For now both the theses, the revised first one and the second one, would be saying exactly the same — excepting that the second thesis would more accurately explicate what precisely is "actually experienced" as a particular case of the Idea of Truth viz. the agreement between opinion and fact. Then everything would be clear, but unfortunately also pretty trivial.

[10] *Logical Investigations*, I, pp. 194f.

I do not think we would be doing Husserl a service by reconstructing his theory in this way. For we neglect thereby a series of important differences between Husserl's theory of truth and the traditional correspondence theory. We have therefore the task of determining more closely the peculiarities of Husserl's theory of truth and evidence.

The correspondence theory of truth has, as against its interesting philosophical rivals, the advantage that it can be immediately tied to the natural linguistic usage and widely diffused notions. There is also no doubt that Husserl's theory is closer to the correspondence theory than to the other theories of truth. For Husserl also a judgment is true if its sense agrees with the existing state of affairs. But as contradistinguished from the conventional correspondence theory, Husserl holds besides that it is possible that this agreement may be experienced. If some one, for example, assures us that he has experienced the truth of the judgment '2+2=4,' we would find his statement rather curious. Certainly in some cases analogous locutions are usual. One can say that he has experienced the truth of a statement, saying or maxim, when after initial doubts one has been confronted with the, generally painful, fact that the statement in question is, after all, true. It is in this sense that Goethe's Helena in the second part of *The Faust* (verse 9939/40) says : "Ein altes Wort bewährt sich leider auch an mir : dass Glück und Schönheit dauerhaft sich nicht vereinen." We would not be surprised if Helena also said that she had experienced the truth of this saying. But what one means when one says so, is certainly not what Husserl has in view. Helena does not mean that she has experienced the bodily presence of the ideal state of affairs "Schönheit und Glück sind auf die Dauer unverträglich," that she compared it to her opinion about the matter and experienced the agreement of both. What she means rather is that she has been through a series of experiences which have convinced her that the old saying is after all true. Her experiences confirm the old saying as true.

Generally the truth of a proposition is ascertained, not experienced. Husserl can speak of the 'experience' of truth in his sense, because he maintains that we may have a relation to ideal states of affairs which correspond to the relation which we have to the objects, things or facts that we perceive. But precisely for that reason the analogy between perception and evident judgment cannot strictly be carried through. For evidence is not simply perception of this ideal state of affairs, but the experience of the agreement between this state of affairs and the opinion which is expressed in the judgment. Evident judgment accordingly is something thoroughly complex. It is composed of, first, the act of judging, secondly the percep-

·tion of a state of affairs (real or ideal), thirdly the insight that the opinion expressed in the judgment corresponds to the perceived state of affairs.

The evident judgment combines all these in one indissoluble unity. So far, according to Husserl's theory, there is no strict analogy between perception and evident judgment. For perception itself is a simple phenomenon which is not composed of a representation, the perception of the object, and the insight that the representation in fact corresponds to the object. Of course, we can, in the domain of perception in the wider sense, construct more complicated cases which are composites of perceptions, representations and judgments. There is the case of confrontation of a witness with someone who is suspected of an offence. A person may compare his memory images with a visual impression and find out if he experiences agreement between them, and then arrive at the judgment that the person he is seeing is in fact the offender. The evident judgment is then not merely a different judgment as against the non-evident judgment, but possesses an inner complexity which essentially distinguishes it from mere opinion and supposition. As contrasted with it, the perceptual phenomenon is usually not a complex of different acts of representation, judgment and perception. It is not therefore possible to compare, as Husserl does, perception with evident judgment and mere representations with non-evident judgments. Rather, the connective link between perception (in the ordinary sense) and evident judgment lies, at best, in the fact that an evident judgment contains within itself a partial aspect which, according to Husserl, is a special sort of perception, i.e. the perception of ideal states of affairs and objects. In view of these explanations, we may be justified in saying that Husserl's argument about the relation of evidence and truth is involved in a peculiar circularity : it refers to evidence in order to establish the thesis that there exist ideal objects such as pure meanings. This justification can refer to evidence only if evidence guarantees truth. That again is established by Husserl by means of the proposition that evidence itself already includes the perception of ideal states of affairs and objects. In order to justify the belief in the existence of such a region of ideal essences, Husserl must already presuppose them. In any case, Husserl's peculiar manner of establishing the existence of ideal objects already presupposes their existence. His proof, upon examination, is seen to be merely a closer elaboration of his thesis.

These discussions should be sufficient to show that the further consequences that Husserl draws from his thesis must be questionable. For example, he contends that on the assumption of the analogy between evident judgment and perception, it becomes easily intelligible how an evident judgment can guarantee its own truth. Just as nothing can be seen where nothing is, just as there cannot be perception of a thing if the perceived thing does not exist, similarly if a state of affairs does not hold good it cannot also be seen. Only if the state of affairs obtains precisely as the judgment supposes it to be, it can be seen or seen insightfully. Since the evident judgment as such essentially includes such an act of mental perception (for evidence is the experience of agreement between the seen state of affairs and the opinion) an evident judgment can at all come into being only where the conditions of the truth of the judgment are already fulfilled. One needs as little to wonder that there are true judgments which are not evident. For the being of an object and its being-perceived are different things. Similarly, the existence of a state of affairs is essentially different from the grasping of it. Evidence guarantees truth, because truth is a necessary, though not sufficient, condition for there being evidence.

All this may seem very illuminating, but upon closer scrutiny it becomes questionable. Certainly there is a sense in which I cannot perceive what does not exist, and I cannot call a judgment 'evident' if it is not true. But that does not mean that I can simply look at the perceptual act itself or the evident judgment itself, and find out whether it is in fact a perception or it is in fact an evident judgment. This shows that there is a systematic ambiguity in the terms 'evident' and 'perception,' which it is difficult to get rid of. In one sense, these terms are used to describe phenomena, in another sense to determine facts. If I say with Husserl, and with justification, that the object is bodily given in perception, this is all right so long as I want to describe thereby the mere phenomenon as such. If I perceive something, then the perceived is bodily present before me — but only as a phenomenon. For there are also, in such cases, illusions; for example, illusion of motion that we all know from our everyday experience. One perceives the phenomenal movement of the train in which one is sitting, while in reality it is the other train that is moving. On the other hand, it also happens that one thinks one is only imagining something which one in fact is seeing. This sort of case happens in day to day life, when, for example, one does not "believe his eyes" — e.g. when one sees someone on the street, whom one takes, on good grounds, as living in a foreign country. In a well-known psychological experiment, subjects were required to imagine an apple as vividly as possible and then to project this image upon a screen. The subjects did not notice that during the experiment the *perceivable* picture of an apple was projected on the screen, so that they mistook their images for perceptions. In cases such as these, that which is, phenomenally speaking, an imagination, can be, in fact, a perception, and *vice versa*.

The same holds good for judgmental evidence. Phenomenally speaking, we cannot separate evidence from the conviction that the judgment is true; in fact however actual evidence and truth of a judgment are inseparably connected. But the transition from phenomenal evidence to actual truth is, as before, unjustified.

What Husserl attempts in this thesis may be better characterised as building a bridge across from phenomenal evidence to actual truth of judgments. One may therefore call his theory of truth a radicalisation of the correspondence theory. According to the correspondence theory truth of a judgment consists in its agreement with a fact. It does not say, over and above this, how such an agreement is to be ascertained; and one may, without contradiction, assume that a proposition is true, but that it can be, with certainty, determined as being in fact true or false only in the context of experience. Similarly, one may, without contradiction, say both that perception, as perception, makes being accessible to us, but also that it is always possible to doubt the perceptual character of a given act, which doubt can be resolved with satisfaction only in the larger context of other perceptions. Husserl is in this regard more radical : perception, for him, guarantees reality, evidence guarantees truth. According to him, a particular judgment is not only either true or false but also can — as this particular judgment (in so far as it is an evident judgment) — guarantee its own truth. There can be no doubt that scientists and philosophers would have reasons to be happy if what Husserl says were true. This explains why the early Husserl and his followers, in so far as they did follow him, overlooked the fact that the daring bridge called evidence, which was intended to connect judgment with fact, had the drawback, rather unfortunate in a bridge, that it ended on the same bank of the river from which it began. Less metaphorically expressed : they did not see that evidence presupposes experienced truth, that experienced truth as little guarantees actual truth as experienced movement is the same actual movement.

Concerning the notion of 'evidence' (or 'perception') one has two different options : either one regards evidence as a phenomenal character of certain judgments, in which case it is inseparably bound up with the conviction that the judgment under consideration is true, but not with its actual truth for which it may be a symptom and nothing more. Or, one so defines evidence that it coincides with the consciousness of actual truth of the judgment. In that case, whether a judgment possesses evidence can be decided only in the context of a totality of experience, or a theory; or in the context of an appropriate epistemological position, it can never be finally decided. The third alternative, obviously taken up by Husserl, is not open to us :

one cannot regard evidence as the phenomenal character of the evident judgment, and at the same time maintain that evidence, so understood, can guarantee the actual truth of the evident judgment.

4.   This entire train of thought seems to set up insurmountable difficulties for a theory of evidence of the kind developed by Husserl. It acquires a special importance for Husserl-interpretation through the fact that he may well have taken his so-called "turn towards idealism" under the influence of the sort of arguments which were developed above against his thesis regarding the relation between truth and evidence. We said at the beginning that when he wrote the *Logical Investigations* he tried to explicate the evident character of evident judgments by reducing evidence to truth. In view of the difficulties of such a reduction, he could have found it more promising to reverse the reduction procedure and instead to dissolve truth into a hierarchy of evidences. This is exactly the thesis which we find in the passages on evidence in the *Ideas* [11] and especially in the *Cartesian Meditations*.[12]

The special character of logic as a science can be correctly understood, according to the early Husserl, only by interpreting logic as a science which studies objective facts, namely the relations of ideal objects, ideal unities of meaning and the like, which we grasp by a kind of intuitive insight. Husserl felt obliged to give reasons for his belief that there exists such a domain of ideal meanings. He believed that this existence thesis could be justified by appealing to the character of evidence of judgments concerning such objects. An exact analysis of the evident character of judgment should yield that every evident judgment possesses objective validity. But the difficulties of such an interpretation, which has been developed very impressively in the *Logical Investigations*, did not escape Husserl, especially as the difficulties were pointed out to him by colleagues, highly regarded by him, such as Wundt, Stumpf, Külpe and Natorp. Scientificality remained for Husserl the first requirement for every serious philosophy, and scientificality lies, for him, only in the stringent and indubitable truth of philosophical assertions. Husserl was therefore led to a new mode of thinking, which not only is comparable to that of Descartes, but which Husserl explicitly referred back to Descartes. In 1907, the formula "dissolution of being into consciousness" first appeared in Husserl's writings, with explicit

---

[11] *Ideas*, pp. 365ff. Cp. also E. Husserl, *Idea of Phenomenology* (E. Tr. by W. P. Alston & G. Nakhnikian), pp. 46ff. This text of 1907 is an important first stage of the "idealistic' theory of evidence of the *Ideas* of 1913.

[12] *Cartesian Meditations*. E. Tr. by D. Cairns, §§ 24-29, pp. 57-64.

reference to Descartes as his predecessor.[13] Husserl's enigmatic turn to idealism, indicated by this formula, can, in any case, be partly comprehended if we presuppose that Husserl took the turn under the pressure of the very same difficulties that presented themselves against his theory of evidence. In place of the problem of how to know a presupposed objective reality, there emerged the problem of the constitution of an entire re-unified world of intentional objects of a pure consciousness. Evidence which for the early Husserl was the bridge between act and object and guaranteed truth, is neither suited nor needed for building such a bridge, once the Cartesian foundation has been adopted in its Husserlian form. The gap between act and object which earlier had to be bridged, is now made to vanish: we have the world already in our cogitations, and phenomenology can now be described as a description and analysis of the constitution of the world in our acts of consciousness.

It is clear that truth or the true actuality of objects is to be obtained only from *evidence*, and that it is evidence alone by virtue of which an *"actually" existing*, true, rightly accepted object of whatever form or kind *has sense for us* — and with all the determinations that for us belong to it under the title of its true nature. Every rightness comes from evidence, therefore from our transcendental subjectivity itself; every imaginable adequation originates as our verification, is our synthesis, has in us its ultimate transcendental basis.[14]

It is only in the framework of a strictly idealistic position that it is possible to maintain, without contradiction, an identity between evidence and truth. One may wonder at the price Husserl has paid in consequence — for saving his evidence theory of truth. The price seems too high; and we would therefore prefer to reject the attractive thesis according to which evidence is perception of truth.

---

[13] The formula quoted by Walter Biemel in his introduction to the *Idea of Phenomenology* (*Husserliana*, II) — "Dissolution of being into consciousness" — is not taken from the published text. For the exact reference, Mr. Biemel directed me, in a most friendly manner, to Dr. Karl Schumann of the Husserl Archive in Louvain. According to his friendly communication (letter of 3.7.71) Husserl has, in the inner cover of manuscript B II 1, as indication of the content of the notes contained in it, entered the following note in September 1908 : "Being of nature 'dissolving itself in' consciousness." However, neither B II 1 or B II 2 which shows a similar entry contains a text which is, in its contents, appropriate to this formula. One may suppose that the missing pages were annexed to the manuscript K II 1 (indicated as 'duplicate') by Husserl. One finds there the following sentence : "And if it belongs to the immanent essence of such consciousness-structure that the 'object' is thought, posited, and finally is determined and known in an acceptable manner, then the objective being 'dissolves into' the structures of consciousness which themselves are subject to essential laws." (K II 1/12a-b). I thank Dr. Schumann for his ready help and permission to publish his findings here.

[14] *Cartesian Meditations*, p. 60.

THE TASK AND THE SIGNIFICANCE OF THE *LOGICAL INVESTIGATIONS**

by

EDMUND HUSSERL

A complete transformation of the inner and as quickly also of the outer situation of Dilthey took place about the turn of the century. In the year 1900-01 appeared my *Logical Investigations* which were the results of my ten year long efforts to clarify the Idea of pure Logic by going back to the sense-bestowing or cognitive achievements being effected in the complex of lived experience of logical thinking. To put it exactly, the specific investigations of the second volume were concerned with the turning back of intuition upon the logical experiences which take place in us when we think but which we are not able to see, which we do not have in the field of attentive glance when we perform the act of thinking in the naturally original manner. The thinker does not know anything of his thought-experiences, he knows only of his thoughts (*Gedanken*) which his acts of thinking continually produce. It was necessary to bring this hidden life of thought under our grasp through subsequent reflection and to identify it through faithfully descriptive concepts; it was also necessary to solve the problem that arises for the first time : namely, to make it intelligible, how in the achievements of this inner logical experience there takes place the formation of all those spiritual forms which emerge in statement-making, judging thought as concepts, judgments, inferences etc., and which find their general expression, their universal objective, and spiritual expression in the fundamental concepts and principles of logic.

(a) *Criticism of psychologism; the essence of irreal (ideal) objects and of irreal (ideal) truths*

The *Logical Investigations* were preceded by an important preparatory work, which was concerned with a pure apprehension of these sense-formations

---

* E. tr. by J. N. Mohanty. Reprinted from E. Husserl, *Phänomenologische Psychologie* (*Husserliana* vol. IX) with permission.

themselves and with fighting against all empiricistic and psychological mixing up of the psychological contents of the acts of thinking with the logical concepts and propositions themselves. For example, the proposition that is expressed, which is acquired as the result of logical thinking, contains as a sense-formation, within its own sense, nothing of the act of thinking, as little as the number which is counted in the experience of counting contains anything of the psychic act of counting. Numbers, propositions, truths, proofs and theories in their ideal objectivity, constitute a closed realm of objects — not things, not realities like stones or horses, but still objects. The formal logic systematically founded by Aristotle is, in its central core, a theory of propositions, a discipline which lays down the pure forms of possible propositions and also the formal laws which propositions must satisfy if they are to be true. The entire theory of syllogism belongs to it. Let us now consider the highest fundamental concept of this logical theory, the concept of proposition, with the help of a clarifying example.

Irrespective of whether it is I or someone else who thinks or proves the Pythagorean theorem, the latter itself is a unique member of the realm of propositions. The same is the case with the number 4, irrespective of when and by whom it is thought and brought to givenness in consciousness. A proposition or a number is not a real occurrence in the totality of the world, does not occur then and there in its own individual uniqueness, which, moving or at rest, exercises real causality. That holds good only of the written number, or of the sentence uttered now or at some other time. But the written expression of a number or of a proposition or also the utterance, is not the Pythagorean theorem or the number 4 itself — as had already been seen by Leibniz, had been still earlier seen by the scholastics and consistently worked out by Bolzano. Such irreal or, as one says, ideal objects are, in their numerically identical uniqueness, substrates of true and false judgments, exactly as much as real objects are; conversely, 'object' in the most general and logical sense means nothing other than a something about which meaningful and true statements can be made.

It is useful for our purpose to emphasise here that in the systematic-critical preliminary considerations of the first volume of the *Logical Investigations* two kinds of things were being defended : first, as against logical psychologism it defended the already mentioned irreality, the ideal objective and identical being of such objects as concepts, propositions, inferences, truths, true proofs, etc... This included the thesis that these objects are unities of meaning of such a kind that in the content of the meanings themselves there is nothing of the psychic acts and other subjective experiences which constitute the changing consciousness of the objects concerned, that they are in no way tied to the real men or other subjects. Psychic acts, like their subjects, belong to the real world. Secondly, and in close connection with the above : correlative to the ideal objectivities, there are also pure, ideal truths which say nothing about the world or about anything real. Pure logic, in the theory of syllogism, speaks about pure concepts and pure propositions, just as pure arithmetic states truths and theories about pure numbers of the number series, in whose meaning not the least is said about the spatio-temporal, factual world. Irrespective of whether there is a world or not, irrespective of whether this world remains as it is or not, the truth that $2+2=4$ subsists in itself as a pure truth. It does not contain in its sense the least information about the real facts. The same holds good of the law of non-contradiction and other such laws. Pure ideal truths are "*a priori*," and are seen to be true in the unconditioned necessity of their generality. This generality is in need of a characterisation. Ideal objects are not related to actual facts, but, in accordance with their meaning, are implicitly related to *possible* facts, to ideally possible or ideally conceived facts. Pure arithmetic does not presuppose any of the enumerated things or processes belonging to the real world; nevertheless, every number has a universal extension. Under the idea of '3' fall all conceivable sets in so far as they are enumerable as 3. Accordingly, every arithmetical theorem and the entire arithmetic is *a priori* applicable to every conceivable, and as a further consequence, to every actually given set in its facticity. Likewise, the logic of propositions (the Aristotelian theory of syllogism) is applicable to all imaginable cases in which imagined men or other such rational beings would judge and in their judgments express the corresponding sentences as expressed significations. To every ideal object there thus belongs inseparably an ideal extension, the idea of a totality of imaginable special cases and along with it a validity in general (*eine Überhaupt-Geltung*), a generality which is not restricted by the presupposition of factual singularities or states of affairs. This is what is meant by unconditioned generality. "Prior" to the givenness of a fact and a factual world, we could be *a priori* unconditionally certain of the fact that, what we state as logicians or as arithmeticians must be applicable to everything that may be encountered as the corresponding factual reality.

The generality extends still further insofar as the ideal objects with their extension of possible corresponding singularities could again relate themselves to ideal objects. One can thus count not only possible realities, but also pure numbers themselves; similarly, the ideal truths of logic speak also of propositions in general. But propositions are propositions not only about the earth, the Black forest or the factual nature in which we live, but also about idealities. One can always make statements about statements. The logical laws themselves are propositions about propositions.

If pure logic says that every self-contradictory proposition is false and that every consistent proposition is possible, that holds good also of the propositions which are asserted within logic itself — propositions in which nothing is said about the real world. Let us now sum up : There undoubtedly are *irreal* objectivities and corresponding *irreal* truths with an ideal extension through which they relate to ideal objects but also always to possible realities — be it noted, however, only to ideally possible realities whose factual existence is not presupposed. Corresponding to these, there are sciences of irrealities, "*a priori* sciences" whose Idea theoretically determines a closed domain of ideal objects.

(b) *Investigation into the correlation between ideal objects and psychic meaning-constituting experiences through essential descriptions in reflexive attitude*

But the major themes of the *Logical Investigations* were not these determinations of the *Prolegomena* which was confined to pure logic, but descriptive investigations about psychic experiences with which every sort of ideal objectivities of logic and mathematics are inseparably related. In other words, apart from the necessary extensional relatedness which lies in the very sense of ideal objects and through which every 'number' is related to possible groups of singular objects and especially to possible singular realities, ideal objects have also necessarily another sort of relatedness to possible reality, namely, to psychic subjects and acts. This is the sort of relatedness which played the major role in the fight against psychologism in logic. Precisely that which, in this fight, was to be kept separate in order to avoid corrupting the idealities and in order to reach a pure formal logic parallel to pure mathematics — i.e., the psychology of knowledge was now made the main subject matter of investigation.

Let us reflect on this a little closer : a proposition may say something about stones, heavenly bodies, etc. — i.e., about reality. It does this through its sense (*Sinn*). But whatever the statement may be about, it has infinitely many possibilities of being made by us or by some other conceivable person, of being actually expressed in possible acts of judgment and on the basis of possible subjective experiences of perception, memory or representation. Likewise, nothing about the person who counts and his acts of counting belongs to the sense or content of a pure number. But ideally we can conceive of an arbitrary psychic subject, a given man or an imagined centaur as the one who counts and as counting becomes conscious of the appropriate number. We in fact find ourselves compelled to say that numbers are produced in the act of counting, propositions are produced in the acts of judging.

We face thereby a remarkable situation in connection with the ideal objectivities with which the logician has to do. They have, on the one hand, a peculiar kind of being-for-themselves and also a being-in-themselves; and we have the *a priori* truths relating to them, those of arithmetic and pure logic. This 'in itself' means : they are what they are, irrespective of whether they are counted, thought, judged, known or not. The same is true of every mathematical proposition or of every number. On the other hand, it is unthinkable that such ideal objects could not be apprehended in appropriate subjective, psychic acts and experiences; we even find ourselves compelled to say that the numbers are produced in acts of enumerating, the truth under consideration is subjectively formed in the act of judging.

It is actually this fact, that ideal objects always confront us as subjective structures in productive experiences and acts, which was the source of the then almost universally prevalent psychologisation of ideal objects. Now, even if it was made evident that ideal objects possess their own being, which is in fact being-in-itself, in spite of the fact that they appear in consciousness in the process of their formation, there remained here a great task, never before seriously considered : namely, the task of thematising, for the purpose of enquiry, the correlation between ideal objects of the purely logical domain and the subjective, psychic experiences as constituting acts. If I 'repeat' the same act of production, if I again practise the same acts of enumeration, predication or inference, they are no doubt new psychical acts, but I can evidently recognize that what has come into being in them is identically the same pure number, identically the same truth, etc. But speaking about it in vague and empty generalities does not yield scientific knowledge. What are the hidden psychic experiences like, which are correlated to the idealities under consideration and which must run their course in the manner of completely determinate acts of production so that the subject may thereby be conscious of and have evident knowledge of those idealities as objects?

The proper theme of the *Logical Investigations*, and by suitable extension, of the entire phenomenology has been therewith indicated. You can see that the primary interest in this does not lie with the idealities, and will not rest satisfied in the domain of these idealities. Arithmetic, the *a priori* science of numbers and other pure mathematical structures, is the theme of the mathematicians. It is not otherwise with traditional logic; only here a purification had at first to be accomplished and exhibited : namely, that with regard to the formal-logical there is an exact parallel i.e. a purely logical and ideal objectivity. It became thereby clear that this discipline of pure propositions and truths in general is inseparable from arithmetic and the total formal mathematical analysis, so that under the title "mathesis universalis" an unique science must have to be delimited — as was already recognized by Leibniz, but now for the first time made intelligible. Now generally speaking : one can do mathematics as a mathematician, and the themes in that case are the mathematical idealities purely in themselves and in their ideal relations amongst themselves. As a mathematician, one of course constantly lives through the correlative mathematical activities, but one knows nothing of them; one can know of them first through reflection. In any case, they do not constitute the scientific theme for the mathematician. If however one turns his theoretical interest to the multiplicity of subjective acts, to the entire interconnection of subjective life in and through which the mathematical objects emerge in the mathematician, then the idea of correlation research becomes pertinent. Obviously, it is such that the mathematical also occurs in it, i.e. as the respective ideal structure exactly as it 'emerges' in the experience which forms it and makes it conscious as it is, and in a certain manner participates in temporality and reality without itself being real and consequently a temporally individuated object.

What has been taken up for consideration in special investigations to be concretely worked out was, as may be also said now, a theory of logico-mathematical knowledge, a scientific investigation of mathematical knowledge together with what is known in it, but entirely concretely, demonstrating, step by step, the correlative inner occurrences in psychological reflection, occurrences which make it possible, in logico-mathematical knowledge, for the mathematical to emerge objectively as concept, as proposition, as connectedness of propositions and as a whole science, but also as number, sets, manifold, as the substrate of a theory of manifold, etc.

You would now understand why the *Logical Investigations* called this work concerned with the psychical 'descriptive psychology.' In fact, what the *Investigations* had in view, and necessarily so, was the laying bare of a revealing inner intuition of the acts of thinking hidden for the thinker himself, an essential description moving itself within pure inner intuition and relating to the pure givenness of experience. But on the other hand, the name 'Phenomenology' was selected to indicate the quite novel peculiarity of the method. In fact, an unique method of dealing with the mental emerged here. What was new, for one thing, was the task, and correspondingly the effort to enquire, radically and consistently, back from the categories of objectivities to the correlative modes of consciousness, the subjective acts, act-structures, experiential foundations in which the objectivities of the appropriate sorts come to be objects of consciousness and to evident self-givenness.

Already at the very first go, a new world came to light. One observed with astonishment, what immeasurable multiplicity of differences in inner life made its appearance purely intuitively and was made accessible to a rigorous scientific treatment, only if one had the courage exclusively to interrogate consciousness itself in a consistently undertaken inner intuition, and to observe how it is made possible that such objectivities come to be made conscious, how consciousness, as a process of achieving objectivity, looks like in itself.

I must however add that an extension of the sphere of the problem had immediately to be made. The same problems which arose here in the context of mathematical and logical idealities had evidently to be raised in connection with all idealities, also for the real objects of knowledge. They could have been formulated also from these latter contexts which were only in part considered in the *Logical Investigations*.

(c) *A closer characterization of the reflection which is decisive for phenomenology (performance of reflection in stages)*

With a view to further characterize the peculiarity of the problem orientation and the method of logical clarification, the following has to be noted : the regressive inquiry from the objectivities under consideration to the subjective experiences and active formings by a subject who is conscious of such objectivities, was from the beginning determined by a certain leading intention which (surely, in so far as I had not achieved reflective clarity about it) had not yet found expression in the form of clarified thoughts and claims.

For, the highest stage of reflective clarity about the significance of the methodological procedure was achieved for the first time much later — indeed, through reflection on that which had been, in the *Investigations*, felt as the deepest need and had made fulfilling achievements possible.

In the first place, what was aimed at was a pure intuition and not a theoretical and hypothetical construction in the manner of naturalistic psychology. Logical thinking itself as well as the contents of such thinking, the conceptual contents and the objectivities with which such thinking is concerned precisely as they become objects of consciousness, were to be brought to givenness and faithfully described purely in accordance with the subjective and changing modes in which they 'appear' in it. 'Description' meant not merely expression of the intuited in concepts constructed originally out of such intuition, but also as far-reaching an analysis as possible of the intuited with its moments to be intuitively displayed. To illustrate all this : if I judge or ascertain that a straight line is uniquely determined by two points, I live through this act or experience, ascertaining also in a certain manner that I am conscious of this act, though I am not directed towards it by way of judging. But quite evidently, I can retrospectively attend to it and thereby make a reflective judgment. Instead of saying, "Two points uniquely determine a straight line," I then would say, "I judge, I am convinced, I think that ..." Obviously, I can now ask, what does this experience of judging, passively pre-given in its 'how,' look like from close quarters? Does it permit further expansion? Can I determine anything intuitively about it? The same questions arise in every other case. We have here to follow the general typicality of the experience of thinking, in its general and yet purely intuitive descriptions, that belongs obviously to a psychology based on 'inner experience' which had been in demand and had been attempted already in the beginning of the 18th century in Locke's *Enquiry*. But owing to deep-seated reasons, it never could equally well come to achieve systematic and pure descriptions — neither with regard to the acts of experience and thought, nor with regard to acts of valuation, volition and action, and also with regard to their fantasized neutral correlates. The reason lay partly in that one rather too hastily sought after an explanatory achievement in psychology after the model of explanations in the natural sciences, and therefore was quickly led beyond the domain of pure intuition and the pure givenness in inner experience.

Of special importance is the fact, first noticed much later, that reflective experience, the so-called 'inner,' itself has many strata and depth dimensions, and that it is exceedingly difficult to take recourse to it effectively in order to go beyond the most superficial. In fact, one did not have any idea at all of the depths and mediations involved. One did not therefore realize that inner reflection is not a simple reflection which immediately led to the concrete data of inner life at any moment. The concrete data, rather, let themselves be apprehended only through many stages of reflection, so that inner experience is a process of revealing, that is to be achieved through ever new acts of reflection. The need for a pure and systematically advancing description and the conviction that it denotes a large field of difficult and philosophically as well as psychologically basic work, grew soon after the flowering of experimental psychology. The motives lay in logic, ethics, aesthetics, also in the normative philosophical sciences and in the rational criticism connected with them. One should at first get to know the cognitive life itself, as also the volitional and evaluative lives, in inner experience, then construct clear concepts out of that knowledge — in order to arrive at an epistemology, value-theory and theory of will. In other words, one has to acquire, from within, a clear understanding of how truth arises as the achievement of 'rational' knowing, how genuine 'value' arises in the achievement of 'rational' evaluation, how ethical goodness arises as the subjective achievement of ethically correct volition.

(d) *Brentano as the pathfinder for investigations into inner experience —*
   discovery of intentionality as the basic character of the psychic

Attempts to reform, above all, logic and epistemology and also ethics and aesthetics were the order of the day. Brentano participated in them in his own way, and especially in his Vienna lectures he energetically defended the thesis that all healthy reform in this field leads back to a purely descriptive analysis of the logical as well as of all other data of consciousness in general in inner experience, at first in inner perception. From there he required of psychology in general, to which all such analysis has to be assigned, that it develop a purely descriptive psychology which is to be the foundation of all explanatory theories, and which he later called 'Psychognosie.'

   Although Brentano was very severely attacked in his own time, he has, in this regard, provided an extraordinarily strong incentive not only in Germany, but also in England and in general in the international sphere. Of special significance was a general point of view for psychological description which he developed from inner intuition : we designate it today by the word 'Intentionality.' For the first time, the fundamental essence of psychic life was thereby formulated in its central feature : consciousness is consciousness of something. This was laid down on a purely descriptive basis as the essential character of psychic life which was captured directly from the evidence of inner experience.

   One could not get away from the knowledge that intentionality is a basic property of mental life, which is quite immediately and evidently given prior to all theory. When I perceive a house, I would perhaps say to myself that there is a house out there and there is within me a psychic experience of perceiving, perhaps a perceptual image as a distant effect of the house itself upon my psycho-physical subjectivity. But whatever may be the case with this causal relation, and irrespective of whatever there may be to say against it, it should be made evident that in the perceptual experience itself there is a relation to consciousness or a relation of consciousness to the house which is being perceived in it. It may be that I later on rightly realize that I have been subject to an illusion. Nevertheless I had the consciousness of "the house as being there"; descriptively there is nothing in it to distinguish it from any other perception. When the house is a mere hallucination, one cannot naturally speak of an external-internal psycho-physical causality. But it is clear that that momentary experience in itself is not merely a subjective experience, but is also perception of this house. The relatedness to an object belongs descriptively to the experience, no matter whether the object actually exists or not. Likewise, if I imagine a centaur, the experience of the fiction itself is still fantasy of such and such centaur. In the experience which we call memory, there is similarly a relatedness to the past, in love a relatedness to the beloved, in hatred a relatedness to the hated, in willing a relatedness to that which is willed.

The scholastics had already recognized intentionality. They distinguished between the truly actual objects which exist in themselves and the merely intentional objects as meant within the act of meaning, as experienced within the act of experiencing, as judged within the act of judging. It was implied therein that mental life has in itself the property of relating itself to an objectivity. However, it would be fundamentally wrong to hold that Brentano has merely rediscovered an old scholastic doctrine. His great discovery and his true originality lie in this, that — guided by the idea of a descriptive psychology which he conceived, from a naturalistic standpoint, to be the basis of an explanatory psychology in the scientific style — he sought for a descriptive principle of distinction between the physical and the psychic, and was led thereby first to assert that intentionality is the descriptively identifiable essential feature of the specifically mental life. That apparently is only a very small slant of the scholastic doctrine of intentionality. But such seemingly small slants make history and decide the fate of science. It was the fruitful and now obvious consequence of this descriptive determination, that psychology had first to raise itself to be a purely descriptive science of psychic life, and that as so delimited it was to be nothing other than a descriptive science of intentionality, of the manifold formations of consciousness as consciousness of something, with all the intuitively distinguishable contents belonging to it.

Surely, this doctrine, in spite of its evidently descriptive rootedness in mental life, was full of the greatest difficulties and obscurities : how is one to deal with consciousness as such in an enquiry into inner experience, how to undertake intentional analysis, what sort of generality is possible and should be sought for in this domain, how from this starting point one has to ground psychology as a science of the psycho-physical, real mental life — all this was in darkness. Naturally, the dominant psychology reacted generally in the negative. In spite of this one could not totally avoid the influence of Brentano. There were researchers free from preconceptions, who could not, after Brentano's discovery, shut their eyes to the given fact that intentionality is the fundamental property of mental life, prior to all theory, in immediate, inner experiential evidence.

Once seen clearly, intentionality had to be a psychological theme, namely, the central theme for psychology. We find accordingly that since the seventies, at first within Germany and later on outside, there have been many prominent psychologists who, in their descriptions, wanted to make allowance for intentionality. At the same time, the more general claim of a descriptive psychology as the most basic discipline within psychology found various supporters. Dilthey does not seem to have been influenced by Brentano in this matter. Rather he seems to have been led to the idea of a pure description entirely on his own, guided by his own area of interest in the *Geisteswissenschaften*. It is remarkable that the central significance of intentionality does not play any role in his thinking.

On the other hand, the *Logical Investigations* are fully influenced by Brentano's suggestions, as should be readily understandable in view of the fact that I was a direct pupil of Brentano. And yet the idea of a descriptive psychology has undergone, in the *Investigations*, a new change and also an essential transformation through an essentially new method, so much so that Brentano himself did not recognize it as the fruition of his own ideas. While Brentano restricted himself to his own mode of thinking, it was quite different with Dilthey, who accepted the *Logical Investigations* with great joy, although it arose without any relation to his writings, and saw in it a first concrete working out of his *Ideas towards a Descriptive and Analytical Psychology*. Dilthey himself first brought out this relationship, for unfortunately under the influence of Ebbinghaus's adverse criticism I had not thought it necessary to read Dilthey's great work — and all the more, since in those years I had no sensitivity at all for the significance of Dilthey's writings. The strong tendency towards positivism to be found in his later work *Introduction to the Geisteswissenschaften* shocked me in view of my inner struggle to overcome positivism in principle. I was at first greatly surprised to hear from Dilthey personally, that phenomenology and particularly the descriptive analysis of the second, specifically phenomenological part of the *Logical Investigations* were in essential harmony with his *Ideas* and could be regarded as a first basic step towards an actual working out of his ideal of psychology carried out with a fruitful method. Dilthey had always laid the greatest importance on this convergence of our investigations in spite of their fundamentally different starting points, and in his old age had taken up again, with youthful enthusiasm, the investigations in the theory of the *Geisteswissenschaften* which he had abandoned. Its result was the last and the best of his books on this theme (whose publication he sadly enough predeceased) i.e. *Der Aufbau der geschichtlichen Welt* (of 1910) which appeared in the *Abhandlungen* of the Berlin Academy. The more I have progressed in the development of the phenomenological method and the phenomenological analysis of the mental life, the more I have been led to recognize that Dilthey was right in his so strange judgment on the inner unity of phenomenology and descriptive-analytical psychology. His writings contain a genial pre-view and a first stage of phenomenology. They are in no way antiquated, even today they are rich in most valuable concrete suggestions for work in Phenomenology which is methodologically advanced and, in its entire problematic, differently structured. I would therefore very much recommend a study of all the writings of this extraordinary person. They contain true treasures of intuitive demonstrations (*Aufweisungen*) and descriptions of historical interconnections; and in general wherever there is pure description in true adequacy to givenness to actual intuition, there after all is an already prepared field for fruitful work for the phenomenologist. But one cannot get from them a development of that purely inner-directed psychology which Dilthey always cherished but which he could not carry through in the form of a rigorous science with conceptually rigorous method and decisively established statements. It should well be noted that however pleasing the later great influences of Dilthey may have been, an external imitation of his style may indeed have unfavorable consequences.

The psychology which I am going to introduce in some of its main features will not therefore immediately carry the stamp of Dilthey's, but shall be a phenomenological psychology — as I have already announced.

(e) *Further development of the thoughts about intentionality in the logical investigations. The character of consciousness as achievement. Transition from a pure descriptive psychology to an a priori (eidetic-intuitive) psychology and its significance for theory of knowledge*

It will not be possible, in this introduction, to characterise in every respect all that methodologically opens up for the first time in the *Logical Investigations*. I can only clarify a few things here, and to begin with, as follows : Brentano never went beyond an external classificatory-descriptive treatment of intentional experiences, or what amounts to the same, of the modes of consciousness. He never saw and never took up the great task of starting from the basic categories of objects regarded as possible objects of consciousness, particularly of cognitive consciousness, and then enquiring back into the entire multiplicity of possible modes of consciousness through which we become conscious of such objectivities and can, in principle, become conscious of them, in order to be able, from there onwards through further investigation, to explain the teleological function of these modes of consciousness for the synthetic truth-accomplishments of reason. It is only through this formulation of the problem (however incomplete a form it still had in the *Logical Investigations*) that it was possible to gain a deep and penetrating insight into consciousness and its achievements. In fact, now for the first time it became clear that consciousness was not merely an empty, even if many-colored, having-conscioused (*Bewusst-haben*), but also a process of accomplishing which is operative in many demonstrable forms and corresponding syntheses, but everywhere intentional, goal-directed and directed towards the idea of truth. I may also say that a transcendental doctrine of consciousness was for the first time possible, and along with it it was possible to gain an innermost understanding of the process of apperception, as taking place in psychological inwardness, of objects of all categories. It was also possible to gain an innermost understanding of all validating achievements — logical, axiological and practical.

It is in such work that consciousness or intentionality first revealed its true essence. Prior to it, psychology — and even now, the entire scientifically oriented psychology — was dominated by a certain conception of mental life which, as is evident, looks upon it as an analogue of physical processes of nature i.e. as an ever changing complex of elements. One accordingly took it as his task to reduce the complexes to their elements and their elementary forms of combination and the corresponding causal laws. As against this, I now emphasized that this entire conception was meaningless, that the synthesis of consciousness was totally different from external combination of natural elements, that it belonged to the essence of the life of consciousness to conceal within itself, in place of spatial outsidedness, being-inside-one-another and being-through-one-another, and in place of spatial totality, an intentional involvedness, motivatedness, being-contained-in-one-another through meaning — and all this in a manner which has no analogue, according to form and principle, in the physical realm. Brentano's thought was still, in the sense explicated, naturalistic. He had not yet seen something like intentional implication and intentional analysis as analysis of continuously developing sense-giving. With this is indicated what constitutes the radically different character of every intentional psychology of the inner, of every descriptive-analytical psychology in the true sense — which is so different from experimental, psycho-physical and other varieties of external psychology which comprehends only the inductive and outer realm of the objectified mental being.

There is still another, and perhaps the most important and essential novelty of the psychological-phenomenological method which I have not yet indicated and which for the first time appeared in the *Logical Investigations* and thoroughly determined their mode of enquiry. It became clear very soon that a descriptive investigation having the sort of goal as the *Logical Investigations* had, could not by any means have the character of a merely empirical psychological enquiry, it could not be descriptive in the sense of a psycho-physical psychology or in the sense of a naturalistic psychology. The exclusive theme of the *Logical Investigations* was the psychical modes which are correlative to the objectivities (and especially the logical-ideal ones) which are intended, psychical modes in whom, purely in the immanence of psychical life, concepts, judgments and theories form themselves as ideal, identical unities of sense together with the modes of being merely supposed or of being evidently true, as the case may be.

The psychology of the last thousand years was to be, and in fact was, in all its historically changing forms, an empirical science of human and animal mental life. But if one goes back from the ideal objectivities to the consciousness wherein they are subjectively formed, one can soon convince oneself of the fact that the inner passivities and activities in which they form themselves subjectively and come to evident givenness and can be made intuitively clear through methodical reflection and phenomenological analysis, are not empirical contingencies of human act-experiences, contingent facticities which could be thought of as being different from what they are. On the other hand, it is evident that if at all things like numbers, mathematical sets, propositions, theories and such others shall be subjectively given, or should be objects of consciousness in subjective experiences, these experiences which are necessary for that purpose must in all cases have an identical structure. In other words, as thinking subjects whether we consider us men or we posit angels, devils or gods, or any being which enumerates, counts and mathematicises — the inner act or life of counting and mathematical thinking, if something logico-mathematical is to come out of it, should, with *a priori* necessity, have always the same essential structure. To the *a priori* of pure logic and pure mathematics, to this region of unconditionally necessary and universal truths, there corresponds a correlative psychical *a priori* i.e. a region of unconditionally necessary and universal truths which pertain to mathematical experience, mathematical representations, thinking, connecting, etc. viz. a multiplicity of psychical acts of a subject in general (in so far as it has to be conceived as such in pure ideality) which apprehends the mathematical as such. If we understand the logical-mathematical objectivity as being such as can necessarily be made inter-subjectively insightful, then we may have to substitute for the particular subject the communicative subjectivity and its socialised life.

But the same holds good for all investigations into psychic correlations concerning objects of every region and category, and it holds good not with an empty generality, not with a signification and assertion that is removed from facts, but in a determinate specificity which corresponds to determinate objects and relates to correlative revealing intuitions. With this, at the same time, there opens up a novel idea of psychology — novel not merely by virtue of its concretely and universally apprehended theme of object-consciousness correlation, but also because of the fact that it is to be an *a priori*, not empirical, psychology. It is to be *a priori* in the same straight-forward sense in which mathematics is an *a priori*, non-empirical science, or as we shall call it, an eidetic science; herein is manifest a peculiarity which has its evidence prior to all 'theories' of *a priori* knowledge i.e. prior to all epistemological interpretations. Instead of the actual human subjects living on this earth in this world, this psychology deals with the ideal essence of a mathematicising and, in general, of a knowing subjectivity as such, which has to be clarified in phenomenological exemplary intuition, but in an ideally possible, unconditioned generality. As against this, it is of no significance to say that already Lotze had noticed the *a priori* within the region of immanent sense qualities and that logic, in spite of all unclarity about its noetic-noematic interpretation, was nevertheless accepted as an *a priori* discipline. One had not, with that, brought about an actual beginning of a phenomenological *a priori* psychology and one did not have any idea even of its possibility. The same holds good also of Brentano.

In olden days, viz. in the Leibniz-Wolffian schools of the 18th century, there had been much talk of *a priori* psychology. Kant's *Critique* put an end to it. But that psychology was ontological-metaphysical. Unlike this new one, that psychology was not purely intuitive and descriptive and yet at the same time *a priori*, and it did not therefore ascend from intuitive concrete data to intuitive necessities and generalities. In the systematic and concrete expositions to which we shall soon proceed, this new psychology would receive a clarification which would make it fully self-evident. Such an *a priori* (eidetic-intuitive) psychology was possible only after the methods of intentional analysis and intentional implication had been concretely laid down and in parts developed — but that again, to begin with, in naive intuitiveness and prior to all questions about their empirical or *a priori* significance. You should however note that the descriptive psychological analyses of the *Logical Investigations* gave it an essentially different character from the descriptive and analytical psychology which Dilthey had required in the interests of historical and systematic sciences of the mind (*Geisteswissenschaften*) and also from Brentano's psychognosy. The *Logical Investigations* also gave a descriptive analytical psychology in the interests of psychology itself, but also, as Dilthey on his part did, for the foundations of a theory of reason. But this psychology had an essentially different form, according to the novel starting point and goals which led up to it. From the very beginning, it was not aiming at a new foundation for psychology. The aim was rather purely epistemological. As against formal logic as an *a priori* science of the essential structures and essential laws of certain ideal objectivities, a science was required which would undertake a systematic clarification of the subjective acts of thinking in which these thoughts are subjectively formed, and particularly of the specific rational acts in which such thoughts assume the normative form of self-evident truth in the sense of over-subjective validity.

The same is also expressed differently when I say that it was concerned with a preliminary, concretely executed attempt at a theory of knowledge which, though, was certainly limited, in its theme, to the formal logical sphere of reason, but extended by the nature of things to the formal-mathematical domain. For the first time it was evident that a theory of reason understood as a system of rational activities being performed within the thinking subjectivity, could be brought into existence neither through the sort of vague empirical or *a priori* discussions removed from facts which were usual, nor through a merely empirical descriptive psychology based on inner experience. It became rather clear that there should come into being, in place of empirical psychology, a novel, purely *a priori* and yet at the same time descriptive science of the psychical, namely a science which makes it intelligible with unconditioned and directly intuited necessity, how psychic life, especially cognitive life, purely in itself and in accordance with its own *a priori* essential structure, performs intentional accomplishments — in particular, accomplishments belonging to the type 'ideal validity,' which is what is called 'true being' and 'truth.'

Although originally nothing was thought about a reform of the existing psychology, it was however afterwards absolutely clear to me that herein lay the beginning of a new sort of psychology, and in fact a new form of the old idea of an *a priori* psychology — exactly as the old idea of an *a priori* ontology was revived in the *Prolegomena* and in the third and the fourth Investigations in a new non-metaphysical form.

Along with this there came about a noteworthy change in the historical relation between psychology and theory of knowledge. On the one hand, there was, since centuries, and in a great many changing forms, an empirical psychology (at present in so successful a form as that of experimental psychology), a psychology which always laid claim to comprehend epistemology within itself, or at least to provide it with its foundation. On the other hand, since Kant, a transcendental epistemology came into being with revolutionary consequences and validity — an epistemology which sharply rejected all empirico-psychological foundation and fought it as psychologism and yet did not know, as distinguished from psycho-physical psychology, any other *a priori* psychology which could serve as the necessary foundation. Psychology, like all other objective sciences, should therewith retain its right to autonomous being.

Now it was something historically novel that an epistemological investigation into the logico-mathematical, undertaken entirely independently of traditional empirical psychology, should press forward towards a methodical reform of psychology and should formulate anew the problem of the relation between epistemology and psychology. These concretely executed epistemological-logical investigations had tried to make use of a psychological analysis, though of a new *a priori* kind. An *a priori* science of the mental, constructed on the basis of pure inner intuition, as it emerged here in its real beginnings, would not possibly be without any significance for a strictly scientific, empirical psychology, exactly as an *a priori* science of space and of the formal idea of nature in general could not be without significance for an empirical science of nature.

Brentano and also Dilthey had already realized that traditional empiricism and epistemological psychologism did contain a lasting core of truth, namely that a theory of knowledge must be formulated in an intuitive ana-

lysis of knowing and a rational theory of ethics in an intuitive analysis
of moral consciousness, and so in a descriptive psychology. But as long
as this analysis was regarded as empirical, the objections raised by the anti-
psychologists could not be met. How could a theory of knowledge, a science
of the *a priori* principles which are to render the possibility of objective
rational accomplishments intelligible, be founded on psychology, itself an
empirical science? Besides, the supporting descriptions or 'psychogenetic'
investigations would be necessarily useless and would be unable to lead
to an understanding of the logical and the ethical, because they could not
possibly arrive at any pure intentional analysis. Had they been able to do
that, then the pure psychological *a priori* would have easily dawned on
them — towards which the obvious reference back to the problem of constitution did supply the stimulus.

(f) *The consequent extension and deepening of the formula of the
problems of the* Logical Investigations. *Exhibition of the necessity
of an epistemological foundation for the* a priori *sciences through
transcendental phenomenology — the science of transcendental
subjectivity*

Surely, the horizons which opened up for a new theory of knowledge as
well as for theories of all other forms of reason on the one hand, and for
an *a priori* psychology on the other, had to be further traversed before
a complete clarity could be achieved regarding the future tasks for investigations in the theory of reason in psychology. In the *Logical Investigations*,
in any case, the highest stage of fundamental clarity had by no means been
reached. It is only in the course of the progress of the investigations beyond
the limited sphere of the problems of the *Logical Investigations*, in the
consequent extension of it into a problem which comprehends the totality
of all possible objects in general and the totality of all possible modes of
consciousness in general, or of possible subjectivity in general — that the
most fundamental clarifications could first come into being. What inevi-
tably presented itself, arising out of the needs stimulated by the formal
universality of *mathesis universalis*, for a universal extension of the *Logical
Investigations*, was the extension of *a priori* and formal logic and mathematics into the idea of a comprehensive system of *a priori* sciences for every
conceivable category of objects, and highest of all, the demands of a
universal *a priori* of possible worlds in general besides those of formal
mathematics; but on the other hand, and correlatively, the extension of

a pure *a priori* consideration of the cognitive consciousness concerned with the formal generalities alone to cognitive consciousness that is rich in content and that is directed towards every specific category of objectivities in general; and finally, from that point onwards, an *a priori* pure theory of consciousness, in its full universality, had to develop, which would comprehend every kind of evaluating, thinking, willing consciousness and therefore consciousness of every type and therefore the entire concrete subjective life in all forms of its intentionality, and opened up all the problems of the constitution of the world and the unity of conscious subjectivity, individual and personal as well as social.

SUGGESTIONS FOR FURTHER READING

Logical Works of Husserl (other than the *Logische Untersuchungen*)

1. *Philosophie der Arithmetik*, I. Psychologische und logische Untersuchungen, Halle: Pfeffer, 1891; *Husserliana*, Bd. XII, edited by L. Eley, The Hague: Martinus Nijhoff, 1970.
2. "Folgerungskalkül und Inhaltlogik," *Vierteljahrsschrift für wissenschaftliche Philosophie*, Vol. 15, 1891, 168-189, 351-356.
3. "Besprechung: E. Schröder, Vorlesungen über die Algebra der Logik, I," *Göttingische Gelehrte Anzeigen*, 1891, 243-278.
4. "Psychologische Studien zur elementaren Logik," *Philosophische Monatshefte*, Vol. 30, 1894, 159-191.
5. "Bericht über deutsche Schriften zur Logik aus dem J. 1894," *Archiv für systematische Philosophie*, Vol. 3, 1897, 2; 6-244.
6. "Bericht über deutsche Schriften zur Logik 1895-1898," *Archiv für syst. Phil.*, Vol. 9, 1903, 113-132, 237-259, 393-408, 523-543.
7. "Bericht über deutsche Schriften zur Logik 1895-1899," *Ibid.*, Vol. 10, 1904, 101-125.
8. "Selbstanzeige" (of the *Logische Untersuchungen*), *Vierteljahrsschrift für wissenschaftliche Philosophie*, Vol. 24, 100, 511; Vol. 25, 1901, 260-263.
9. *Formale und Transzendentale Logik*, Halle: Max Niemeyer, 1929. (*Husserliana*, Vol. XVII edited by P. Janssen, The Hague: Martinus Nijhoff).
10. *Erfahrung und Urteil*. Untersuchungen zur Genealogie der Logik, edited by L. Landgrebe, Prag: Academia Verlag, 1939.

English Translations

Formal and Transcendental Logic, translated by Dorion Cairns, The Hague: Martinus Nijhoff, 1969.

"Outline of a 'Preface' to the Logical Investigations," translated by P. J. Bossert, The Hague: Martinus Nijhoff, 1975.

Experience and Judgment: Investigations in a Genealogy of Logic, translated by James S. Churchill and Karl Ameriks, Evanston: Northwestern University Press, 1973.

Books on Husserl's *Philosophy of Logic*

Bachelard, S. *A Study of Husserl's Formal and Transcendental Logic*, E. tr. by L. E. Embree, Evanston: Northwestern Univ. Press, 1968.

Carr, D. & Casey, E. S. (eds.) *Explorations in Phenomenology*, The Hague : Martinus Nijhoff, 1973 (especially Part Three).

Derrida, J. *Speech and Phenomena* and Other Essays on Husserl's Theory of Signs, E. tr. by D. Allison, Evanston : Northwestern Univ. Press, 1973.

Føllesdal, D. *Husserl and Frege*, Oslo: Ascehoug, 1958.

Levin, D. M. *Reason and Evidence in Husserl's Phenomenology*, Evanston: Northwestern Univ. Press, 1970.

Mohanty, J. N. *Edmund Husserl's Theory of Meaning*, Third Edition (with a new Introduction), The Hague: Martinus Nijhoff, 1976.

Noack (ed.) *Husserl*, Darmstadt: Wissenschaftliche Buchgesellschaft, 1973.

Osborn, A. D. *Edmund Husserl and His Logical Investigations*, Second Edition, Cambridge, Mass.: Edward Brothers, 1949.

Scherer, R. *La Phénoménologie des "Recherches logiques" de Husserl*, Paris: Presses Universitaires de France, 1967.

Sokolowski, R. *Husserlian Meditations: How Words Present Things*, Evanston: Northwestern Univ. Press, 1974.

Tugendhat, E. *Der Wahrheitsbegriff bei Husserl und Heidegger*, Berlin: Walter de Gruyter, 1967.

Reviews of the *Logical Investigations*

Levin, D. M. in *Journal of Philosophy*, LXIX, 1972, 384-398.

Meyn, H. L. in *Metaphilosophy,* IV, 1973, 162-172.

Sokolowski, R. in *Inquiry*, 14, 1971, 318-347.

Unpublished Dissertations bearing on Husserl's Philosophy of Logic:

McIntyre, R. T. *Husserl and Referentiality*: The Role of the Noema as an intensional Entity (Stanford, 1970).

Smith, D.W. *Intentionality, Noemata and Individuation*: The Role of Individuation (Stanford, 1971).

Papers

Aquila, Richard. "Husserl's Critique of Hume's Notion of "Distinctions of Reason," *Philosophy and Phenomenological Research*, 20, 1959, 213-221.

Biemel, Walter (ed.). "Dilthey-Husserl Briefwechsel," *Revista de Filosofia de la Universidad de Costa Rica*, I, 1957, 101-124.

Cairns, Dorion. "The Ideality of Verbal Expressions," *Philosophy and Phenomenological Research*, 1, 1941, 435-456.

— "Some Results of Husserl's Logical Investigations," *Journal of Philosophy*, 26, 1939, 236-239.

Church, Alonzo. "Review of Marvin Farber, *Foundation of Phenomenology*", *Journal of Symbolic Logic*, 9, 1944, 64-65.

Dupré, Louis. "The Concept of Truth in Husserl's *Logical Investigations*," *Philosophy and Phenomenological Research*, 24, 1963, 345-354.

Eley, Lothar. "Afterword to Husserl's *Experience and Judgment*: Phenomenology and Philosophy of Language" in Husserl, *Experience and Judgment*.

— "Life-World Constitution of Propositional Logic and Elementary Predicate Logic" in Tyminiecka (ed.) *Analecta Husserliana*, II, 333-353.

Findlay, J. N. "Meaning and Intention," *Indian Journal of Philosophy*, I.

Fels, H. "Bolzano und Husserl," *Philosophisches Jahrbuch der Görresgesellschaft*, 1925, 510-418.

Føllesdal, D. "Husserl's Notion of Noema," *Journal of Philosophy*, 66, 1969, 680-687.

Fulton, S. "Husserl's Significance for the Theory of Truth," *Monist*, 45, 1935, 264-306.

Gotesky, R. "Husserl's conception of 'logic as Kunstlehre' in the *Logische Untersuchungen*," *Philosophical Review*, 47, 1938, 375-389.

Gurwitsch, A. "Substantiality and Perceptual Coherence: Remarks on H. B. Veatch's *Two Logics*," *Research in Phenomenology*, II, 1972, 29-46.

— "Reflections on Mathematics and Logic" in: *Phenomenology and the Theory of Science*, Evanston: Northwestern University Press, 1974.

Hein, K. F. "Husserl's Criterion of Truth," *Journal of Critical Analysis*, 3, 1971, 125-136.

Husserl, E. "Über psychologische Begründung der Logik" — Ein unveröffentlichter Eigenbericht Husserls, *Zeitschrift für philosophische Forschung*, 13, 1959, 346-348.

Küng, Guido. "World as Noema and as Referent," *Journal of the British Society for Phenomenology*, 3, 1972, 5-26.

— "Husserl on Pictures and Intentional Objects," *Review of Metaphysics*, XXVI, 1973, 670-680.

Levin, D. M. "Husserl's Notion of Self-evidence" in: Edo Pivcevic (ed.), *Phenomenology and Philosophical Understanding*, Cambridge University Press, England, 1975.

McCarthy, I. A. "Logic, Mathematics and Ontology in Husserl," *Journal of the British Society for Phenomenology*, III, 1972.

Mohanty, J. N. (ed.), "Frege-Husserl Correspondence," *Southwestern Journal of Philosophy*, V, 1974, 83-95.

— "On Husserl's Theory of Meaning," *Southwestern Journal of Philosophy*, V, 1974, 229-244.

Moneta, Giuseppina C. "The Foundations of Predicative Experience and the Spontaneity of Consciousness," in L. Embree (ed.), *Life-World and Consciousness*, Essays for Aron Gurwitsch, Evanston: Northwestern University Press, 1972.

Parrit, H. "Husserl and Neo-Humboldtians on Language," *International Philosophical Quarterly*, 12, 1972, 43-68.

Pietersma, H. "Husserl and Frege," *Archiv für Geschichte der Philosophie*, 49, 1967, 298-323.

Pumahka, K. "Methods and Problems in Husserl's Transcendental Logic," *International Logic Review*, 2, 1971, 202-218.

Schuewer, A. "Remarks on the Idea of Authentic Thinking in Husserl's *Logical Investigations*," *Research in Phenomenology*, I, 1971, 17-32.

Smith, D. W. & McIynter, R. T. "Intentionality via Intensions," *Journal of Philosophy*, 68, 1971, 541-560.

Solomon, R. C. "Sense and Essence: Husserl and Frege," *International Philosophical Quarterly*, 10, 1970, 378-401.

Thiele, Joachim. "Ein Brief Edmund Husserls an Ernst Mach," *Zeitschrift für philosophische Forschung*, 19, 1965.

Tragesser, R. S. "Some Observations concerning Logics and Concepts of Existence," *Journal of Philosophy*, LXIX, 1972, 375-383.

Tugendhat, E. "Phänomenologie und Sprachanalyse" in: R. Bubner (ed.), *Hermeneutik und Dialektik*, II, Tübingen: J. C. B. Mohr, 1970, 3-23.

Welton, D. "Intentionality and Language in Husserl's Phenomenology," *Review of Metaphysics*, 27, 1973, 260-298.

Wundt, W. "Psychologismus und Logizismus," in: Wundt, W. *Kleine Schriften*, Leipzig, 1910-21, Vol. I, 1910. (Contains Wundt's reply to Husserl's criticism of Wundt in the *Prolegomena*.)